FREEMASONRY

WRITTEN BY:

DR. JAMES WILSON

PLANO, TEXAS

SEPTEMBER, 1903

STONE GUILD PUBLISHING
PLANO, TEXAS
HTTP://WWW.STONEGUILDPUBLISHING.COM/

2009

SGP

First Paperback Edition 2009

ISBN-13 978-1-60532-056-4
ISBN-10 1-60532-056-0

10 9 8 7 6 5 4 3 2

PREFACE.

As the most fertile source of instruction in Freemasonry is to be found—alone—in its Traditions and Mythical Legends, which—symbolically—teach of the origin and design of Ancient Craft Masonry, I have collated from the most authentic authors what every Mason must know before he can have that high appreciation of our ancient and honorable order to which it is entitled, and which alone can make it as intelligent and interesting to him as it was designed and deserves to be.

And feeling confident that this book will supply a long felt want existing among the greater majority of the craft on the subject of Ancient Craft Masonry, and, therefore, be duly appreciated, I remain,

Fraternally yours,
JAMES WILSON, M. D.
Plano, Texas.

FREEMASONRY

ANCIENT CRAFT MASONRY.—This is the name given to the three symbolic degrees of Entered Apprentice, Fellow Craft, and Master Mason. The degree of Royal Arch is not generally included under this appellation, although, when considered (as it really is) a complement of the third degree, it must, of course, constitute a part of Ancient Craft Masonry.

In the article of union between the two Grand Lodges of England, adopted in 1813, it is declared that "pure Ancient Masonry consists of three degrees and no more; viz., those of the Entered Apprentice, the Fellow Craft, and the Master Mason, including the Supreme Order of the Holy Royal Arch."

ANCIENT MASONS.—Ancients was the name assumed by the schismatic body of Masons who in 1838 seceded from the regular Grand Lodge of England, and who at the same time insultingly bestowed upon the adherents of that body the title of Moderns.

Thus Dermot, in his Ahiman Rezon, divides the Masons of England into two classes, as follows:

The Ancients, under the name of Free and Accepted Masons; the Moderns, under the name of Freemasons of England. And through the similarity of names, yet they differ exceedingly in makings, ceremonies, knowledge, Masonic language, and installations. So much so, that they always have been, and still continue to be, two distinct societies, directly independent of each other."

To understand, therefore, anything of the meaning of these two terms, we must be acquainted with the history of the schism of the self-styled Ancients from the legal Grand Lodge of England.

No Masonic student should be ignorant of this history, and I propose, therefore, says Dr. Mackey, to give a brief sketch of it in the present article.

"In the year 1738, a number of brethren in London, having become dissatisfied with certain transactions in the Grand Lodge of England, separated themselves from the regular Lodges, and began to hold meetings and initiate candidates without the sanction and authority of the Grand Lodge." Preston, who has given a good account of the schism, does not, however, state the cause which led to the dissatisfaction of the recusant brethren. But Theory attributes it to the fact that the Grand Lodge had introduced some innovations, altering the rituals and suppressing many of the ceremonies which had long been in use. This is also the charge made by Dermott. It is certain that changes were made, especially in some of the modes of recognition; and these changes, it is believed, were induced by the publication of a spurious revelation by the notorious Samuel Prichard. Preston himself acknowledged that innovations took place, although he attributes them to a time subsequent to the first secession. Just about this time some dissensions had occurred between the Grand Lodge at London and that at York, and the seceding brethren, taking advantage of this condition of affairs, assumed, but without authority from the Grand Lodge of York, the name of Ancient York Masons. Matters were, however, subsequently accommodated; but in the next year the difficulties were renewed, and the Grand Lodge persisting in its innovations and ritualistic changes, the seceding brethren declared themselves independent, and assumed the appellation of Ancient Masons, to indicate their adhesion to the ancient forms, while, for a similar purpose, they denominated the members of the regular Lodges, Modern Masons, because, as was contended, they had adopted new forms and usages. The seceders established a new Grand Lodge in London, and, under the claim that they were governed by the Ancient York Constitutions, which had been adopted at that city in the year 926, they gained over many influential persons in England, and were even recognized by the Grand Lodges of Scotland and Ireland. The Ancient York Lodges, as they were called, greatly increased in England, and become so popular in America that a majority of the Lodges and provincial Grand Lodges established in this country during the eighteenth century derived their warrants from the Grand Lodge of Ancient York Masons.

In the year 1756, Laurence Dermott, then Grand Secretary, and subsequently the Deputy Grand Master of the schismatic Grand Lodge, published a Book of Constitutions for the use of the Ancient Masons, under the title of "Ahiman Rezon," which work went through several editions, and became the code of Masonic law for all who adhered, either in England or America, to the Ancient York Grand Lodge, while the Grand Lodge of Masons, or the regular Grand Lodge of England, and its adherents, were governed by the regulations contained in Anderson's Constitutions, the first of which had been published in 1723.

The dissensions between the two Grand Lodges of England lasted until the year 1813, when the two bodies become consolidated under the name and title of the United Grand Lodge of Ancient Freemasons of England.

Four years afterwards a similar and final reconciliation took place in America, by the union of the two Grand Lodges in South Carolina. At this day, all distinction between the Ancients and Moderns has ceased, and it lives only in the memory of Masonic students.

ANTEDILUVIAN MASONRY.—Among the traditions of Masonry, which, taken literally, become incredible, but which, considered allegorically, may contain a profound meaning, not the least remarkable are those which relate to the existence of a Masonic system before the Flood.

Without regarding uncertain accounts, we may safely conclude the Old World, that lasted 1656 years, could not be ignorant of Masonry.

Dr. Oliver has devoted the twenty-eighth lecture in his historical landmarks to an inquiry into the nature and design of Freemasonry before the Flood, but he admits that any evidence of the existence at that time of such an institution must be based on the identity of Freemasonry and morality. We may safely assume, he says, that whatever had for its object and end an inducement to the practice of that morality which is founded on the love of God, may be identified with primitive Freemasonry.

The truth is, that antediluvian Masonry is alluded to only in what is called the "ineffable degrees," and that its only important tradition is that of Enoch, who is traditionally supposed to be its founder, or, at least, its' great hierophant.

APOCALYPSE, MASONRY OF THE.—The adoption of St. John the Evangelist as one of the patrons of our Lodges has given rise among the writers of Freemasonry, to a variety of theories as to the original cause of his being thus connected with the Institution.

Several traditions have been handed down from remote periods, which claim him as a brother, among which the Masonic student will be familiar with that which represents him as having assumed the government of the Craft, as Grand Master, after the demise of John the Baptist. There is something, both in the life and in the writing of St. John the Evangelist, which closely connects him with our mystic Institution.

He may not have been a Freemason in the sense in which we now use the term; but it will be sufficient if it can be shown that he was familiar with other mystical institutions which are generally admitted to have been more or less intimately connected with Freemasonry by deriving their existence from a common origin. Such a society was the Essenian Fraternity, a mystical association of speculative philosophers among the Jews, whose organization very clearly resembles that of the Freemasons, and who are even supposed by some to have derived their tenets and their discipline from the builders of the Temple.

As Oliver observes, their institution "may be termed Freemasonry, retaining the same form, but practiced under another name." Now there is little doubt that St. John was an Essene. Calmet positively asserts it; and the writings and life of St. John seem to furnish sufficient internal evidence that he was originally of that brotherhood.

Mackay says: "But it seems to me that St. John was more particularly selected as a patron of Freemasonry in consequence of the mysterious and emblematic nature of the Apocalypse, which evidently assimilated the mode of teaching adopted by the Evangelist to that practiced by the Fraternity."

If anyone who has investigated the ceremonies performed in the Ancient Mysteries, the spurious Freemasonry, as it has been called of the Pagans, will compare them with the mystical machinery used in the Book of Revelations, he will find himself irresistibly led to the conclusion that St. John the Evangelist was intimately acquainted with the whole process of initiation into these mystic associations, and that he has selected its imagery for the groundwork of his prophetic book.

"The whole machinery of the Apocalypse," says Mr. Faber, "from beginning to end, seems to me very plainly to have been borrowed from the machinery of the Ancient Mysteries; and this, if we consider the nature of the subject, was done with the very strictest attention to poetical decorum."

St. John himself is made to personate an aspirant about to be initiated, and accordingly, the images presented to his mind's eye closely resemble the pageants of the Mysteries both in nature and in order of succession.

The prophet first beholds a door opened in the magnificent temple of heaven; and into this he is invited to enter by the voice of the one who plays the hierophant, here he witnesses the unsealing of the sacred book, and forthwith he is appalled by a troop of ghastly apparitions, which flit in horrid succession before his eyes. Among these are preeminently conspicuous a vast serpent, the well-known symbol of the great father; and two portentous wild beasts, which severally come up out of the sea, and out of the earth, such hideous figures correspond with the canine phantoms of the orgies, which seem to rise out of the ground, and which the polymorphic images of the hero God who was universally deemed the offspring of the sea.

Passing these terrific monsters in safety, the prophet constantly attended by his angel hierophant, who acts the part of an interpreter, is conducted into the presence of a "female," who is described as closely resembling the great mother of pagan theology, like Isis emerging from the sea and exhibiting herself to the aspirant. Apuleius, this female divinity, up borne by the marine wild beast, appears to float upon the surface of many waters. She is said be an open and systematic harlot, just as the great mother was the declared female principle of fecundity; and as she was always propitiated by literal fornication reduced to a religious system, and as the initiated were made to drink a prepared liquor out of a sacred goblet, so this harlot is represented to intoxicate the Kings of the Earth with the golden cup of her prostitution. On her forehead the very name of Mystery is inscribed, and the label teaches us that, in point of character, she is the great universal Mother of Idolatry.

The nature of the mystery, the officiating hierophant, undertakes to explain, and an important prophecy is most curiously and artfully veiled under the very language of the orgies.

To the sea-born great father was ascribed a three fold state; he lived, he died, and he revived, and these changes of condition were duly exhibited in the Mysteries.

To the sea-born wild beast is similarly ascribed a threefold state; he lives, he died, he revives; while dead, he lies floating on the mighty ocean, just like Horus, or Osiris, or Siva, or Vishnou. When he revives again, like those kindred deities, he emerges from the waves; and, whether dead or alive, he bears seven heads and ten horns, corresponding in number with the seven ark-preserved "Rishis" and the ten aboriginal patriarchs.

Nor is this all; as the worshipers of the great father bore his special mark or stigma, and were distinguished by his name, so the worshipers of the maritime beast equally bears his mark and is equally decorated by his appellation.

At length, however, the first of the doleful part of these sacred mysteries draws to a close, and the last or joyful part is rapidly approaching. After the prophet has beheld the enemies of God plunged into a dreadful lake or inundation of liquid fire, which corresponds with the infernal lake or deluge of the orgies, he is introduced into a splendidly illuminated region especially adorned with the characteristics of that paradise which was the ultimate scope of the ancient aspirants, "while without the holy gate of admission are the whole multitude of profane, dogs, and sorcerers and whoremongers, and murderers, and idolaters, and whosoever loved and makes a lie."

Such was the image of the Apocalypse, in close resemblance to the machinery of the Mysteries, and the intimate connection between their system and that of Freemasonry very naturally induced our ancient brethren to claim the patronage of an apostle so preeminently mystical in his writings, and whose last and crowning work bore so much of the appearance in an outward form of a ritual of initiation.

PRIMITIVE FREEMASONRY.—The primitive Freemasonry of the Antedeluvians is a term for which we are indebted to Dr. Oliver, although the theory was broached by earlier writers, and among them, the Chevalier Ramsay. The theory is that the principles and doctrines of Freemasonry existed in the earliest ages of the world, and were believed and practiced by the primitive people, or priesthood, under the name of purer primitive

Freemasonry, and that this Freemasonry, that is to say, the religious doctrine inculcated by it, was, after the Flood, corrupted by the pagan philosophers and priests, and, receiving the title of Spurious Freemasonry, was exhibited in the Ancient Mysteries. The Noachide, however, preserved the principles of the Primitive Freemasonry, and transmitted them to succeeding ages, when at length they assumed the name of Speculative Masonry.

The Primitive Freemasonry was probably without ritual or symbolism, and consisted only in a series of abstract propositions derived from antediluvian traditions. Its dogmas were the unity of God and the immortality of the soul. Dr. Oliver, who gave this system its name, describes it in the following language: "It included a code of simple morals. It assured men that they who did well would be approved of God; and if they followed evil courses, sin would be imputed to them, and they would thus become subject to punishment." "It detailed the reasons why the seventh day was consecrated and set apart as a Sabbath, or day of rest, and showed why the bitter consequences of sin were visited upon our first parents as a practical lesson that it ought to be avoided."

"But the great object of this Primitive Freemasonry was to preserve and cherish the promise of a Redeemer, who should provide a remedy for the evil that their transgression had introduced into the world, when the appointed time should come."

In his history of initiation he makes the supposition that the ceremonies of this Primitive Freemasonry would be few and unostentatious, and consisted, perhaps, like that of admission into Christianity, of a simple lustration conferred alike on all, in the hope that they would practice the social duties of benevolence and good will to man, and unsophisticated devotion to God.

He does not, however, admit that the system of Primitive Freemasonry consisted only of those tenets which are to be found in the first chapters of Genesis, or that he intends in his definition of the science to embrace so general and indefinite a scope of all the principles of truth and light, as Preston has done in his declaration that "From the commencement of the world we may trace the foundation of Masonry!" On the contrary, Dr. Oliver supposes that this Primitive Freemasonry included a particular and definite system, made up of legends and symbols, and confined to those who were initiated into its mysteries.

The knowledge of these mysteries was, of course, communicated by God himself to Adam, and from him traditionally received by his descendants, through the patriarchal line.

This view of Oliver is sustained by the remarks of Rosenberg, a learned French Mason, in an article in the Freemasons' Quarterly Review, on the Book of Raziel, an ancient Kabbalistic work, whose subject is "these divine mysteries."

"This book," says Rosenberg "informs us that Adam was the first to receive the mysteries. Afterwards, when driven out of paradise, he communicated them to his son Seth. Seth communicated them to Enoch, Enoch to Methuselah, Methuselah to Lamech, Lamech to Noah, Noah to Shem, Shem to Abraham; he to

Isaac; he to Jacob; he to Levi; he to Kelboth; he to Amram; he to Moses; he to Joshua; he to the elders; the elders to the prophets, and they to the wise men, and then from one to another down to Solomon.

Such then was the pure and primitive Freemasonry, the first system of mysteries which, according to modern Masonic writers of the school of Oliver, has descended, of course with various modifications, from age to age, in a direct and uninterrupted line, to the Freemasons of the present day.

PROGRESSIVE MASONRY.—Freemasonry is undoubtedly a progressive science, and yet the fundamental principles of Freemasonry are the same now as they were at the very beginning of the Institution. Its landmarks are unchangeable; in them there can be no alteration, no diminution nor addition. When, therefore, we say that Freemasonry is progressive in its character, we of course do not mean to allude to this unalterable part of its constitution; but there is a progress under which every science must undergo, and which many of them have already undergone, to which the science of Freemasonry is subject.

Thus, we say of Christianity that it is a progressive science. Two hundred years ago all its principles, so far as they were known, were directed to such futile inquiries as the philosopher's stone and the elixir of immortality. Now these principles have become more thoroughly understood, and more definitely established, and the object of their application is more noble and philosophical. The.

writings of the chemists of the former and the present period sufficiently indicate this progress of the science.

And yet the elementary principles of chemistry are unchangeable; its truths were the same then as they are now. Some of them were at that time unknown, because no mind of sufficient reason had discovered them; but they existed as truths from the very creation of matter, and now they have only been developed and invented.

So it is with Freemasonry; it, too, has had its progress. Masons are now expected to be more learned than formerly, in all that relates to the science of the Order, its origin, its history, its subjects, are now considered worthy of the attentive consideration of its disciples.

The rational explanation of our ceremonies and symbols, and their connection with ancient systems of religion and philosophy are now considered as necessary topics of inquiry for all who desire to distinguish themselves as proficient in Masonic science.

In all these things, we see a great difference between the Masons of the present and former days. In Europe a century ago, such inquiries were considered as legitimate subjects of Masonic study. Hutchison published in 1760 in England his admirable work entitled. "The Spirit of Freemasonry," in which the deep philosophy of the Institution was fairly developed with much learning and ingenuity. Preston's illustrations of Masonry printed at not a much later period also exhibit the system treated in many places in a philosophical manner. Lawrie's History of Freemasonry, published in Scotland, about the end of the last century, is a work containing much profound historical and antiquarian research.

And in the present century, the works of Oliver alone would be sufficient to demonstrate to the most cursory observer that Freemasonry has a claim to be ranked among the learned institutions of the day.

In Germany and France, the press has been borne down with the weight of abstruse works on our Order, written by men of the highest literary pretensions. It is only within a few years that Masonry has begun to assume the exalted position of a literary Institution in which the labors of our trans-Atlantic brethren had long ago placed it.

SPURIOUS FREEMASONRY.—For this term, and for the theory connected with it, we are indebted to Dr. Oliver, whose speculations led him to the conclusion that in the earlier ages of the world there were two systems of Freemasonry, the one of which, preserved by the patriarchs and their descendants, he called Primitive or Pure Freemasonry of antiquity. To comprehend this system of Oliver, and to understand his doctrine of the declension of the spurious from the primitive Freemasonry, we must remember that there were two races of men descended from the loins of Adam, whose history is as different as their characters were dissimilar. There was the virtuous race of Seth and his descendants, and the wicked one of Cain. Seth and his children down to Noah preserved the dogmas and instructions, the legends and symbols which had been received from their common progenitor, Adam; but Cain and his descendants, whose vices at length brought on the destruction of the earth, totally forgot, or greatly corrupted them.

Their Freemasonry was not the same as that of the Sethites; they distorted the truth, and varied the landmarks to suit their own profane purposes. At length the two races became blended together, the descendants of Seth becoming corrupted by their frequent communications with those of Cain, adopted their manners and soon lost the principles of the Primitive Freemasonry, which at length were confined to Noah and his three sons, who alone, in the destruction of a wicked world, were thought worthy of receiving mercy.

Noah consequently preserved the system, and was the medium of communicating it to the post-deluvian world. Hence, immediately after the Deluge, Primitive Freemasonry was the only system extant.

But this happy state of affairs was not to last. Ham, the son of Noah, who had been accursed by his father for his wickedness, had long been familiar with the corruptions of Cain, and the gradual deviations from truth which, through the influence of evil example, had crept into the system of Seth. After the deluge, he propagated the worst features of both systems among his immediate descendants.

Two sects or parties, so to speak, now arose in the world; one which preserved the great truths of religion, and consequently of Masonry, which has been handed down from Adam, Enoch and Noah;

and another, which deviated more and more from the pure original source.

On the dispersion at the Tower of Babel, the schism became still wider, and more irreconcilable. The legends of Primitive Freemasonry were altered, and its symbols perverted to a false worship.

The mysteries were dedicated to the worship of false gods, and the practice of idolatrous rites; and in the place of the pure and primitive Freemasonry, which continued to be cultivated among the patriarchal descendants of Noah, was established those mysteries of paganism to which Dr. Oliver has given the name of the "Spurious Freemasonry."

It is not to Dr. Oliver, nor to any very modern writer, that we are indebted for the idea of Masonic schism in this early age of the world. The doctrine that Masonry was lost, that is to say, lost in its purity, to the larger portion of mankind, at the Tower of Babel, is still preserved in the ritual of Ancient Craft Masonry. And in the degree of Noachites, a degree which is attached to the Scottish Rite, the fact is plainly alluded to, as, indeed, the very foundation of the degree.

Two races of Masons are there distinctly named; the Noachites, and the Hiramites; the former were the conservators of the Primitive Freemasons, as the descendants of Noah; the latter were the descendants of Hiram, who was himself of the race which had fallen into Spurious Freemasonry, but had reunited himself to the true sect at the building of King Solomon's Temple. But the inventors of the degree do not seem to have had any very precise notions in relation to this latter part of the history.

The mysteries, which constituted what has been called Spurious Freemasonry, were all more or less identical in character, varying in a few unimportant particulars attributable to the influence of local causes. Their great similarity in all important points shows their derivation from a common origin.

In the first place, they were communicated through a system of initiation, by which the aspirant was gradually prepared for the reception of their final doctrines; the rites were performed at night, and in the most retired situations, in caverns or in the deep recesses of groves and forests, and the secrets were only communicated to the initiated after the administration of an obligation.

Thus, Formicus tells us "when Orphius explained the ceremonies of his mysteries to candidates, he demanded of them, at the very entrance, an oath, under the solemn sanction of religion, that they would not betray the rites to profane ears."

And hence, as Warburton says from Horus Apollo, the "Egyptian hieroglyphic for the mysteries was a grasshopper, because that insect was supposed to have no mouth."

The ceremonies were all of a funeral character. Commencing in representations of a lugubrious description, they celebrated the legend of the death and burial of some mystical being, which was the especial object of their love and admiration. But these rites thus beginning in lamentation and typical of death, always ended in joy. The object of their sorrow was restored to life and immortality, and the latter part of the ceremonial was descriptive of his Resurrection. Hence, the great doctrines of the Mysteries were the immortality of the soul, and existence of a God.

Such, then, is the theory on the subject of what is called "Spurious Freemasonry," as taught by Oliver and the disciples of his school. Primitive Freemasonry consisted of that traditional knowledge and symbolic instruction which has been handed down from Adam, through Enoch, Noah, and the rest of the patriarchs, to the time of Solomon.

Spurious Freemasonry consisted of the doctrines and initiations practiced at first by the antediluvian descendants of Cain, and, after the dispersion at Babel, by the pagan priests and philosophers in their mysteries.

SPECULATIVE MASONRY.—The lecturers of the symbolic degrees instruct the neophyte in the difference between the operative and speculative divisions of Masonry. They tell him "we work in speculative Masonry, but our ancient brethren wrought in both operative and speculative." The distinction between an operative art and a speculative science is, therefore, familiar to all Masons from their early instructions.

To the Freemason this operative art has been symbolized in that intellectual deduction from it which has been correctly called speculative Masonry. At one time, each was an integral part of one identical system. Not that the period ever existed when every operative Mason was acquainted with or initiated into the speculative sciences. Even now, there are thousands of skilful artisans who know as little of that as they do of the Hebrew language which was spoken by its founder.

But operative Masonry was, in the inception of our history, and is, in some measure, even now, the skeleton upon which was strung the living muscles and tendons and nerves of the speculative system. It was the block of marble, rude and unpolished it may have been, from which was sculptured the life-breathing statue; that is, so far as the scientific application and the religious consecration of the rules and principles, the language, the implements and materials of operative Masonry have been introduced into the speculative science of the Order; or, in plainer words, while the body of speculative Masonry may be found in the Middle Ages, we must look to a far remoter period for that principle of the Fatherhood of God and the brotherhood of man which develops the great doctrine of the purification of the heart and the immortality of the soul—speculative Masonry, or Free Masonry, being a system of ethics, must therefore, like all other ethical systems, have its distinctive doctrines. These may be divided into three classes; viz., the moral, the religious, and the philosophical.

First. The Moral Doctrines.—These are dependent on and spring out of its character as a social institution. Hence among its numerous definitions, is one that declares it to be a "science of morality." And morality is said to be symbolically one of the precious jewels of a Master Mason.

The object of Freemasonry in this moral point of view is to carry out to their fullest practical extent those lessons of mutual love and mutual aid that are essential to the very idea of a brotherhood. There is a socialism in Freemasonry, from which spring all Masonic virtues.

> "That virtue has not left mankind,
>   Her social maxims prove;
> For stamped upon the Mason's mind
>   Are unity and love."

Thus the moral design of Freemasonry, based upon its social character, is to make men better to each other, to cultivate brotherly love and to inculcate the practice of all those virtues which are essential to the perpetuation of a brotherhood.

A man is bound by the old charges, to obey the moral law, and of this law the very keystone is the divine precept, the "Golden Rule" of our Lord, to do unto others as we would they should do unto us. To relieve the distressed, to give good council to the erring, to speak well of the absent, to observe temperance in the indulgence of appetite, to bear evil with fortitude, to be prudent in life and conversation, to dispense justice to all men, are duties that are inculcated on every Mason by the moral doctrines of his Order. These doctrines of morality are taught in all the old constitutions of the Craft.

Second. The religious doctrines of Freemasonry are very simple and self-evident. They are darkened by no perplexities of sectarian theology, but stand out in the broad light, intelligible and acceptable by all minds, for they ask only for a belief in God and in the immortality of the soul. He who denies these tenets can be no Mason.

For the religious doctrines of the Institution significantly impress them in every part of its ritual. The neophyte no sooner crosses the threshold of the Lodge but he is called upon to recognize, as his first duty, an entire trust in the superintending care and love of the Supreme Being, and the series of initiation into symbolic Masonry terminates by revealing the awful symbol of a life after death and the entrance upon immortality.

Now, this and the former class of doctrines are intimately connected and mutually dependent. For we must first know and feel the universal fatherhood of God before we can rightly appreciate the universal brotherhood of man.

Third. The philosophical doctrines of Freemasonry are scarcely less important, although they are less generally understood than either of the preceding class. The object of these philosophical doctrines is very different from that of either the moral or the religious.

For the moral and religious doctrines of the Order are intended to make men virtuous, while its philosophical doctrines are designed to make them zealous Masons. He who knows nothing of the philosophy of Freemasonry will be apt to become in time lukewarm and indifferent; but he who devotes himself to its contemplation will find an ever-increasing ardor in its study.

Now, these philosophical doctrines are
developed in that symbolism which is the especial
characteristic of Masonic teaching, and relate
altogether to the lost and recovered word, the
search after divine truth, the time and manner of
its discovery, and the reward that awaits the
faithful and successful searcher. Such a philosophy
far surpasses the abstract quiddities of
metaphysicians. It brings us into close relations to
the profound thought of the ancient world, and
makes us familiar with every subject of mental
science that lies within the grasp of the human
intellect, so that in conclusion we find that the
moral, religious and philosophical doctrines of
Freemasonry respectively relate to the social, the
eternal and intellectual progress of man.

Finally, it must be observed that while the old
operative institution abundantly taught in its
constitutions the moral and religious doctrines of
which we have been treating, it makes no reference
to the philosophical doctrines, and we find nothing
of this symbolic philosophy in the old operative
Masonry. And we may lay it down as an axiom,
that the philosophic doctrines of the Order are
altogether a development of the system, solely, of
speculative Masonry.

VISIBLE MASONRY.—In a circular published
March 18, 1775, by the Grand Orient of France,
reference is made to two divisions of the Order,
namely, visible and invisible Masonry. Did we not
know something of the Masonic contentions then
existing in France between the Lodges and the
supreme authority, we should hardly comprehend

the meaning intended to be conveyed by these words. By "invisible Masonry" they denoted that body of intelligent and virtuous Masons who, irrespective of any connection with dogmatic authorities, constituted "a mysterious and invisible society of true sons of light," who, scattered over the two hemispheres, were engaged with one heart and soul in doing everything for the glory of the Grand Architect and the good of the fellow-men. By "visible Masonry" they meant the congregation of Masons into Lodges, which were often affected by the contagious vices of the age in which they lived.

The former is perfect; the latter continually needs purification. The words were originally invented to affect a particular purpose, and to bring the recusant Lodges of France into their obedience. But they might be advantageously preserved, in the technical language of Masonry, for a more general and permanent object.

Invisible Masonry would then indicate the abstract spirit of Masonry as it has always existed, while visible Masonry would refer to the concrete form which it assumes in Lodge and Chapter organizations, and in different rites and systems.

The latter would be like the material church, or church militant; the former like the spiritual church, or church triumphant. Such terms might be found convenient to Masonic scholars and writers.

LITERATURE OF MASONRY.—Freemasonry has its literature, which has been rapidly developed in the last few decades of the present century far more than in any preceding one.

This literature is not to be found in the working of its degrees, in the initiation of its Lodges, in the diffusion of its charities, or in the extension of its fraternal ties. Of all these, although necessary and important ingredients of the Order, its literature is wholly independent.

This is connected with its ethics as a science of moral, social, and religious philosophy; with its history and archaeology, as springing up out of the past times; with its biography, as the field in which men of intellect have delighted to labor; and with its bibliology, as the record of the results of that labor.

It is connected, too, incidentally, with many other arts and sciences. Mythology affords an ample field for discussion in the effort to collate the analogies of classic myths and symbols with its own. Philosophy submits its laws for application to the origin of its mystic words, all of which are connected with its history. It has, in fine, its science and its philosophy, its poetry, and romance.

No one who has not studied the literature of Masonry can ever dream of its beauty and extent; no one who has studied it can have failed to receive the reward that it bestows.

ORIGIN OF FREEMASONRY.—The origin and source whence first sprang the institution of Freemasonry such as we now have it, has given rise to more difference of opinion and discussion among Masonic scholars, than any other topic in the literature of the Institution. Hence the charge that "The absurdities and puerilities of Freemasonry are fit only for children, and are unworthy of the time and attention of wise men."

Such is the language of its adversaries, and the apothegm is delivered with all that self-sufficiency which shows that the speaker is well satisfied with his own wisdom, and is very ready to place himself in the category of those wise men whose opinion he invokes. This charge of a puerility of design and object of Freemasonry is worth investigation.

Is it then possible that those scholars of unquestioned strength of intellect and depth of science, who have devoted themselves to the study of Masonry and who have in thousands of volumes given the result of their researches, have been altogether mistaken in the direction of their labors, and have been seeking to develop, not the principles of philosophy, but the mechanism of a toy? Or is the assertion that such is the fact a mere sophism, such as ignorance is every day uttering, and a conclusion to which men are more likely to arrive when they talk of that of which they know nothing, like the critic who reviews a book that he has never read, or the skeptic who attacks a creed that he does not comprehend?

Such claims to an inspired infallibility are not uncommon among men of unsound judgment.

Thus, when Gall and Spurzheim first gave to the world their wonderful discoveries in reference to the organization of the functions of the brain— discoveries which have since wrought a marked revolution in the science of anatomy, physiology and ethics—the Edenburg reviews attempted to demolish these philosophers and their new system, but succeeded only in exposing their own ignorance of the science they were discussing.

Time, which is continually evolving truth out of every intellectual conflict, has long since shown that the German philosophers were right, and that their Scottish critics were wrong. How common is it, even at this day, to hear men deriding alchemy as a system of folly and imposture, cultivated only by madmen and knaves, when the researches of those who have investigated the subject without prejudice, but with patient learning, have shown, without any possibility of doubt, that these old alchemists, so long the objects of derision to the ignorant, were religious philosophers, and that their science had really nothing to do with the discovery of the elixir of life or the transmutation of baser metals into gold, but that they, like the Freemasons, with whom they have a strong affinity, concealed under profound symbols, intelligible only to themselves, the search after divine truth and the doctrine of immortal life. Truth was the gold which they eliminated from all mundane things, and the immortality of the soul was the elixir of everlasting life which perpetually renewed youth, and took away the power of death.

So it is with Freemasonry. Those who abuse it

know nothing of its inner spirit, of its profound philosophy, of the pure religious life that it inculcates.

To one who is at all acquainted with its organization. Freemasonry presents itself under two different aspects:

Fist as a secret society, distinguished by a peculiar ritual.

And secondly, as a society having a philosophy on which it is founded, and which it proposes to teach its disciples.

These, by way of distinction, may be called the ritualistic and the philosophical elements of Freemasonry.

The ritualistic element of Freemasonry is that which relates to the due performance of the rites and ceremonies of the Order.

Like the rubrics of the church, which indicate when the priest and congregation shall kneel and when they shall stand, it refers to questions such as these: What words shall be used in such a place, and what ceremony shall be observed on such an occasion? It belongs entirely to the inner organization of the institution, or to the manner in which its services shall be conducted, and is interesting or important only to its own members.

The language of its ritual, or the form of its ceremonies, has nothing more to do with the philosophic designs of Freemasonry than the rubrics of a church have to do with the religious creed professed by that church; it might at any time be changed in its most material points, without in the slightest degree affecting the essential character of the institution.

A great many theories have been advanced by Masonic writers as to the real origin of the Institution, as to the time when and the place where it first took its birth. Writers on the history of Freemasonry have at different times attributed its origin to the following sources, in the following order, viz.: To the patriarchal religion, to the Ancient Pagan Mysteries, to the Temple of King Solomon, to the Crusaders, to the Knights Templar's, to the Roman Colleges of Architecture, to the operative Masons of the Middle Ages, to the Rosecrucians of the sixteenth century. To Oliver Cromwell, for the advancement of his political schemes; to the Pretender for the restoration of the House of Stuart to the British throne; to Sir Christopher Wren, at the building of St. Paul's Cathedral; to Dr. Dedaquliers and his associates in the year 1717. But whatever theory may be selected, and wheresoever, on whensoever it may be supposed to have received its birth, one thing is certain, namely, that for generations past and yet within the records of history, it has, unlike other mundane things, presented to the world as unchanged organization—in teaching divine truth by a mythical initiation and secret symbols. Take, for instance, the theory which traces it back to one of the most recent periods, that, namely, which places the organization of the Order of Freemasons at the building of the Cathedral of Strasburg, in the year 1275. During all the time that has since elapsed, full six hundred years, how has Freemasonry presented itself? Why as a brotherhood organized and controlled by a secret discipline, engaged in important agricultural labors, and combining with its operative tasks speculations of great religious import, if we see any change, it is simply this, that when the necessity no longer existed, the operative element was laid aside, and the speculative only was retained, but with a scrupulous preservation (as if it were for purposes of identification) of the technical language, the rules and regulations, the working-tools and the discipline of the operative art. The material only on which they wrought was changed. The disciples and followers of Erwin of Steinbach, the master builder of Strasburg, were engaged, under the influence of a profoundly religious sentiment, in the construction of a material edifice to the glory of God. The more modern workers in Freemasonry are under the same religious influence, engaged in the construction of spiritual temples.

But this is not all; this society, or brotherhood, or con-fraternity, as it might more appropriately be called, is distinguished from all other associations by the possession of certain symbols, myths, and, above all else, a golden legend, all of which are directed to the purification of the heart, to the elevation of the mind, and to the development of the great doctrine of immortality.

Now, the question when and where these symbols, myths and legends arose is one that is well worth the investigation of all Masons, because it is intimately connected with the history of the human intellect, as well as of the origin of Ancient Craft Masonry. Did the stonemasons and building corporations of the Middle Ages invent them?

Certainly not, for they are found in organizations that existed ages previously.

The Greeks of Eleusis taught the same dogma of immortal life in the same symbolic mode, and their legend, if it differed from the Masonic in its accidents, was precisely identical in its substance. For Hiram there was Dionysus, for the acacia the myrtle; but there were the same mourning, the same discovery, the same rejoicing because what had been lost was found, and then the same ineffable light, and the same sacred teaching of the name of God and the soul's immortality.

And so as an ancient orator, who had passed through one of these old Greek Lodges—for such without much violence of language they may be called—declared that those who have endured the initiation into these mysteries entertain better hopes both of the ends of life and of the eternal future.

Is not this the very object and design of the legend of the Master's degree? And this same peculiar form of symbolic initiation is to be found among the old Egyptians and in the Island of Samothracia, thousands of years before the light of Christianity dawned upon the world to give the seal of its Master and Founder of the divine truth of the Resurrection.

This will not, it is true, prove the descent of Freemasonry, as now organized—because it has ever been a progressive institution in perfecting its organization—from the religious mysteries of antiquity, although this is one of the theories of its origin entertained and defended by scholars of no mean pretension.

But it will prove an identity of design in the moral and intellectual organization of all these institutions and it will give the Masonic student subjects for profound study when he asks the interesting question: Whence came these symbols, myths and legends? Who invented them? How and why have they been preserved?

Looking back into the remotest days of recorded history, he finds priesthood in an island of Greece, and another on the banks of the Nile, teaching the existence of a future life by symbols and legends, which conveyed the lesson in a peculiar mode.

And now, after thousands of years have elapsed, we find the same symbolic and legendary mode of instruction, for the same purpose, preserved in the depository of what is comparatively a modern institution.

And between these two extremes of the long past and the present now, we find the intervening period occupied by similar associations, succeeding each other from time to time, and spreading over different countries, but all engaged in the same symbolic instruction, with substantially the same symbols and the same mythical history.

Does not all this present a problem in moral and intellectual philosophy, and in the archaeology of ethics which is well worthy of an attempted solution? How unutterably puerile seem the objections of a few contracted minds, guided only by prejudice, when we consider the vast questions of deep interest that are connected with Freemasonry as a part of those great brotherhoods that have filled the world for so many ages. So far back, indeed, that some philosophic historians have supposed that they must have derived their knowledge of the doctrines which they taught in their mystic assemblies from direct revelation through an ancient priesthood that gives no other evidence of its former existence but the results which it produced.

Man needs something more than the gratification of his animal wants. The mind requires food as well as the body, and nothing can better give that mental nutriment than the investigation of subjects which relate to the progress of the intellect and the growth of the religious sentiment.

Looking, then, upon Freemasonry as one of those associations which furnish the evidence and the example of the progress of man in intellectual, moral and religious development, it may be well claimed for it that its design, its history, and its philosophy, so far from being puerile, are well entitled to the respect of the world, and are worth the careful research of scholars.

ETHICS OF FREEMASONRY.—As Freemasonry claims to be a religion, in so far as it is founded on a recognition of the relations of man and God, and a philosophy in so far as it is engaged in speculations on the nature of man, as an immortal, social and responsible being, the ethics of Freemasonry will be both religious and philosophical.

The symbolism of Masonry, which is its peculiar

mode of instruction, inculcates all the duties which we owe to God, as being His children, and to men as being their brethren. "There is," says Dr. Oliver, "scarcely a point of duty or morality which man has been presumed to owe to God, his neighbor, or himself under the patriarchal, the Mosaic, or the Christian dispensations, which, in the construction of our symbolical system, has been left untouched."

Hence, he says that those symbols all unite to form "a code of moral and theological philosophy," the term of which expression would have been better if he had called it "a code of philosophical and theological ethics."

At a very early period of his initiation the Mason is instructed that he owes a threefold duty—to God, his neighbor, and himself, and the inculcation of these duties constitutes the ethics of Freemasonry.

Now, the Tetragammaton, the letter G. and many other symbols of like character impressively inculcate the lesson that there is a God in whom "we live, and move, and have our being," and of whom the apostle, quoting from the Greek poet, tells us that "we are his offspring." To him, then, as the Universal Father, do the ethics of Freemasonry teach us that we owe the duty of loving and obedient children.

And then the vast extent of the Lodge, making the whole world the common home of all Masons, and the temple in which we all labor for the building up of our bodies as a spiritual house, are significant symbols, which teach us that we are not only the children of the Father, but fellow-workers, laboring together in the same task and owing a common servitude to God as the Grand Architect of the universe—the Algabil or Master Builder of the world and all that is therein; and thus those symbols of a joint labor, for a joint purpose, tell us that there is a brotherhood of man; to that brotherhood do the ethics of Freemasonry teach us that we owe the duty of fraternal kindness in all its manifold phases.

And so we find that the ethics of Freemasonry are really founded on the two great ideas of the universal fatherhood of God, and the universal brotherhood of man.

TRADITION.—There are two kinds of tradition in Masonry:

First. Those which detail events either historically, authentic in part or in whole, or consisting altogether of arbitrary fiction, and intended simply to convey an allegorical or symbolic meaning, and are synonymous with legend, or a mental representation of a truth.

Second. The traditions which control and direct the usage of the "Fraternity" and constitute the unwritten law, and are almost wholly applicable to its ritual. Although they are sometimes of use in the interpretation of doubtful points in its written law, for between the written and unwritten law the latter is always paramount in Masonry. And Cicero has wisely said, that "a well constituted commonwealth must be governed, not by the written law alone, but also by the unwritten law or traditions of usage."

This maxim is not less true in Masonry, no matter what change may be made in its statutes and regulations of to-day and its recent customs. There is no danger of losing the identity of its modern with its ancient form and spirit while its traditions are recognized and maintained. Thus we can understand how important those traditions of Masonry which prescribe its ritual observances and ancient landmarks should be thoroughly understood, because it is only by attention to them that uniformity in the esoteric instruction and work of the Order can be preserved. Therefore, our ancient landmarks we are carefully to observe, and not suffer them on any pretense to be infringed or countenance any deviation from our established customs.

For the treachery of memory, the weakness of judgment and the fertility of the imagination will lead men to forget, to diminish, or to augment the teaching of any system not prescribed within certain limits by a written rule.

But it is a matter of congratulation that the variation of the phraseology of the lectures, or in the forms and ceremonies of initiation, so long as they do not trench the foundation of symbolism on which the sciences and philosophy of Masonry are built, can produce no other effect than a temporary inconvenience, for a variation in the ritual can never be such as to destroy the true identity of the institution; its profound dogmas of the "unity of God and the eternal life," and of the universal "brotherhood of man" taught in its symbolic method, will forever shine out pre-eminently above all temporary changes of phraseology. If uniformity of work is never attained, uniformity of design, and uniformity of character will forever preserve Freemasonry from disintegration, for it was founded upon a principle implanted in man by Jehovah Himself that is as immortal as the human soul.

While the traditions that have been orally handed down to us from our forefathers from generation to generation clearly demonstrate and verify the fact that from the very beginning of the race there existed a disposition of the "human heart to nourish the belief in a future life, and the immortality of the soul.

LANDMARKS.—In the discussion of the question what are and what are not the landmarks of Masonry, there has been much diversity of opinion among Masonic writers. Until the year 1858 no attempt had been made by any Masonic writer to distinctly enumerate the landmarks of Freemasonry, and to give to them a comprehensible form.

In October of that year, Dr. Mackey published in the American Quarterly Review of Freemasonry an article on "The Foundation of Masonic Law," which contained a distinct enumeration of the landmarks. It has since been very generally adopted by the Fraternity. According to this recapitulation, the result of much labor and research, the landmarks are twenty-five in number, the general principles of which are as follows:

1. The marks of recognition are, of all the landmarks, the most legitimate and unquestioned. They admit of no variation.

2. The division of symbolic Masonry into three degrees, is a landmark that has been better

preserved than almost any other, although even here the mischievous spirit of innovation has left its traces, and by the disruption of its concluding portion from the third degree, a want of uniformity has been created in respect to the final teaching of the Master's order, and the Royal Arch of England, Scotland, Ireland and America, and the "higher degrees" of France and Germany, are all made to differ in the mode in which they lead the neophyte to the great consummation of all symbolic Masonry. In 1813 the Grand Lodge of England vindicated the ancient landmarks, by solemnly enacting that Ancient Craft Masonry consisted of the degrees of Entered Apprentice, Fellow Craft and Master Mason, including the Holy Royal Arch.

3. The legend of the third degree is an important landmark, the integrity of which has been well preserved. There is no rite of Masonry practiced in any country or language, in which the essentials of this legend are not taught. The lectures may vary, and indeed are continually changing, but the legend has ever remained substantially the same. And it is necessary that it should be so, for the legend of the Temple Builder constitutes the very essence and identity of Masonry. Any rite which should exclude it, or materially alter it, would at once, by that exclusion or alteration, cease to be a Masonic rite.

4. The government of the Fraternity by a presiding officer called a "Grand Master" is a fourth landmark of the Order.

Many persons suppose that the election of the Grand Master is held in consequence of a law or regulation of the Grand Lodge. Such, however, is not the case. The office is indebted for its existence to a landmark of the Order.

Grand Masters, or persons performing the functions under a different but equivalent title, are to be found in the records of the Institution long before Grand Lodges were established; and if the present system of legislative government by Grand Lodges were to be abolished, a Grand Master would still be necessary.

5. The prerogative of the Grand Master to preside over every assembly of the Craft, wheresoever and whensoever held, is a fifth landmark.

6. The prerogative of the Grand Master to grant dispensations for conferring degrees at irregular times is another landmark, which Dr. Mackey considers very important. This prerogative, he says, the Grand Master possessed before the enactment of the law requiring probation, and as no statute can impair his prerogative, and he still retains the power.

7. The prerogative of the Grand Master to give dispensations for opening and holding Lodges is another landmark.

8. The prerogative of the Grand Master to make Masons at sight is a landmark closely connected with the preceding one; but used only under extraordinary circumstances.

9. The necessity for Masons to congregate in Lodges is another landmark. It is not to be understood by this that any ancient landmark has directed that permanent organization of subordinate Lodges which constitutes one of the features of the Masonic system as it now prevails. But the landmarks of the Order always prescribed that

Masons should from time to time congregate together for the purpose of labor and that these congregations should be called Lodges.

10. The government of the Craft, when so congregated in a Lodge, by a Master and two Wardens, is also a landmark. The presence of a Master and two Wardens is as essential to the valid organization of a Lodge as a warrant or charter is at the present day.

11. The necessity that every Lodge, when congregated, should be duly tiled is an important landmark of the Institution which is never neglected.

12. The right of every Mason to be represented in all general meetings of the Craft, and to instruct his representatives, is a twelfth landmark.

13. The right of every Mason to appeal from the decision of his brethren in Lodge convened, to the Grand Lodge of Masons, is a landmark highly essential to the preservation of justice and the prevention of oppression.

14. The right of every Mason to visit and sit in every regular Lodge is an unquestionable landmark of the Order. This right, may of course, is forfeited by various circumstances.

15. It is a landmark of the Order that no visitor unknown to the brethren present, or to some one of them, as a Mason, can enter a Lodge without first passing an examination according to ancient usage.

16. No lodge can interfere with the business of another Lodge.

17. It is a landmark that every Freemason is amenable to the laws and regulations of the Masonic jurisdiction in which he resides, and this although

he may not be a member of any Lodge.

18. Certain qualifications of candidates for initiation are derived from a landmark of the Order. "Only candidates may know that no Master should take an Apprentice unless he has sufficient employment for him, and unless he be a perfect youth," having no maim or defect in his body that may render him incapable of learning the art of serving his Master's Lord and of being made a brother.

19. A belief in the existence of God as the Grand Architect of the universe is one of the most important landmarks of the Order. It has always been admitted that a denial of the existence of a Superintending Power is an absolute disqualification for initiation.

20. Subsidiary to this belief in God, as a landmark of the Order, is the belief of a resurrection to a future life.

21. It is a landmark that a "Book of the Law" shall constitute an indispensable part of the furniture of every Lodge. It is not absolutely required that everywhere the Old and New Testament shall be used. The "Book of the Law" is that volume which, by the religion of the country, is believed to contain the revealed will of the Grand Architect of the universe; hence in all Lodges in Christian countries, the "Book of the Law" is composed of the Old and New Testaments; where Judaism is the prevailing faith, the Old Testament alone would be sufficient; and in Mohammedan countries and among Mohammedan Masons, the Koran might be substituted. The

landmark, therefore, requires that a "Book of the Law," a religious code of some kind, purporting to be an exemplar of the revealed will of God, shall form an essential part of the furniture of every Lodge.

22. The Equality of all Masons is another landmark of the Order, which implies that, as children of one great Father, we meet in the Lodge upon the level; that on that level we are all traveling to one predestined goal, from which there is no return.

23. The secrecy of the institution is another and most important landmark. The form of secrecy is a form inherent in it, existing with it from its very foundation, and secured to it by its ancient landmarks.

24. The foundation of a speculative science upon an operative art, and the symbolic use and explanation of the terms of that art, for the purpose of a religious or moral teaching, constitutes another landmark of the Order.

25. The last and crowning landmark of all is that these landmarks can never be changed. As they were received from our predecessors, we are bound by the most solemn obligations of duty to transmit them to our successors.

I think another important landmark was never to confer a degree in day-time. In the Ancient Mysteries they were always conferred at night.

GEOMETRY.—In the modern rituals, geometry is said to be the basis on which the superstructure of Masonry is erected, and in the old constitutions of the mediaeval Freemasons of England, the most prominent place of all the sciences is given to geometry, which is made synonymous with Masonry.

Thus, in the Halliwell MS., which dates not later than the latter part of the fourteenth century, the constitutions of Masonry are called "the constitution of the art of geometry according to Euclid," the words geometry and Masonry being, used indifferently throughout the document; and in the Harleian MS. it is said, "Thus the Craft geometry was governed there, and that worthy Master (Euclid) gave it the name of Geometry, and it is called Masonry in this land long after." In another part of the same MS. it is thus defined: "The fifth science is called Geometry, and it teaches a man to mete and measure of the earth and other things, which science is Masonry."

The Egyptians were undoubtedly one of the first nations who cultivated geometry as a science. "It was not less useful and necessary to them," as Goquest observes, "in the affairs of life, than agreeable to their speculative philosophical genius." From Egypt, which was the parent both of the science and the mysteries of the pagan world, it passed over into the other continents; and geometry and operative Masonry have ever been found together, the latter carrying into execution those designs which were first traced according to the principles of the former.

Speculative Masonry is, in like manner, intimately connected with geometry, in deference to our operative ancestors, and, in fact, as a necessary result of our close connection with them. Speculative Masonry derives its most important symbols from this parent science.

Hence, it is not strange that Euclid, the most famous of geometricians, should be spoken of in all the old records as a founder of Masonry in Egypt, and that a special legend should have been invented in honor of his memory.

EUCLID, LEGEND OF.—All the old manuscript constitutions contain the well-known "legend of Euclid," whose name is presented to us as Worthy Clerk Euclid" in every conceivable variety of corrupted form. The Dowland manuscript, although apparently written in the seventeenth century, is believed on good authority to be only a copy, in more modern and more intelligible language, of an earlier manuscript of the year 1530, in the following words:

"Moreover, when Abraham and Sarah his wife went into Egypt, there he taught the seven sciences to the Egyptians, and he had a worthy scoller that height Ewclyde and he learned right well, and was a master of all the vii sciences liberal. And in his days it befell that the lord and the estates of the realms had soe many sons that they had gotten some by their wives and some by other ladies of the realm; for that land is a hot land and a plenteous of generation. And they had not competent live ode to find with their children; wherefore they made much care.

"And the king of the land made a great council and a parliament, to-wit, how they might find their children honestly as gentlemen; and they could find no manner of good way. And then they did cry through the entire realm, if there were any man could inform them, that he should be so rewarded for his travail that he should hold him pleased.

"After that the cry was made, then came this worthy Clerk Eweclyde, and said to the king and to all his great lords: if ye will take me your children to govern, and to teach them one of the seven sciences, wherewith they may live honestly as gentlemen should, under a condition that yee will grant me and them a commission that I may have power to rule them after the manner that the science ought to be ruled. And that the king and all his counsel granted to him anon, and sealed their commission.

"And thus this worthy took to him these lords' sons and taught them the science of Geometry in practice, for to work in stones all manner of worthy work that belonged to building churches, temples, castles, towers and manors, and all other manner of buildings, and he gave them in charge on this manner."

Here follows the usual "charges" of a Freemason as given in all the old constitutions; and then the legend concludes in these words: "And thus was the science grounded there; and that worthy master Ewclyde gave it the name of Geometry. And now it is called through all this land Masonry."

This legend, considered historically, is certainly

very absurd, and the anachronism which makes
Euclid the contemporary of Abraham adds, if
possible, to the absurdity. But, interpreted as all
Masonic legends should be interpreted, as merely
intended to convey a Masonic truth in symbolic
language, it loses its absurdity, and becomes
invested with an importance that we should not
otherwise attach to it.

Euclid is here very appropriately used as a type
of geometry, that science of which he was so
eminent a teacher, and the myth or legend then
symbolizes the fact that there was in Egypt a close
connection between that science and the great
moral and religious system which was among the
Egyptians, as well as other ancient nations what
Freemasonry is at the present day—a secret
institution, established for the inculcation of the
same principles, and inculcating them in the same
symbolic manner. So interpreted, this legend
corresponds to all the developments of Egyptian
history, which teaches us how close a connection
exists in that country between the religious and
scientific systems.

Thus Kennick (Anct. Egypt, i. 383) tells us that
"When we read of foreigners (in Egypt) being
obliged to submit to painful and tedious ceremonies
of initiation, it was not that they might learn the
secret meaning of the rites of Osiris or Isis, but
that they might partake of the knowledge of
astronomy, physics, geometry and theology."

This is a myth or legend that is almost wholly
unhistorical, and which has been invented only for
the purpose of enunciating and illustrating a

particular thought or dogma, and therefore is clearly a "philosophic myth."

ESSENES.—Lawrie, in his History of Freemasonry, in replying to the objection, that if the Fraternity of Freemasons had flourished during the reign of Solomon, it would have existed in Judea in after ages, attempts to meet the argument by showing that there did exist after the building of the Temple, an association of men resembling Freemasons in the nature, ceremonies and object of the institution. The association to which he here alludes is that of the Essenes, whom he subsequently describes as an ancient fraternity originating from an association of architects who were connected with the building of Solomon's Temple.

Lawrie evidently seeks to connect historically the Essenes with the Freemasons, and to impress his readers with the identity of the two institutions. "I am not prepared," says Dr. Mackey, "to go so far; but there is such a similarity between the two, and such remarkable coincidences in many of their usages, as to render this Jewish sect an interesting study to every Freemason to whom, therefore, some account of the usages and doctrines of this holy brotherhood will not, perhaps, be unacceptable.

At the time of the advent of Jesus Christ there were three religious sects in Judea—the Pharisees, the Sadduces, and the Essenes; and to one of these sects every Jew was compelled to unite himself. The Savior has been supposed by many writers to have been an Essene, because, while repeatedly denouncing the errors of the two other sects, he has nowhere uttered a word of censure against the Essenes, and because, also, many of the precepts of the New Testament are to be found among the laws of this sect.

In ancient authors such as Josephus, Philoporphyry, Eusilius and Pliny, who have had occasion to refer to the subject, the notices of this singular sect have been so brief and unsatisfactory that modern writers have found great difficulty in properly understanding the true character of Essenism. And yet our antiquaries never weary of the task of investigation. They have at length, within a recent period, succeeded in eliciting from the collations of all that has been previously written on the subject, very correct details of the doctrines and practices of the Essenes. Of these writers, probably none have been more successful than the laborious German critics Frankel and Rappaport. Their investigations have been ably and thoroughly condensed by Dr. Christian D. Ginsburg, whose essay on "The Essenes, Their History and Doctrines," has supplied the most material facts contained in the present article.

It is impossible to ascertain the precise date of the development of Essenism, as a distinct organization. The old writers are so exaggerated in their statements that they are worth nothing as historical authorities. Philo says, for instance, that Moses himself instituted the order; and Josepnus, that it existed ever since the ancient time of the fathers; while Pliny asserts with mythical liberality, that it has continued for thousands of ages. Dr. Ginsburg thinks that Essenism was a gradual development of the prevalent religious notions out of Judaism, a theory which Dr. Dollin ger repudiates.

But Rappaport, who was a learned Jew, thoroughly conversant with the Talmud and other Hebrew writings, and who is hence called by Ginsburg "the Corypheus of Jewish critics," asserts that the Essenes were not a distinct sect, in the strict sense of the word, but simply an order of Judaism, and that there never was a rupture between them and the rest of the Jewish community.

This theory is sustained by Frankel, a learned German, who maintains that the Essenes were simply an intensification of the Pharisaic sect, and that they were the same as the Chasidion, whom Lawrie calls the Kassideans, and of whom he speaks as the guardians of King Solomon's Temple. If this view be the correct one—and there is no good reason to doubt it—then there will be another feature of resemblance and coincidence between the Freemasons and the Essenes; for, as the latter was not a religious sect, but merely a development of Judaism, an order of Jews entertaining no heterodox opinions, but simply carrying out the religious dogmas of their faith with an unusual strictness of observance, so are the Freemasons not a religious sect, but simply a development of the religious idea of the age. The difference, however, between Freemasonry and Essenism lies in the spirit of universal tolerance prominent in the one and absent in the other. Freemasonry is Christian as to its membership in general, but recognizing and tolerating in its bosom all other religions. Essenism, on the contrary, was exclusively and entirely Jewish in its membership, its usages, and its doctrines.

The Essenes are first mentioned by Josephus as existing in the days of Jonathan the Macalaean, one hundred and sixty-six years before Christ. The Jewish historian repeatedly speaks of them at subsequent periods; and there is no doubt that they constituted one of the three sects which divided the Jewish religious world at the advent of our Savior, and of this sect he is supposed, as has been already said, to have been a member.

The Essenes were so strict in the observance of the Mosaic laws of purity, that they were compelled for the purpose of avoiding contamination, to withdraw altogether from the rest of the Jewish nation and to form a separate community, which thus became a brotherhood.

The distinctive ordinances of the brotherhood and the mysteries connected with the Tetragrammaton and the angelic worlds were the prominent topics of Sabbatical instruction. In particular did they pay attention to the mysteries connected with the Tetragrammaton, or the Shemhamphorash, the expository name, and the other names of God which played so important a part in the mystical theosophy of the Jewish Kabbalists, a great deal of which has descended to the Freemasonry of our own day.

Lawrie, in his History of Freemasonry, gives, on the authority of Pictet of Basnage, and of Philo, the following condensed usages of the Essenes:

"When a candidate was proposed for admission the strictest scrutiny was made into his character. If his life had hitherto been exemplary, and if he appeared capable of curbing his passions and regulating his conduct according to the virtuous though austere maxims of their order, he was presented, at the expiration of his novitate, with a white garment as an emblem of the regularity of his conduct and the purity of his heart.

"A solemn oath was then administered to him, that he would never divulge the mysteries of the order that he would make no innovations on the doctrines of the society, and that he would continue in that honorable course of piety and virtue which he had begun to pursue.

"Like Freemasons, they instructed the young member in the knowledge which they derived from their ancestors. They admitted no women into their order. They had particular signs for recognizing each other, which have a strong resemblance to those of Freemasons. They had colleges or places of retirement, where they resorted to practice their rites and settle the affairs of the society.

"They abolished all distinctions of rank; and if preference was ever given, it was given to piety, liberality, and virtue. Treasurers were appointed in every town, to supply the wants of indigent strangers."

Lawrie thinks that this remarkable coincidence between the chief features of the Masonic and Essenan fraternities, can be accounted for only by referring them to the same origin; and to sustain this view, he attempts to trace them to the Kassideans, or Assideans, more properly the Chasidim, "an association of architects who were connected with the building of Solomon's Temple." But, aside from the consideration that there is no evidence that the Chasidim were a body of architects—for they were really a sect of Jewish Puritans, who held the Temple in especial honor—we can not conclude, from a mere coincidence of doctrines and usages, that the origin of the Essenes and the Freemasons is identical. Such a course of reasoning would place the Pythagorans in the same category, a theory that has been rejected by the best modern critics.

The truth appears to be that the Essenes, the school of Pythagoras, and the Freemasons, derive their similarity from that spirit of brotherhood which has prevailed in all ages of the civilized world, the inherent principle of which, as the results of any fraternity—all the members of which are engaged in the same pursuit and assenting to the same religious creed—are brotherly love, charity, and that secrecy which gives them their ties, ancient or modern, these "remarkable cointies, ancient and modern, these "remarkable coincidences" will be found.

ROMAN COLLEGES OF ARTIFICERS.—It was the German writers on the history of the Institution, such as Krause, Heldman and some others, who first discovered, or at least first announced to the world the connection that existed between the Roman Colleges of Architecture and the Society of Freemasons.

The theory of Krause on the subject is to be found principally in his well known work entitled "Dei Dreialtesten Kunsterkunden." He there advances the doctrine that Freemasonry as it now exists, is indebted for all its characteristics, religious and social, political and professional, its interior organization, its modes of thought and action, and its very design and object, to the Collegia Artificum of the Romans, passing with but little characteristic changes through the "Architectural Gilds" of the Middle Ages up to the English organization of the year 1717. So that he claims an almost absolute identity between the Roman Colleges of Numa, seven hundred years before Christ, and the Lodges of the nineteenth century. We need not, according to his view, go any farther back in history, nor look to any other series of events, nor trouble ourselves with any other influences for the origin and the character of Freemasonry.

This theory, which is, perhaps, the most popular one on the subject, requires careful examination, and in the prosecution of such an inquiry the first thing to be done will be to investigate the true character and condition of these Roman Colleges.

It is to Numa, the second king of Rome, those historians, following after Plutarch, ascribe the first organization of the Roman Colleges; although, as Numan reasonably conjectures, it is probable that similar organizations previously existed among the Alban population, and embraced the resident Tuscan artificers. But it is admitted that Numa gave to them that form which they always subsequently maintained.

Numa, on ascending the throne, found the citizens divided into various nationalities, derived from the Romans, the Sabines, and inhabitants of neighboring smaller and weaker towns, who by choice or compulsion had removed their residence to the bank of the Tiber. Hence resulted a disseverance of sentiment and feeling, and constant tendency to disunion. Now, the object of Numa was to obliterate these contending elements and to establish a perfect identity of national feeling, so that, to use the language of Plutarch, "the distribution of the people might become a harmonious mingling of all with all."

For this purpose, he established one common religion, and divided the citizens into curias and tribes, each curias and tribe being composed of an admixture indifferently of Romans, Sabines, and the other denizens of Rome.

Directed by the same political sagacity, he distributed the artisans into various guilds or corporations under the name of colleges. To each collegium was assigned the artisans of a particular profession, and each had its own regulations, both secular and religious. These colleges grew with the growth of the republic, and although Numa had originally established but nine, namely, the College of Musicians, of Goldsmiths, of Carpenters, of Dyers, of Shoemakers, of Farmers, of Smiths, of Potters, and a ninth, composed of all artisans not embraced under either of the preceding heads, they were subsequently greatly increased in number. Eighty years before the Christian era they were abolished or sought to be abolished by a decree of the Senate, who looked with jealousy on their political influence, but thirty years afterwards they were revived and new ones established by a law of the tribune Clodius, which repealed the senatus consultum. They continued to exist under the Empire, were extended into the provinces, and even outlasted the Roman power.

And now let us inquire into the form and organization of these colleges, and, in so doing, trace the analogy between them and the Masonic Lodges, if any such analogy exists.

The first regulation, which was an indispensable one, was that no college could consist of less than three members. So indispensable was this rule, that the expression, "Three make a college," became a maxim of the civil law. So rigid, too, was the application of this rule, that the body of consuls, although calling each other "colleges" and possessing and exercising all collegiate rites, were, because they consisted only of two members, never legally recognized as a college. The reader will very readily be struck with the identity of this regulation of the colleges and that of Freemasonry, which with equal rigor requires three Masons to constitute a Lodge. The college and the Lodge each demanded three members to make it legal; a greater number might give it more efficiency, but it could not render it more legitimate. This then is the first analogy between the Lodges of Freemasons and the Roman Colleges. These colleges had their appropriate officers, who very singularly were assimilated in stations and duties to the officers of a Masonic Lodge. Each college was presided over by a chief or president, whose title of Magister is exactly translated by the

English word Master. The next officers were the Decuriones. They were analogous to the Masonic "Wardens," for each Decurio presided over a section or division of the colleges, just as in the most ancient English and in the present Continental ritual, we find the Lodge divided into two sections or "columns," over each of which one of the Wardens presided, through whom the commands of the Master were extended to "the brethren of his column." There was also in the colleges a Scribe, or "Secretary," who recorded its proceedings; a Thesaurensis or "Treasurer," who had charge of the common chest; a Tabularius, or Keeper of the Archives, equivalent to the modern "Archivist;" and lastly, as these colleges combined a peculiar religious worship with their operative labors, there was in each of them a Sacerdos, or Priest, who conducted the religious ceremonies, and was thus exactly equivalent to the "Chaplain" of a Masonic Lodge. In all this we find another analogy between these ancient institutions and our Masonic bodies.

Another analogy will be found in the distribution or division of classes in the Roman Colleges. As the Masonic Lodges have their Master Masons, their Fellow Crafts, and their Apprentices, so the colleges had their Seniores, "Elders," or chief men of the trade, and their journeymen and apprentices. The members did not, it is true, like the Freemasons, call themselves "brothers," because this term, first adopted in the guilds or corporations of the Middle Ages, is the offspring of a Christian sentiment; but as Krause remarks, these colleges were in general conducted after the pattern or model of a family; and hence the appellation of "brother" would now and then be found among the family appellations.

The partly religious character of the Roman Colleges of Artificers constitutes a very peculiar analogy between them and the Masonic Lodges. The history of these colleges shows that an ecclesiastical character was bestowed upon them at the very time of their organization by Numa. Many of the workshops of these artificers were erected in the vicinity of temples, and their cura, or place of meeting, was generally in some way connected with a temple. The deity to whom such temple was consecrated was peculiarly worshiped by the members of the adjacent college, and became the patron god of their trade or art. In time when the pagan religion was abolished and the religious character of these colleges was changed the pagan gods gave way, through the influence of the new religion, to Christian saints, one of whom was always adopted as the patron of the modern guilds, which in the Middle Ages took the place of the Roman Colleges; and hence the Freemasons derive the distinction of their Lodges to Saint John from a similar custom among the corporations of builders.

These colleges held secret meetings, in which the business transacted consisted of the initiation of neophytes into their fraternity, and of mystical and esoteric instructions to their apprentices and journeymen. They were in this respect secret societies like the Masonic Lodges.

Finally, it is said by Krause, that these colleges of workmen made a symbolic use of the implements of their art or profession; in other words, that they cultivated the science of symbolism, and in this respect, therefore, more than in any other, is there a striking analogy between the Collegiate and the Masonic Institutions.

The statement can not be doubted, for as the organization of the colleges partook—as has already been shown—of a religious character, and, as it is admitted that all the religion of paganism was eminently and almost entirely symbolic, it must follow that any association which was based upon or cultivated the religious mystological sentiment must cultivate also the principle of symbolism.

In this form, the organization, the mode of government, and the usages of the Roman Colleges, there is an analogy between them and the modern Masonic Lodges which is evidently, according to their history, more than accidental. It may be that long after the dissolution of the colleges, Freemasonry, in the establishment of their Lodges, designedly adopted the collegiate organization as a model after which to frame its own system; or it may be that the resemblance has been the result of a slow but inevitable growth of a succession of associations arising out of each other, at the head of which stands the Roman Colleges.

We have now reached recent historical ground, and can readily trace these associations of builders to the establishment of the Grand Lodge of England at London, in 1717, when the Lodges abandoned their operative characters and became exclusively speculative (see Revival).

The record of the continued existence of Lodges of Free and Accepted Masons, from that day to this, in every civilized country of the world, is in the hand of every Masonic student. To repeat it would be a tedious work of supererogation.

And now what is the necessary deduction? It cannot be denied that Krause is correct in his theory that the incunabula—the cradle or birthplace—of the modern Masonic Lodges, is to be found in the Roman Colleges of Architects.

That theory is correct, if we look only to the outward form and mode of working of the Lodges. To the colleges are they indebted for everything that distinguishes them as a guild or corporation.

But when we view Freemasonry in a higher aspect, when we look at it as a science of symbolism—which none can deny—the whole of which symbolism is directed to but one point, namely, the elucidation of the great doctrine of the immortality of the soul, and the teaching of the two lives, the present and the future, we must go beyond the Colleges of Rome, which were only operative associations, to that other type to be found in the Ancient Mysteries, where precisely the same doctrine was taught, precisely in the same manner. Krause does not, it is true, altogether omit a reference to the Priests of Greece, who, he thinks, were in some way the original whence the Roman Colleges derived their existence; but he has not pressed the point with the pertenacity which its importance requires. He gives in his theory a preeminence to the colleges to which Dr. Mackey says, "they are not in truth entitled."

REVIVAL.—The occurrences which took place in the city of London in the year 1717, when that important body which has since been known as the Grand Lodge of England was organized, had been always known in Masonic history as the "Revival of Masonry." Anderson, in the first edition of the "Constitutions," published in 1723, speaks of the brethren having revived the drooping Lodge of London, but he makes no other reference to the transaction. In his second edition, published in 1738, he is more diffuse, and the account there given is the only authority we possess of the organization made in 1717. Preston and all subsequent writers have derived their authority from Anderson. The transactions are thus detailed by Preston, whose account is preferred, as containing a more succinct form of all that Anderson has more profusely detailed:

"On the occasion of George I., the Masons in London and its environs, finding themselves deprived of Sir Christopher Wren and their annual meetings discontinued, resolved to cement themselves under a new Grand Master, and to revive the communications and annual festivals of the Society. With this view, the Lodges at the Goose and Gridiron, in St. Paul's Churchyard; the Crown, in Parker's Lane; the Apple-Tree Tavern, in Charles Street, Convent Garden; and the Rummer and Grape Tavern, in Channel Row, Westminster, the only four Lodges in being in the south of England at that time, with some other old brethren, met at the Apple-Tree Tavern, above mentioned, in February, 1717, and having voted the oldest Master Mason then present into the chair, constituted themselves a Grand Lodge, pro tempore, in due form. At this meeting it was resolved to hold quarterly communications of the Fraternity, and to hold the next annual assembly and feast on the 24th of June, at the Goose and Gridiron, in St. Paul's Churchyard (in compliment to the oldest Lodge, which then met there), for the purpose of electing a Grand Master among themselves, till they should have the honor of a noble brother at their head. Accordingly, on St. John the Baptist day, 1717, in the third year of the reign of King George I., the assembly and feast were held at the said house. When the oldest Master Mason and the Master of a Lodge, having taken the chair, a list of proper candidates for the office of Grand Master was presented, and the names being separately proposed, the brethren by a great majority of hands elected Mr. Anthony Sayer Grand Master of Masons for the ensuing year, who was forthwith invested by the said oldest Master, installed by the Master of the oldest Lodge and duly congratulated by the assembly, who paid him homage.

The Grand Master then entered on the duties of his office, appointed his Wardens, and commanded the brethren of the four Lodges to meet him and his Wardens quarterly in communication, enjoining them at the same time to recommend to all the Fraternity a punctual attendance on the next annual assembly and feast."

Recently this claim that Masonry was not for the first time organized, but renewed, in 1717, has been attacked by some of the modern iconoclasms, who refuse credit to any traditional, or even to any record which is not supported by other contemporary authors. Chief among these is Bro. W. P. Buchan, of England, who in his numerous articles in the London Freemason (1871 and 1872) has attacked the antiquity of Freemasonry, and refused to give it an existence anterior to the year 1717. His exact theory is that "Our system of degrees, words, grips, signs, etc., was not in existence until about A. D. 1717." He admits, however, that certain of the "elements or ground work" of the degrees existed before that year, but not confined to the Masons, being common to all the guilds. He thinks that the present system was indebted to the inventive genius of Anderson and Desaguliers, and he supposes that it was simply "a reconstruction of an ancient society, viz., of some form of old pagan philosophy." Hence, he contends that it was not a "revival," but only a "renaissance," and he explains his meaning in the following language:

"Before the eighteenth century we had a renaissance of pagan architecture; then, to follow suit, in the eighteenth century we had a renaissance in a new form of pagan mysticism; but for neither are we indebted to the operative Masons, although the operative Masons were made use of in both cases."

Buchan's theory has been attacked by Bros. William J. Hughan and Chalmers I. Patton. That he is right in his theory, that the three degrees of Master, Fellow Craft and Apprentice were unknown to the Masons of the seventeenth century, and that these classes existed only as a gradation of rank, will be very generally admitted.

But there is unquestionable evidence that the modes of recognition, the method of government, the legends, and much of the ceremonial of initiation, were in existence among the operative Masons of the Middle Ages, and were transmitted to the speculative Masons of the eighteenth century.

The work of Anderson, of Desaguliars, and their contemporaries, was to improve and to enlarge, but not to invent.

The Masonic system of the present day has been the result of slow but steady growth, just as the lectures of Anderson, known to us from their publication in 1725, were subsequently modified and enlarged by the successive labors of Clare, of Dunckerlay, of Preston and of Hemming; did he and Desaguliers submit the simple ceremonial which they found at the recognition of the Grand Lodge in 1717, to a similar modification and enlargement?

ANTIQUITY OF FREEMASONRY.—Dr. Mackey, in his Encyclopedia of Freemasonry, says: "Years ago, in writing an article on this subject, under the impression made upon me by the fascinating theories of Dr. Oliver, though I never completely accepted his views, I was led to place the organization of Freemasonry, as it now exists, at the beginning of Solomon's Temple. Many years of subsequent research have led me greatly to modify the views I had previously held. Although I do not rank myself among those modern iconoclasts who refuse credence to every document whose authenticity, if admitted, would give to the Order a birth anterior to the beginning of the last century,

I confess that I can not find any incontrovertible evidence that would trace Masonry, as now organized, beyond the building corporations of the Middle Ages.

"In this point of view I speak of it only as an architectural brotherhood, distinguished by signs, by words, and by brotherly ties which have not been essentially changed, and by symbols and legends which have only been developed and extended, while the association has undergone a transformation from an operative to a speculative science."

"But then these building corporations did not spring up in all their peculiar organization different, as it was, from that of other guilds, like Antochthones from the soil. They, too, must have had an origin and an archetype, from which they derived their peculiar character. And I am induced, for that purpose, to look to the Roman Colleges of Artificers, which were spread over Europe by the invading forces of the Empire. But these have been traced to Numa, who gave to them that mixed practical and religious character which they are known to have possessed, and in which they were initiated by the mediaeval architects."

"We must therefore look at Freemasonry in two distinct points of view: First, as it is a society of speculative architects, engaged in the construction of spiritual temples, and in this respect a development from the operative architects of the tenth and succeeding centuries, who were themselves offshoots from the Traveling Masons of Como, who traced their origin to the Roman Colleges of Builders. In this direction, I think the line of descent is plain, without any demand upon our credulity for assent to its credibility."

But Freemasonry must be looked at also from another standpoint. Not only does it present the appearance of a speculative science based upon an operative art, but it also very significantly exhibits itself as the symbolic expression of a religious idea, in other and plainer words. We see in it the important lesson of eternal life, taught by a legend, which, whether true or false, is used in Masonry as a symbol and an allegory.

But whence came this legend? Was it invented in 1717, at the revival of Freemasonry in England? We have evidence of the strongest circumstantial character, derived from the Sloan Manuscript No. 3,329, recently exhumed from the shelves of the British Museum, that this very legend was known to the Masons of the seventeenth century at least.

Then did the operative Masons of the Middle Ages have a legend also? The evidence is that they did. The Compagnons de la Tour, who was the offshoots of the old Masters' Guilds, had a legend. We know what the legend was, and we know that its character was similar to, although not in all the details precisely the same as the Masonic legend. It was, however, connected with the Temple of Solomon. It is not the form of the legend, but the spirit and symbolic design, with which we have to do.

The legend of the third degree, as we now have it, is intended by a symbolic representation, to teach the resurrection from death, and the divine dogma of a future life. All Masons know its character, and it is neither expedient nor necessary to dilate upon it. But can we find such a legend elsewhere? Certainly we can. Not, indeed, the same legend, not the same details; but a legend with the same spirit and design. A legend funeral in character, celebrating death and resurrection, solemnized in lamentation and terminating in joy. Thus, in the Egyptian Mysteries of Osiris, the image of a dead man was borne in a coffin by a profession of initiates and the enclosure in the coffin or interment of the body was called the aphonism, or disappearance, and the lamentations for him formed the first part of the Mysteries. On the third day after the interment, the priests and initiates carried the coffin, in which was also a golden vessel, down to the river Nile. Into the vessel they poured water from the river, and then with the cry of "We have found him; let us rejoice," they declared that the dead Osiris, who had descended into Hades, had returned from thence, and was restored again to life, and the rejoicing which ensued constituted the second part of the Mysteries.

The analogy between this and the legend of Freemasonry must be at once apparent. Now just such a legend, everywhere differing in particulars, but everywhere coinciding in general character, is to be found in all the old religions—sun worship, in tree worship, in animal worship it was often permitted. It is true, from the original design, sometimes it was applied to the death or winter and the birth of spring; sometimes to the setting and the subsequent rising of the sun, but always indicating a loss and a recovery.

Especially do we find this legend of the third degree in a purer form in the Ancient Mysteries. At Samothrace, at Eleusis, at Byblos—in all places where the ancient religions and mythical rites were celebrated—we find the same teaching of eternal life inculcated by the representation of an imaginary death and apotheosis. And it is this legend, and this legend alone, that connects speculative Masonry with the Ancient Mysteries of Greece, of Syria, and of Egypt.

"The theory, then, that I advance," says Dr. Mackey, "on the subject of the antiquity of Freemasonry is this: I maintain that in its present peculiar organization it is the successor, with certainty, of the building corporations of the Middle Ages, and through them, with less certainty but wit great probability, of the Roman Colleges of Artificers. Its connection with the Temple of Solomon as its birthplace may have been accidental—a mere arbitrary selection by its inventors—and bears, therefore, only an allegorical meaning or it may be historical, and to be explained by the frequent communications that at one time took place between the Jews and the Greeks and the Romans. This is a point still open for discussion. The historical materials upon which to base an opinion are, as yet, too scanty.

"But I am inclined, I confess, to view the Temple of Jerusalem and the Masonic traditions connected with it as a part of the great allegory of Masonry. But in the other aspect in which Freemasonry presents itself to our view and to which I have already adverted, the question of antiquity is more easily settled.

"As a brotherhood composed of symbolic Maters, and Fellows, and Apprentices—those building spiritual temples as these built material ones—its age may not exceed five or six hundred years; but as a secret association containing within itself the symbolic expression of a religious idea, it connects itself with all the Ancient Mysteries, which with similar secrecy, gave the same symbolic expression to the same religious idea.

"These mysteries were not the cradle of true Masonry; they were only its analogues. But I have no doubt that all of the Mysteries had one common source, perhaps as has been suggested, some ancient body of priests; and I have no more doubt that Freemasonry has derived its legend, its symbolic mode of instruction, and the lesson for which that instruction was intended, either directly or indirectly from the same source, in this view the Mysteries become interesting to the Mason as a study, and in this view only.

"And so, when I speak of the antiquity of Freemasonry, I must say if I would respect the axioms of historical science, that its body came out of the Middle Ages, but that its spirit is to be traced to a far remoter period."

LEGEND.—Strictly speaking, a legend (from the Latin "legendus," "to be read") should be restricted to a story that has been committed to writing, but by good usage the word has been applied more extensively, and now properly means a narrative, whether true or false, that has been traditionally preserved from the time of its first oral communication; such is the definition of a Masonic legend.

The authors of the Conversations Lexicon, referring to the monkish lives of the saints which originated in the twelfth and thirteenth centuries, say that the "title legend was given to all fictions which made pretensions to truth." Such a remark, however correct it may be in reference to these monkish narratives, which were often invented as ecclesiastical exercises, is by no means applicable to the legends of Freemasonry. These are not necessarily fictitious, but are either based on actual historical facts which have been but slightly modified, or they are the offspring and expansion of some symbolic idea, in which latter respect they differ entirely from the monastic legends, which often have only the fertile imagination of some studious monk for the basis of their construction.

The instructions of Freemasonry are given to us in two modes, by symbol, and by legend. The symbol is a material and the legend a mental representation of a truth. The sources of neither can be in every case authentically traced. Many of them come to us, undoubtedly from the old operative Masons of the mediaeval guilds. But whence they got them is a question that naturally arises, and which still remains unanswered. Others have sprung from a far earlier source; perhaps as Crewzer has suggested in his Symbolic, from an effort to engraft higher and purer knowledge on an imperfect religious idea. If so, then the myths of the Ancient Mysteries, and the legends and traditions of Freemasonry would have the same remote and the same final cause; they would differ in construction, but would agree in design. For instance, the myth of Adonis in the Syrian mysteries, and the legend of Hiram Abif in the third degree, would differ very widely in their details, but the object of each would be the same, namely, to teach the doctrine of the resurrection from death to eternal life. The legends of Freemasonry constitute a considerable and very important part of its ritual; without them, its most valuable portions as a scientific system would cease to exist. It is in fact in the traditions and legends of Freemasonry, more even than in its material symbols that we are to find the deep religious instructions which the Institution is intended to inculcate. It must be remembered that Freemasonry has been defined to be "a system of morality veiled in allegory and illustrated by symbols." Symbols, then, alone do not constitute the whole of the system; allegory comes in for its share, and this allegory, which veils the divine truths of Masonry, is presented to the neophyte in the various legends which have been traditionally presented in their Order.

They may be divided into three classes:

First. Mythical legend.

2. The philosophical legend.

3. The historical legend.

And these classes may be divided as follows:

First. The myth may be engaged in the transmission of a narrative of early deeds and events having a foundation in truth, which truth, however, has been greatly distorted and perverted by the omission or introduction of circumstances and personages, and then it constitutes a mythical legend.

Second. Or it may have been invented and adopted as the medium of enunciating a particular thought, or of inculcating a certain doctrine, when it becomes a philosophical legend.

Third, or lastly, the truthful elements of actual history may greatly predominate over the fictitious and invented materials of the myth; and the narrative may be in the main made up of facts, with a slight coloring of imagination, when it forms a historical legend.

ALLEGORY.—A discourse or narrative, in which there is a literal and a figurative sense, a patent and a connected meaning; the literal or patent sense being intended; by analogy or comparison, to indicate the figurative or concealed one, its derivation from the Greek "means" to say something different—that is, to say something where the language is one thing and the meaning another, exactly expresses the character of an allegory. It has been said that there is no essential difference between an allegory and a symbol. There is not in design, but there is in their character. An allegory may be interpreted without any previous conventional agreement, but a symbol cannot. Thus, the legend of the third degree is an allegory, evidently to be interpreted as teaching a restoration to life without any previous understanding. The sprig of acacia is a symbol of the immortality of the soul, but this we know only because such meaning had been continually determined. When the symbol was first established it is evident, then, that an allegory whose meaning is obscure is imperfect. The enigmatical meaning should be easy of interpretation. All the legends of Freemasonry are more or less allegorical, and whatever truth there may be in some of them in a historical point of view, it is only as allegories or legendary symbols that they are of importance.

The English lectures have, therefore, very properly defined Freemasonry to be "a system of morality veiled in allegory and illustrated by symbols."

The allegory was a favorite figure among the ancients, and in the allegorizing spirit are we to trace the connection of the entire Greek and Roman mythology. Not less did it prevail among the older Aryan nations, and its abundant use is exhibited in the religion of Brahma and Zoroaster. The Jewish Rabbins were generally addicted to it, and carried its employment, as Maimonides intimates, sometimes to an excess. Their Midrash, or system of commentaries on the sacred book, is almost altogether allegorical. Aben Ezra, a learned Rabbi of the twelfth century, says: "The Scriptures are like bodies and allegories are like the garments with which they are clothed. Some are thin, like fine silk, and others are coarse, and thick, like sackcloth."

Our Lord, to whom this spirit of Jewish teaching in his day was familiar, inculcated many truths in parables, all of which were allegories, the primitive fathers of the Christian church were thus infected, and Oregon, who was especially addicted to the habit, tells us that all the pagan philosophers should be read in this spirit.

Of modern allegorizing writers, the most interesting to Masons, are Lee, the author of The Temple of Solomon portrayed by Scripture light, and John Bunyan, who wrote Solomon's Temple spiritualized.

MYTHOLOGY.—Literally, the science of myths and this is a very appropriate definition, for mythology is the science which treats of the ancient pagans, which was almost altogether founded on myths, or popular traditions and legendary tales, and hence Keighly says that "mythology may be regarded as the repository of the early religions of the people." Its interest to a Masonic student arises from the constant antagonism that existed between its doctrines and those of the primitive Freemasonry of antiquity, and the light that the mythological mysteries throw upon the ancient organizations of speculative Masonry.

MYTH.—The word "myth," from the Greek, "mythos," a story, in its original acceptance, signified simply a statement or narrative of an event, without any necessary implication of truth or falsehood; but, as the word is now used, it conveys the idea of a personal narrative of remote date, which, although not necessarily untrue, is certified only by the internal evidence of the tradition itself.

This definition, which is substantially derived from Mr. Grote (History of Greece), may be applied without modification to the myths of Freemasonry, although intended by the author only for the myths of the ancient Greek religion.

The myth, then, is a narrative of remote date, not necessarily true or false, but whose truth can only be certified by internal evidence.

The word was first applied to those fables of the pagan gods which have descended from the remotest antiquity, and in all of which there prevails a symbolic idea, not always, however, capable of a positive interpretation. As applied to Freemasonry, the words myth and legend are synonymous.

From this definition it will appear that the myth is really only the interpretation of an idea. But how we are to read these myths will best appear from these nobles words of Max Muller (science of Song): "Everything is true, natural, significant, if we enter with a reverent spirit into the meaning of ancient art, and ancient language; everything becomes false, miraculous and unmeaning, if we interpret the deep and mighty words of the seers of old in the shallow and feeble sense of modern chroniclers."

A fertile source of instruction in Masonry is to be found in its traditions and mythical legends; not only those which are incorporated into its ritual and are exemplified in its ceremonies, but those also which, although forming no part of the Lodge lectures, have been orally transmitted as portions of its history, and which, only within a comparatively recent period, have been committed to writing.

But for the proper appreciation of these traditions, some preparatory knowledge of the general character of Masonic myths is necessary. Neither if all the details of these traditions be considered as asserted historical facts, seeking to convey nothing more nor less than historical information, then the improbabilities and anachronisms, and other violations of historical truth which distinguish many of them, must cause them to be rejected by the scholar as absurd impostures. But there is another and more advantageous view in which these traditions are to be considered. Freemasonry is a symbolic institution; everything in and about it is symbolic, and nothing more eminently so than its traditions. Although some of them, as for instance the legend of the third degree—have in all probability a deep substratum of truth lying beneath; over this there is superposed a beautiful structure of symbolism. History has perhaps first suggested the tradition, but then the legend, like the myths of the ancient poets, becomes a symbol, which is to enunciate some sublime philosophical or religious truth. Read in this way and in this way only, the myths or legends and traditions of Freemasonry will become intelligent and interesting.

MYTH, HISTORICAL.—A historical myth is a myth that has a known and recognized foundation in historical truth, but with the admixture of a preponderating amount of fiction in the introduction of personages and circumstances. Between the historical myth and the mythical history, the distinction cannot always be preserved, because we are not always able to determine whether there is preponderance of truth or of fiction in the legend or narrative under consideration.

A myth or legend, in which the historical and truthful greatly preponderate over the inventions of fiction, may be called a mythical history. Certain portions of the legend of the third degree have such a foundation in fact that they constitute a mythical history, while other portions, added evidently for the purpose of symbolism, and are simply a historical myth.

A philosophical myth or legend is almost wholly unhistorical. Invented only to enunciate a particular thought or dogma. The legend of Euclid is certainly a philosophical myth.

LEGEND OF ENOCH.—Though the Scriptures furnish but a meager account of Enoch, the traditions of Freemasonry clearly connect him by numerous circumstances with the early history of the Institution. In the very commencement of our inquiries, we shall find circumstances in the life of this great patriarch that shows forth, as it were, something of that mysticism with which the traditions of Masonry have connected him. His name in the Hebrew language, "Henoch," signifies to initiate and to instruct, and seems intended to express the fact that he was, as Oliver remarks, the first to give a decisive character to the rite of initiation, and to add to the practice of divine worship the study and application of human science. In confirmation of this view, a writer says on this subject, that "It seems probable that Enoch introduced the speculative principles into the Masonic creed, and that he originated its exclusive

character," which theory must be taken, if it is
accepted at all, with very considerable modification.

The Oriental writers abound in traditional
evidence of the venerable patriarch; one tradition
states he received from God the gift of wisdom and
knowledge, and that God gave him thirty volumes
from heaven, filled with all the secrets of the most
mysterious sciences." The Rabbins maintain that
he was taught of God and Adam how to sacrifice,
and how to worship the Deity aright. The Greek
Christians supposed him to have been identical
with the first Egyptian Hermes, who dwelt at Sais.
They say that he foretold the deluge that was to
overwhelm his descendants, and that he built the
pyramids, engraving thereon figures of artificial
instruments and the elements of the sciences,
fearing lest memory of man should perish in that
general destruction. In the study of the sciences, in
teaching them to his children and his contemporaries,
and in instituting the rites of initiation. Enoch is
supposed to have passed the years of his peaceful,
his pious and his useful life, until the crimes of
mankind had increased to such a height that, in the
expressive words of Holy Writ: "Every imagination
of the thoughts of man's heart was only evil
continually." It was then according to a Masonic
tradition that Enoch fled to the solitude of Mount
Moriah, and devoted himself to prayer and pious
contemplation. It was on that spot—then first
consecrated by this patriarchal hermitage and
afterwards to be made still more holy by the sacrifices
of Abraham, of David, and of Solomon—that we are
informed that the Shekinah or Sacred Presence

appeared to him and gave him those instructions which were to preserve the wisdom of the antediluvians to their posterity when the world, with the exception of but one family, should have been destroyed by the forthcoming flood. The circumstances which occurred at that time are recorded in a tradition which forms what has been called the great Masonic "Legend of Enoch," and which runs to this effect:

Enoch being inspired by the Most High, and in commemoration of a wonderful vision, built a temple under ground, and dedicated it to God. His son, Methuselah, constructed the buildings, although he was not acquainted with his father's motives for the erection.

This temple consisted of nine brick vaults situated perpendicularly beneath each other, communicating by apertures left in the arch of each vault. Enoch then caused a triangular plate of gold to be made, each side of which was a cubit long; he encircled it with the most precious stones, and encrusted the plate upon a stone of agate of the same form; on the plate he engraved in ineffable characters the true name of Deity, and placing it on a cubical pedestal of white marble, he deposited the whole within the deepest arch. When this subterranean building was completed, he made a door of stone, and attaching to it a ring of iron, by which it might be occasionally raised, he placed it over the opening of the uppermost arch, and so covered it over that the aperture could not be discovered. Enoch himself was not permitted to enter it but once a year, and on the death of

Enoch, Methusalah and Lamech, and the destruction of the world, all knowledge of this temple, and of the sacred treasures which it contained, was lost, until in after times, it was accidentally discovered by another worthy of Freemasonry, who, like Enoch, was engaged in the erection of a temple on the same spot.

The legend goes on to inform us that after Enoch had completed the subterranean temple, fearing that the principles of those arts and sciences which he had cultivated with so much assiduity would be lost in the general destruction of which he had received a prophetic vision, he erected two pillars—the one of marble, to withstand the influence of fire, and the other of brass, to resist the action of water; on the pillars of brass he engraved the history of the creation, the principles of the arts and sciences, and the doctrines of speculative Freemasonry as they were practiced in his time; and on the one of marble he inscribed characters in hieroglyphics, importing that near the spot where they stood, a precious treasure was deposited in a subterranean vault.

Josephus gives an account of these pillars. He ascribes them to the children of Seth, which is by no means a contradiction of the Masonic tradition, since Enoch was one of these children. He also informs us that they remain in the land of Syria to this day. Masonic tradition informs us that Enoch delivered up the government of the Craft to his grandson Lamech, and disappeared from earth.

This legend, says Dr. Mackey, never formed any of the old systems of Masonry, and was first introduced from Talmudic and Rabbinical sources into the high degrees, where, however, it is really to he viewed rather as symbolical as as historical. Enoch himself is but the symbol of initiation, and his legend is intended symbolically to express the doctrine that the true word or divine truth was preserved in the ancient institutions.

LEGEND OF NOAH.—In all the old Masonic manuscript constitutions that are extant, Noah and the flood play an important part of the "legend of the Craft," hence, as the Masonic system became developed, the patriarch was looked upon as what was called a patron of Masonry. And this connection of Noah with the mystic history of the Order was rendered still closer by the influence of many symbols borrowed from the Arkete worship, one of the most predominant of the ancient faiths. So intimately were incorporated the legends of Noah with the legends of Masonry, that Freemasons began at length to be called, and are still called "Noachide," or the descendants of Noah, a term first applied by Anderson, and very frequently used at the present day. It is necessary; therefore, that every scholar who desires to investigate the legendary system of Freemasonry should make himself acquainted with the Noachic myths, upon which much of it is founded.

Dr. Oliver, it is true, accepted them all with a childlike faith, but it is not likely that the skeptical inquirers of the present day will attribute to them any character of authenticity. Yet they are interesting because they show us the growth of legends out of symbols, and they are instructive because they are for the most part symbolic.

The "legend of the Craft" tells us that the three sons of Lamech and his daughter Naamah "did know that God would take vengeance for sin, either by fire or water; wherefore, they wrote these sciences which they had found in two pillars of stone, that they might be found after the flood." Subsequently, this legend took a different form, and to Enoch was attributed the precaution of burying the stone of foundation in the bosom of Mount Moriah, and of erecting the two pillars above it.

The first Masonic myth referring to Noah, that presents itself, is one which tells us that while he was piously engaged in the task of exhorting his contemporaries to repentance, his attention had often been directed to the pillars which Enoch had erected on Mount Moriah. By diligent search he at length detected the entrance to the subterranean vault, and on pursuing his inquiries, discovered the stone of foundation, although he was unable to comprehend the mythical character there deposited. Leaving these, therefore, where he had found them, he simply took away the stone of the foundation, on which they had been deposited, and placed it in the Ark as a convenient altar.

Another myth preserved in one of the degrees, informs us that the Ark was built of cedars which grew upon Mount Lebanon, and that Noah employed the Sidonians to cut them down, under the superintendence of Japhet. The successors of these Sidonians, in after times, according to the same tradition, were employed by King Solomon to fell and prepare cedars on the same mountain for his stupendous Temple. The record of Genesis lays the foundation for another series of symbolic myths connected with the dove, which has thus been introduced into Masonry.

After forty days, when Noah opened the windows of the Ark, that he might learn if the waters had subsided, he dispatched a raven, which returning, gave him no satisfactory information. He then sent forth a dove three several times, at an interval of seven days between each excursion. The first time, the dove finding no resting place, quickly returned; the second time she came back, bringing in her mouth an olive leaf, which showed that the waters must have sufficiently abated to have exposed the tops of the trees; but on the third departure, the dry land being entirely uncovered, she returned no more.

In the Arkite rites, which arose after the dispersion of Babel, the dove was always considered a sacred bird in commemoration of its having been the first discoverer of land; its name which in Hebrew is "Ionah," was given to one of the earliest nations of the earth; and the emblem of peace and good fortune, it became the bird of Venus.

Modern Masons have commemorated the messenger of Noah in the honorary degree of "Ark and Dove," which is sometimes conferred on Royal Arch Masons.

On the 27th day of the second month, equivalent to November 12, in the year of the world 1657, Noah, with his family left the Ark; it was exactly one year of 365 days, or just one revolution

of the sun, that the patriarch was enclosed in the
Ark. This was not unobserved by the descendants
of Noah, and hence, in consequence of Enoch's life
of 365 days, and Noah's residence in the Ark for
the same, apparently mystical period, the
Noachites confounded the worship of the solar orb
with the idolatrous adoration which they paid to
the patriarchs who were saved from the deluge.
They were led to this, too, from an additional
reason, that Noah, as the restorer of the human
race, seemed in some sort, to be a type of the
regenerating powers of the sun.

So important an event as the deluge must have
produced a most impressive effect upon the
religious dogmas and rites of the nations which
succeeded it, consequently we shall find some
allusion to it in the annals of every people, and
some memorial of the principal circumstances
connected with it, in their religious observances.

At first, it is to be supposed that veneration for
the character of the second parent of the human
race must have been long preserved by his
descendants. Nor would they have been unmindful
of the proper reverence due to that sacred vessel—
sacred in their eyes—which had preserved their
great progenitor from the fury of the waters. "They
would long cherish," says Atwood, "the memory of
those worthies who were rescued from the
common lot of utter ruin; they would call to mind,
with the extravagance of admiration, the means
adopted for their preservation; they would adore
the wisdom which contrived, and the goodness
which prompted the execution of such a plan." So
pious a feeling would exist and be circumscribed

within its proper limits of reverential gratitude while the legends of the deluge continued to be preserved in their purity, and while the divine preserver of Noah was remembered as the one god of his posterity.

But, when, by the confusion and dispersion at Babel, the true teachings of Enoch and Noah were lost, and idolatry or polytheism was established for the ancient faith, then Noah became a god, worshiped under different names in different countries, and the Ark was transformed into the Temple of the Deity. Hence arose the peculiar systems of initiations which, known under the name of the "Arkite rites," formed a part of the worship of the ancient world, and traces of which are to be found in almost all the old systems of religion.

It was in the six hundredth year of his age that Noah with his family was released from the Ark. Grateful for his preservation; he erected an altar and prepared a sacrifice of thank-offerings to the Deity. A Masonic tradition says that for this purpose he made use of that stone of foundation which he had discovered in the subterranean vault of Enoch, and which he had carried with him into the Ark. It was at this time that God made his covenant with Noah, and promised him that the earth should never again be destroyed by a flood. Hence, too, he received these commandments for the government of himself and his posterity which have been called "The Seven Precepts of Noachide," and which were preserved as the constitutions of our ancient brethren, and are as follows:

1. Renounce all idols.
2. Worship the only true God.
3. Commit no murder.
4. Be not defiled by incest.
5. Do not steal.
6. Be just.
7. Eat no flesh with blood in it.

It is to be supposed that Noah and his immediate descendants continued to live for many years in the neighborhood of the mountain upon which the ark had been thrown by the subsidence of the waters. There is indeed no evidence that the patriarch ever removed from it. In the nine hundred and forty-eighth year of his age he died, and, according to the tradition of the Orient lists, was buried in the land of Mesopotamia.

During that period of his life which was subsequent to the deluge, he continued to instruct his children in the great truths of religion. Hence, Masons are sometimes called Noachide, or the Sons of Noah, to distinguish them in a peculiar manner as the preservers of the sacred deposit of Masonic truth, bequeathed to them by their great ancestor, and circumstances intimately connected with the transactions of the immediate descendants of the patriarch are recorded in a degree which has been adopted by the Ancient and Accepted Scottish Rite, under the name of "Patriarch Noachite." The primitive teachings of the patriarch which were simple but comprehensive, continued to be preserved in the line of the patriarchs and the prophets to the days of Solomon, but were soon lost to the other descendants of Noah, by a circumstance to which we must now refer.

After the death of Noah, his sons removed from the region of Mount Ararat, where, until then, they had resided, and "traveling from the East," found a place in the land of Shinar, and dwelt there. Here they commenced the building of a lofty tower. This act seems to have been displeasing to God, for, in consequence of it, He confounded their language, so that one could not understand what another said, the result of which was that they separated and dispersed over the face of the earth, in search of different dwelling places. With the loss of the original language, the great truths which that language had conveyed disappeared from their minds. The worship of the one true God was abandoned. A multitude of deities began to be adored. Idolatry took the place of pure theism, and then arose the Arkite Rites, or the worship of Noah and the Ark; Sabaism, or the adoration of the stars, and other superstitious observances, in all of which, however, the priesthood by their mysteries of initiation into a kind of spurious Freemasonry, preserved, among a multitude of errors, some faint allusions to the truth, and retained just so much light as to make their "darkness visible."

Such are the Noachic traditions of Masonry, which, though if considered as materials of history, would be worth but little, yet have furnished valuable sources of symbolism, and in that way are full of wise instruction.

STONE OF FOUNDATION.—The stone of foundation constitutes one of the most important and abstruse of all the symbols of Masonry. It is referred to in the numerous legends and traditions, not only of the Freemason's, but also of the Jewish Rabbis, the Talmudic writers, and even the Mussulman doctors.

Many of these, it must be confessed, are apparently puerile and absurd; but most of them, and especially the Masonic ones, are deeply interesting in their allegorical signification. The stone of foundation is, properly speaking, a symbol of the higher degrees. It makes its first appearance in the Royal Arch, and forms indeed the most important symbol of that degree.

But it is so intimately connected in its legendary history with the construction of the Solomonic Temple, that it must be considered as a part of Ancient Craft Masonry, although he who confines the range of his investigations to the first three degrees will have no means, within that narrow circuit, of properly appreciating the symbolism of the stone of foundation. As preliminary to the inquiry, it is necessary to distinguish the stone of foundation, both in its symbolism and its legendary history from other stones, which play an important part in the Masonic ritual, but which are entirely distinct from it. Such are the cornerstone, which was always placed in the northeast corner of the building about to be erected, and to which a beautiful reference is made in the ceremonies of the first degree; or the keystone, which constitutes an interesting part of the Mark Master's degree, or lastly, the cape-stone, upon which all the

ritual of the Most Excellent Master's degree is
founded.

These are all, in their proper places, highly
interesting and instructive symbols, but have no
connection whatever with the stone of foundation,
whose symbolism it is our present object to discuss.

The Stone of Foundation has a legendary
history and symbolic signification, which are
peculiar to it, and which differ from the history and
meaning which belong to other stones. But in the
very beginning, as a necessary preliminary to any
investigation of this kind, it must be distinctly
understood that all that is said of the Stone of
Foundation in Masonry is to be strictly taken in a
mystical or allegorical sense.

The Stone of Foundation is supposed, by the
theory which establishes it, to have been a stone
placed at one time within the foundations of the
Temple of Solomon, and afterwards, during the
building of the Second Temple, transported to the
Holy of Holies; it was in form a perfect cube, and
had inscribed upon its upper face, within a delta,
or triangle, the sacred Tetragrammaton, or
ineffable name of God. Oliver, speaking with the
solemnity of a historian, says that Solomon
thought that he had rendered the house of God
worthy, so far as human adornment could effect,
for the dwelling of God, "when he had placed the
celebrated Stone of Foundation on which the
celebrated name was mystically engraved, with
solemn ceremonies.

In that sacred depository of Mount Moriab,
alone with the foundations of Dan and Asher, the
center of the Most Holy place where the ark was

overshadowed by the shekinah of God."

The Mosaic legends of the Stone of Foundation based on rabbinical reveries, are of the most extraordinary character, if they are to be viewed as histories, but readily recognizable with sound sense if looked at only in the light of allegories.

They present an uninterrupted succession of events, in which the Stone of Foundation takes a prominent part, from Adam to Solomon, and from Solomon to Zerubbabel. In the Royal Arch and Select Master's degree of the American Rite, the Stone of Foundation constitutes the most important part of the ritual; in both of these, it is the receptacle of the ark, on which the ineffable name is inscribed.

In the Masonic legend, the Foundation Stone first makes its appearance in the days of Enoch, who placed it in the bowels of Mount Moriah. There it was subsequently discovered by King Solomon, who deposited it in a crypt of the first Temple, where it remained concealed until the foundations of the second Temple were laid, when it was discovered and removed to the Holy of Holies.

But the most important point of the legend of the stone of foundation is its intimate and constant connection with the Tetragrammaton, or ineffable name. It is this name, inscribed upon it within the sacred and symbolic delta, that gives to the stone all its Masonic value and signification. It is upon this fact that it was so inscribed, that its whole symbolism depends.

Looking at these traditions in anything like the light of historical narratives, we are compelled to consider them, to use the plain language of Lee, "but as so many idle and absurd conceits." We must go behind the legend, which we acknowledge at once to be only an allegory, and study its symbolism.

The fact that the mystical stone in all the ancient religions was a symbol of the Deity, leads us necessarily to the conclusion that the Stone of Foundation was also a symbol of Deity. And this symbolic idea is strengthened by the Tetragrammaton, or sacred name of God, that was inscribed upon it.

This ineffable name signifies the stone upon which it is engraved as the symbol of the Grand Architect; it takes from it its heathen signification as an idol, and connects it to the worship of the true God. But the Masonic idea is still further to be extended. The great object of all Masonic labor is divine truth. The search for the lost word is the search for truth.

But divine truth is synonymous with God. The ineffable name is a symbol of truth, because God and God alone is truth. It is properly a scriptural idea. If, then, God is truth, and the Stone of Foundation is the Masonic symbol of God, it follows that it must also be the symbol of divine truth. But although the present life is necessarily built upon the foundation of truth, yet we never thoroughly attain it in this sublunary sphere. The Foundation Stone is concealed in the first Temple, and the Master Mason knows it not. He has not the true word. He receives only a substitute.

But in the second Temple of the future life, we

have passed from the grave which had been the end of our labors in the first; we have removed the rubbish, and have found the Stone of Foundation which had been hitherto concealed from our eyes. We now throw aside the substitute for truth, which had contented us in the first Temple, and the brilliant effulgence of the Tetragrammaton and the Stone of Foundation are discovered, and therefore we are the possessors of the true word—of divine truth.

And so the result of this inquiry is, that the Masonic Stone of Foundation is the symbol of divine truth, upon which all speculative Masonry is built, and the legends and traditions which refer to it are intended to describe in an allegorical way the progress of truth in the soul, the search for which is the Mason's labor, and the discovery of which is his reward.

CORNERSTONE, SYMBOLISM OF.—Among the ancients the cornerstone of important edifices was laid with impressive ceremonies. The symbolism of the cornerstone, when duly laid with Masonic rites, is full of significance which refers to its form, to its situation, to its prominence and to its construction.

As to its form, it must be perfectly square on its surfaces, and its solid contents a cube. Now the square is a symbol of morality, and cube of truth. In its situation it lies between the north, the place of darkness, and the east, the place of light, and hence this position symbolizes the Masonic progress from darkness to light and from ignorance to knowledge.

The prominence and durability of the cornerstone, which lasts long after the building in whose foundations it was placed has fallen into decay, is intended to remind the Mason that, when this earthly house of his tabernacle shall have passed away, he has in him a sure foundation of eternal life—a cornerstone of immortality—an emanation of the Divine Spirit, which pervades all nature, and which, therefore, must survive the tomb, and rise triumphant and eternal, above the decaying dust of death and the grave.

The stone, when deposited in its appropriate place, is carefully examined with the necessary implements of operative masonry—the square, the level, and the plumb, themselves all symbolical in Masonry,—and is then declared to be "well formed, true and trusty."

Thus the Mason is taught that his virtues are to be tested by temptation and trial, by suffering and adversity, before they can be pronounced by the Master Builder of Souls to be materials worthy of the spiritual building of eternal life, fitted "as living stones" for that house not made with hands, eternal in the heavens." And lastly, in the ceremony of depositing the cornerstone, the elements of Masonic consecration are produced, and the stone is solemnly set apart by pouring corn, wine and oil upon its surface, emblematic of the nourishment, refreshment and joy which are the rewards of a faithful performance of duty.

In the Old Testament it seems to always have denoted a prince or high personage, and hence the evangelists constantly use it in reference to Christ, who is called the "Chief Cornerstone."

And Christ said to the chief priests and elders: "Did ye never read in the Scriptures, the stone which the builders rejected, the same is become the head of the corner?" In Masonic symbolism, it signifies a true Mason, and therefore it is the first character which the Apprentice is made to represent after his initiation has been completed.

MYSTERIES, ANCIENT.—Each of the pagan gods, says Warburton, had, besides the public and open, a secret worship paid to him, to which none were admitted but those who had been selected by preparatory ceremonies called initiation. This secret worship was termed the Mysteries. And this is supported by Strabo, who says that it was common, both to the Greeks and the Barbarians, to perform their religious ceremonies with the observance of a festival, and they are sometimes celebrated publicly and sometimes in mysterious privacy. Noel thus defines them: "Secret ceremonies, which were practiced in honor of certain gods, and whose secret was known to the initiates alone, who were admitted after long and painful trials, which it was more than their life was worth to reveal."

As to their origin, Warburton is probably not wrong in his statement that the first of which we have any account, are those of Isis and Osiris, in Egypt; for although those of Mithras came into Europe from Persia, they were, it is supposed, carried from Egypt by Zoroaster.

The most important of these mysteries were the Osiric in Egypt, the Mithraic in Persia, the Cabiric in Thrace, the Adonesian in Syria, the Dionysiac and Elusian in Greece, the Scandinavian among the Gothic nations, and the Druidal among the Celts.

In all these mysteries, we find a singular unity of design, clearly indicating a common origin and a purity of doctrine as evidently proving that this common origin was not to be sought for in the popular theology of the pagan world.

The ceremonies of initiation were all funeral in their character. They celebrated the death and resurrection of some cherished being, either the object of esteem as a hero, or of devotion as a god. Subordination of degrees was instituted, and the candidate was subjected to probations varying in their character and severity. The rites were practiced in the darkness of night, and often amid the gloom of impenetrable forests or subterraneous caverns; and the full fruition of knowledge, for which so much labor was endured, and so much danger incurred, was not attained until the aspirant, well tried and thoroughly purified, had reached the place of wisdom and light.

Those mysteries undoubtedly owed their origin to the desire to establish esoteric philosophy in which should be withheld from popular approach those sublime truths which it was supposed could only be entrusted to those who had been previously prepared for their reception. Whence these doctrines were originally derived, it would be impossible to say—possibly from an ancient and highly instructed body of priests, having their origin either in Egypt or in the East, from whom was derived religious, physical and historical knowledge, under the veil of symbols. By this confinement of these doctrines to a system of secret knowledge guarded by the most rigid rites, could they only expect to preserve them from the superstitious innovations and corruptions of the world as it then existed. "The distinguished few," says Oliver, "who retained their fidelity, uncontaminated by the contagion of evil example, would soon be able to estimate the superior benefits of an isolated institution, which offered the advantage of a select society, and keep at an unapproachable distance the profane scoffer, whose presence might pollute their pure devotions and social converse, by contumelious language or unholy mirth." And doubtless the prevention of this intrusion, and the presentation of these sublime truths, was the original object of the institutions of the ceremonies of initiation, and the adoption of other means by which the initiated could be recognized, and the uninitiated excluded. Such was the opinion of Warburton, who says, "the mysteries were at first the retreats of science and virtue till time corrupted them in most of the gods."

The Abbe Robin, in a learned work on the subject, places the origin of the initiates at that remote period, when crimes first began to appear upon earth. The vicious, he remarks, were urged by the terror of guilt to seek among the virtuous for intercessors with the deity. The latter retiring into solitude to avoid the contagion of growing corruption devoted themselves to a life of contemplation and the cultivation of several of the useful sciences.

The periodical return of the seasons, the revolution of the stars, the productions of the earth, and the various phenomena of nature, studied with attention, rendered them useful guides to men, both in their pursuits of industry, and in their social duties. These recluse students invented certain signs to recall to the remembrance of the people the times of their festivals and their rural labors, and hence the origin of the symbols and hieroglyphics that were in use among the priests of all nations.

Having now become guides and leaders of the people, these signs, in order to select as associates of their learned labors and sacred functions, only such as had sufficient merit and capacity, appointed strict courses of trial and examination; and this, our author thinks, must have been the source of initiations of antiquity.

The Maji, Brahmans, Gymnosophists, Druids, and priests of Egypt lived thus in sequestered habitations and subterranean caves, and obtained great reputation by their discourses in astronomy, chemistry and mechanics, by their purity of morals, and by their knowledge of the science of legislation.

It was in these schools, says M. Robin, that the first sages and legislators of antiquity were formed, and in them he supposes the doctrines taught to have been, the unity of God, and the immortality of the soul; and it was from these mysteries and their symbols and hieroglyphics that the exuberant fancy of the Greeks drew much of their mythology.

Warburton deduces from the ancient writers—
from Cicero and Porphyry, from Oregon and Celeus,
and from others—what was the true object of the
mysteries. They taught the dogma of the unity of
God in opposition to the polytheistic notions of the
people, and in connection with this the doctrine of
a future life, and that the initiated should be
happier in that state than all other mortals; that
while the soul of the profane, at their leaving the
body, stuck fast in mire and filth, and remained in
darkness, the souls of the initiated winged their
flight directly to the happy islands and the
habitations of the good. "Thrice happy they," says
Sophocles, "who descended to the shades below
after having beheld those rites, for they alone have
life in Hades, while all others suffer there every
kind of evil." And Isocrates declares, "those who
have been initiated into the mysteries entertain
better hopes as to the end of life and the whole of
futurity."

Others of the ancients have given us the same
testimony as to their "esoteric character." All the
mysteries, says Plutarch, refer to a future life and
to the state of the soul after death. In another
place, addressing his wife, he says, "We have been
instructed in the religious rites of Dionysus that
the soul is immortal, and that there is a future
state of existence." Cicero tells us that in the
mysteries of Ceres at Eleusis, the initiated were
taught to live happily and to die in the hope of a
blessed futurity. And finally Plato informs us that
the hymns of Musaeus which were sung in the
mysteries celebrated the rewards and pleasures of

the virtuous in another life, and the punishments which awaited the wicked. These sentiments so different from the debased polytheism which prevailed among the uninitiated, are the most certain evidence that the mysteries arose from a purer source than that which gave birth to the religion of the vulgar. Taber, finding, as he did, a prototype for every ancient cult in the ark of Noah, it is not surprising that he should apply his theory to the mysteries. "The initiations," he says, "into the mysteries scenically represented the mystic descent into Hades, and the return from thence to the light of day, by which was meant the entrance into the ark, and the subsequent liberation from its dark enclosure. They all equally related to the allegorical disappearance, or death, or descent of the great father, at their commencement; and his invention, or revival, or return from Hades, at their conclusion."

Dollinger says, speaking of the mysteries. "The whole was a drama, the prelude to which consisted in purification, sacrifices and injunctions with regard to the behavior to be observed. The adventures of certain deities, their suffering and joys, their appearance on earth, and relations to mankind, their death or descent to the nether world, their return, or their rising again—all these as symbolizing the life of nature, were represented in a connected series of theatrical scenes. These representations tacked to a nocturnal solemnity, brilliantly got up and accompanies with dancing and song, were eminently calculated to take a powerful hold on the imagination and the heart, and to exhibit in the spectators alternately conflicting sentiments of terror and calm, sorrow and fear and hope. They worked upon them, now by agitating, now by soothing, and meanwhile had a strong hold upon susceptibilities and capacity of individuals, according as their several dispositions inclined them more to reflection and observation or to a resigned credulity."

Bunsen gives the recent, and the most philosophical idea of the character of the mysteries. They did, he says (God in History 2, 3, 4, chapter 6), "Indeed exhibit to the initiated course physical symbols of the generative powers of Nature, and of the universal Nature herself, entirely self-sustaining through all transformations, but the religions element of the mysteries consisted in the relations of the universe to the soul, more especially after death. Thus, even without philosophic proof, we are justified in assuming that the Nature symbolism referring to the zodiac formed a mere framework for the doctrine relating to the soul, and to the ethical theory of the universe; so likewise in the Samothracian worship of the Kabiri, the contest waged by the orb of day was represented by the story of the three brothers—the seasons of the year—one of which is continually slain by the other, but ever and anon rises to life again. But here too the beginning and the end of the worship were ethical. A sort of confession was demanded of the candidate before admission and at the close of the service the victorious god (Dionysus) was displayed as the lord of the spirit. Still less, however, did theorems of natural philosophy form the subject matter of the Elusion mysteries, of which, on the contrary psychical conceptions were the beginning and the end. The predominating idea of these conceptions was that of the soul as a divine, vital force, held captive here on earth and sorely tried; but the initiated were further taught to look forward to a final redemption and blessedness for the good and pious. Eternal torments for the wicked and unjust."

The esoteric character of these mysteries was preserved by the most powerful sanctions. An oath of secrecy was administered in the most solemn form to the initiate, and to violate it was considered a sacrilegious crime, and the prescribed punishment for which was immediate death, and we have at least one instance in Livy of the infliction of the penalty. The ancient writers were therefore extremely reluctant to approach the subject, and Lobeck gives several examples of the cautious manner in which they shrunk from divulging or discussing any explanation of the symbol which had been interpreted to them in the course of initiation. "I would forbid," says Horace, "that any man who would divulge the sacred rites of mysterious Ceres, from being under the same roof with me, or from setting sail with me in the same precarious bark."

On the subject of their relation to the rites of Freemasonry, to which they have in many respects so remarkable a resemblance, that some connection seems necessarily implied, there are five principal theories. The first is that embraced and taught by Dr. Oliver, namely, that they are but deviations from that common source, both of them and Freemasonry, the patriarchal mode of worship established by God himself, with this pure system of truth, he supposes the science of Freemasonry to have been coeval and identical. But the truths revealed by divinity came at length to be doubted or rejected through the imperfection of human reason, and though the visible symbols were retained in the mysteries of the pagan world, their true interpretation was lost.

There is a second theory which, leaving the origin of the mysteries to be sought in the patriarchal doctrines, where Oliver placed it, finds the connection between them and Freemasonry commencing at the building of King Solomon's Temple. Over the construction of this building, Hiram, the Architect of Tyre, presided. At Tyre, the Mysteries of Bachus had been introduced by the Dionysian artificers, and into their fraternity Hiram in all probability had, it is necessarily suggested, been admitted. Freemasonry whose tenets had always existed in purity among the immediate descendants of the patriarchs, added now to its doctrines the guard of secrecy, which, as Dr. Oliver himself remarks, was necessary to preserve them from perversion or pollution.

A third theory has been advanced by the Abbi Robin, in which he connects Freemasonry indirectly with the mysteries through the intervention of the Crusades. He attempts to deduce from the ancient initiations, the Orders of Chivalry, of whose branches, he says, produced the initiation of Freemasonry.

A fourth theory—and this has been recently advanced by the Rev. Mr. King in his treaties on the Gnostics—is that as some of them, especially those of Mithras, were extended beyond the advent of Christianity, and even to the very commencement of the Middle Ages, they were seized upon by the secret societies of that period as a model for their organization, and that through the latter they are able to be traced to Freemasonry. But perhaps, after all, the truest theory is that which would discard all successive links in a supposed chain of descent from the mysteries to Freemasonry and would attribute their close resemblance to a natural coincidence of human thought.

The legend of the third degree and the legend of the Elusinian, the Cabrire, the Dionysian, the Adonic, and all other mysteries are identical in their object, to teach the reality of a future life, and this lesson is taught in all by the use of the same symbolism, and substantially the same scenic representation. And this is not because the Masonic rites are a lineal succession from the Ancient Mysteries, but because there has been at all times a proneness of the human heart to nourish the belief in a future life, and a proneness of the human mind to clothe this belief in a symbolic dress. And if there is any other more direct connection between them, it must be sought for in the Roman Colleges of Architecture, who did most probably exercise some influence over the rising Freemasons of the early ages, and who, as the contemporaries of the mysteries, were, we may well suppose, imbued with something of their organization. These mysteries continued to flourish until long after the Christian era, but they at length degenerated. In the fourth century, Christianity began to triumph. The sun of paganism was setting, and its rites had become contemptible and corrupt, and finally Theodosius, by a general edict of proscription, ordered the whole of the pagan mysteries to be abolished. In the four hundred and thirty-eighth year of the Christian era, and eighteen hundred years after their first establishment in Greece. The mysteries of Miethras which, continually attacked by the fathers of the church, lived until the beginning of the fifth century, were the last of the old mysteries which had once exercised so much influence over the pagan world and the pagan religion.

MITHRAS, MYSTERIES OF.—There are none of the Ancient Mysteries which afford a more interesting subject of investigation to the Masonic scholar than those of the Persian god Mithras, instituted, as it is supposed, by Zeradusht, or Zoroaster, as an initiation into the principles of the religion which he had founded among ancient Persians. They in time extended into Europe and lasted so long that traces of them have been found in the fourth century. "With their penances," says Mr. King, "and tests of the couarge of the candidate for admission, they have been maintained by a constant tradition through the secret societies of the Middle Ages, and the Rosecrusians down to the modern reflex of the latter—the Freemasons."

Of the identity of Mithras with other deities, there have been various opinions. Herodotus says he was the Assyrian Venus and the Arabian Alitta.

Porphyry calls him the Demiurgos and Lord of Generation; the Greeks identify him with Phalus; and Higgins supposed that he was generally considered the same as Osiris. But to the Persians, who first practiced his mysteries, he was a sun god, and worshiped the god of light. He was represented as a young man covered with a Phrygian turban and clothed in mantle of tunic. He presses with his knee upon a bull, one of whose horns he holds in his left hand, while with the right he plunges a dagger into his neck, while a dog standing near laps up the dripping blood. This symbol has been thus interpreted: His piercing the throat with his dagger signifies the penetration of the solar rays into the bosom of the earth, by which action all nature is nourished, the last idea being expressed by the dog licking up the blood as it flows from the wound. But it will be seen hereafter that the last symbol admits of another interpretation. The Mysteries of Mithras were always celebrated in caves. They were divided into seven stages or degrees (Sides says twelve), and consisted of the most rigorous fortitude and courage. Nonnu, the Greek poet, says that these proofs were eighty in number, gradually increasing in severity. No one, says Gregory Nazianzen, could be initiated into the mysteries of Mitchas unless he had passed through all the trials and proved himself passionless and pure. The aspirant at first underwent the purifications by water, by fire, and by fasting, after which he was introduced into the cavern representing the world, on whose walls were inscribed the celestial signs. Here he submitted to a species of baptism, and

received a mark in his forehead. He was presented
with a crown on the point of a sword, which he was
to refuse, and declaring at the same time, "Mithras
alone is my crown." He was prepared by anointing
him with oil, crowning him with olive, and clothing
him with enchanted armor, for the seven stages of
initiation through which he was about to pass.

These commenced in the following manner: in
the first cavern, he heard the howling of wild
beasts, and was enveloped in total darkness,
except when the cave was illuminated by the fitful
glare of terrific flashes of lightning. He was
hurried to the spot whence the sounds proceeded,
and was suddenly thrust by his silent guide
through a door into a den of wild beasts, where he
was attacked by the initiated in the disguise of
lions, tigers, hyenas and other ravenous beasts.
Hurried through this apartment, in the second
chamber he was again shrouded in darkness and
for a time in fearful silence, until it was broken by
awful   peals   of   thunder,   whose   repeated
reverbrations shook the very walls of the cavern,
and could not fail to inspire the aspirant with
terror. He was conducted through four other caverns
in which the methods of exciting astonishment and
fear were ingeniously varied. He was made to swim
over a raging flood, was subjected to a rigorous fast,
exposed to all the horrors of a dreary desert, and
finally, if we trust the authority of Nicratas, after
being severely beaten with rods, was buried for
many days, up to the neck in snow. In the
seventh cavern or Sacellum, the darkness was
changed to light, and the candidate was
introduced in the presence of the Archimagus, or

chief priest, seated on a splendid throne, and surrounded by the assistant dispensers of the mysteries. Here the obligation of secrecy was administered, and he was made acquainted with the sacred words. He received also the appropriate investiture, which, says Maurice, consisted of the Kora, or conical cap, and candy's, or loose tunic of Mithras, on which was depicted the celestial constellations, the zone, or cult, containing a representation of the figures of the zodiac, the pastorial staff, or erasier attending to the influence of the Sun in the labors of agriculture, and the golden serpent, which was placed in his bosom as an emblem of his having been regenerated and made a disciple of Mithras, because the serpent, by casting its silver skin semi-annually was considered in these mysteries as a symbol of regeneration. He was instructed in the secret doctrines of the rites of Mithras, of which the history of the creation, already recited, formed a part.

The mysteries of Mithras passed from Peria to Europe, and were introduced into Rome in the time of Pompey. Here they flourished with various success until the year 378, when they were proscribed by a decree of the Senate, and the sacred cave in which they had been collected was destroyed by the Pretorian prefect.

The Mithraic monuments that are still extant in the museums of Europe evidently show that the immortality of the soul was one of the doctrines taught in the Mithraic institution. The candidate was at one time made to personate a corpse whose restoration to life dramatically represented the resurrection. Figures of this corpse are found in several of the monuments and talismans.

There is circumstantial evidence that there was a Mithraic death in the initiation, just as there was a cabric death in the mysteries of Samothrace, and a Dioneysian in those of Eleusis. Commodus, the Roman Emperor, had been initiated into the Mithraic Mysteries at Rome, and is said to have taken great pleasure in the ceremonies. Lampridius records, as one of the mad freaks of Commodus, that "during the Mithraic ceremonies, when a certain thing was to be done for the sake of impressing terror he polluted the rites by a real murder," an expression which evidently shows that a scenic representation of a fictitious murder formed a part of the ceremony of initiation.

The dog swallowing the blood of the bull was also considered a symbol of the resurrection. It is in the still existing talismans and games, that we find the most interesting memorials of the old Mithraic initiation. One of these is thus described by Mr. C. W. King:

"There is a talisman which, from its frequent repetition, would seem to be a badge of some particular degree amongst the initiated, perhaps of the first admission. A man blindfolded with hands tied behind his back, is bound to a pillow, on which stands a gryphon holding a wheel, the latter a most ancient emblem of the sun. Probably it was in this manner that the candidate was taken by the approach of immediate death, "when the bandage was suddenly removed from his eyes." As Mithras was considered as synonymous with the sun, a great deal of solar symbolism clustered around his name, his doctrines and his initiation.

ADONIS, MYSTERIES OF.—An investigation of the Mysteries of Adonis peculiarly claims the attention of the Masonic student, first because in their symbolism and in the esoteric doctrine, the religious object for which they were intended and the mode in which that object is attained, they have a nearer analogical resemblance to the initiation of Freemasonry than do any of the other mysteries or systems of initiations of the ancient world.

Secondly, because their chief locality brings them into very close connection with the early history and reputed origin of Freemasonry. For they were principally celebrated at Byblos, a city of Phenicia, whose Scriptural name was Gebal, and whose inhabitants were the Giblites or Giblemites who are referred to in the first book of Kings (chapter V., 18) as being the stone-squarer's employed by King Solomon in building the Temple. Hence, there must have evidently been a very intimate connection or at least certainly a very frequent communication between the workers on the first Temple and the inhabitants of Byblos, the seat of the Adonecian Mysteries and the place where the worshipers of that rite were disseminated over other regions of the country.

These historical circumstances invite us to an examination of the system of initiation which was practiced at Byblos, because we may find in it something that was probably suggestive of the

symbolic system of initiation which was
subsequently so prominent a feature in the system
of Freemasonry. Let us first examine the myth on
which the Adonisiac initiation was founded. The
mythological legend of Adonis, is that he was the
son of Myrrha and Cinyras, King of Cyprus, Adonis
was possessed of such surpassing beauty that
Venus became enamored with him, and adopted
him as her favorite. Subsequently Adonis, who was
a great hunter, died from a wound indicted by a
wild boar on Mount Lebanon. Venus flew to the
succor of her favorite, but she came too late. Adonis
was dead. On his descent to the infernal regions,
Prosorpine became, like Venus, so attracted by his
beauty that, notwithstanding the entreaties of the
goddess of love, she refused to restore him to earth.
At length the prayers of the desponding Venus were
listened to with favor by Jupiter, who reconciled the
dispute between the two goddesses, and by whose
decree Proserpine was compelled to consent that
Adonis should spend six months of each year
alternately with herself and Venus. Venus, who was
delighted with the extraordinary beauty of the boy,
put him in a coffer, unknown to all the gods, and
gave him to Proserpine to keep, and to nurture in
the under world. But Proserpine had no sooner
beheld him than she became enamored and refused,
when Venus applied for him, to surrender him to
her rival. The subject was then referred to Jupiter,
who decreed that Adonis should have one-third of
the year to him, should be another third with Venus,
and the remainder of the time with Procerpine.
Adonis gave his own portion to Venus, and lived
happily with her until, having offended Diana, he

was killed by a wild boar.

The mythographer Pharnutus gives still a different story, and says that Adonis was the grandson of Cyniras, and fled with his father, Ammon, into Egypt, whose people he civilized, taught them agriculture and enacted many wise laws for their government. He subsequently passed over into Syria, and was wounded in the thigh by a wild boar, while hunting on Mount Lebanon. His wife, Isis, or Astarte, and the people of Phoenicia and Egypt, supposing that the wound was mortal, profoundly deplored his death, but he afterwards recovered and their grief was replaced by transports of joy. All the myths, it will be seen, agree in his actual or supposed death by violence, in the grief for his loss, in his recovery or restoration to life, and in the consequent joy thereon, And on these facts are founded the Adonisian Mysteries which were established in his honor.

Of these mysteries, we are now to speak.

The Mysteries of Adonis are said to have been first established at Babylon, and thence to have passed over into Syria, their principal seat being at the city of Babylon, in that country. The legend on which the mysteries were founded contained a recital of his tragic death and his subsequent restoration to life, as has just been related. The mysteries were celebrated in a vast temple at Byblos. The ceremonies commenced about the season of the year when the river Adonis began to be swollen by the floods at its source. The Adonis, now called Nahrel Ibeahim, or Abraham's River, is a small river of Syria, which, rising in

Mount Lebanon, enters the Mediterranean a few miles south of Byblos. Maundrell, the great traveler, records the fact which he himself witnessed that after a sudden fall of rain the river, descending in floods, is tinged with a deep red by the soil of the hills in which it takes its rise, and imparts this color to the sea into which it is discharged, for a considerable distance. The worshipers of Adonis were readily lead to believe that this reddish discoloration of the water of the river was a symbol of his blood.

To this Milton alludes when speaking of "Thammuz," which the name was given by the idolatrous Israelites to the Syrian god.

The sacred rites of the Adonisian mysteries began with mourning, and the days which were consecrated to the celebration of the death of Adonis were passed in lugubrious cries and wailings, the celebrants often scourging themselves. On the last of the days of mourning, funeral rites were performed in honor of the god; on the following day the restoration of Adonis to life was announced, and was received with the same enthusiastic demonstrations of joy.

The mythological legend, which has been described in the beginning of this article, was but the esoteric story introduced for the uninitiated. There was also—as there was in all these mystical initiations of the ancients—an esoteric meaning, a sacred and secret symbolism, which constituted the essence of the mysteries, and which communicated only to the initiated. Adonis, which is derived from the Hebrew "Adon," "lord and master," was one of the titles given to the sun; and hence the worship of Adonis formed one of the modifications of that once most extensive system of religion—sun-worship. Godwin, in his Moses Aaron says, "Concerning Adonis, whom sometimes ancient authors call Osiris, there are two things remarkable; aphanimos, the death or loss of Adonis, and heresies, the finding of him again. By the death or loss of Adonis, we are to understand the departure of the sun; by his finding again we are to understand his return. Macrobius, in his Saturnalia, more fully explains the allegory thus: "Philosophers have given the name Venus to the superior or northern hemisphere, of which we occupy a part, and that of Proserpine to the inferior. Hence among the Assyrians and Phoenicians. Venus is said to be in tears when the sun in his annual course through the twelve signs of the zodiac, passes over to our antipodes; for of these twelve signs six are said to be superior and six inferior. When the sun is in the inferior signs and the days are comparatively short, the goddess is supposed to weep for the temporary death or privation of the sun, detained by Proserpine, whom we regard as the divinity of the Southern or antipodal regions. And Adonis is said to be restored to Venus when the sun, having traversed the six inferior signs, enters those of our hemisphere, bringing with it an increase of light and lengthened days. The boar which is supposed to have killed Adonis, is the emblem of winter, for this animal, covered with rough bristles, delights in cold, wet and miry situations, and his favorite food is the acorn, a fruit which is peculiar to winter. The sun is said, too, to be wounded by winter, since at that season we lose its light and heat, which the effects produced by death upon animal beings. Venus is represented on Mount Lebanon in an attitude of grief; her head bent and covered with a veil, is supported by her left hand near her breast, and her countenance is bathed in tears. This figure represents the earth in winter, when, being veiled in clouds and deprived of the sun, its energies have become torpid. The fountains, like the eyes of Venus, are overflowing, and the fields, divested of their flowers, present a joyless appearance. But when the sun has emerged from the Southern hemisphere and passed the vernal equinox, Venus is once more rejoiced, the fields are again embellished with flowers, the grass springs up in the meadows and the trees recover their foliage."

Such is supposed by mythologists in general to have been the esoteric doctrine of the Adonisian initiation, hence said to be a branch of that worship of the sun that at one time was so universally practiced over the world. And as this allegory, when thus interpreted, must nave been founded on the fact that the solar orb disappeared for several months of winter, it follows that the allegory must have been invented by some hyperborean people, to whom only such an astronomical phenomenon could be familiar.

Of all the mythologist, the Abbe Banur is the only one who has approximated to what appears, says Dr. Mackey, to be the true interpretation of the myth. He denies the plausibility of the solar theory, which makes Adonis in his death and resurrection the symbol of the sun's setting and rising, or of his disappearance in winter and his return in summer. He thinks the alternate mourning and joy which characterized the celebration of the mysteries may be explained as referring to the severe but not fatal wound of Adonis, and his subsequent recovery through the skill of the physician Cocytus; or if this explanation be rejected, he then offers another interpretation which is much more, says Mackey, to the truth, thus: "But if any be tenacious of the opinion that Adonis died of his wound, I shall account for that joy which succeeded the morning on the last day of the festival, by saying it imported that he was promoted to divine honors, and that room was no longer left for sorrow; but that having mourned for his death, they were now to rejoice at his deification."

The priests, who would not have been in favor of a tradition which taught that the god whom they had served was subject to death, sought to conceal it from the people, and invented the allegorical explication which I have been refuting.

While, therefore, we may grant the probability that there was originally some connection between the Sabean worship of the sun and the celebration of the Adonisian festival, we can not forget that these mysteries, in common with all the other sacred initiations of the ancient world, have been originally established to promulgate among the initiated the once hidden doctrine of a future life.

The myth of Adonis in Syria, like that of Osiris in Egypt, of Atys in Somothrace, or of Dionysus in Greece, presented symbolically the two great ideas of decay and restoration; sometimes figured as darkness and light, sometimes as winter and summer, sometimes as death and life, but always maintaining, no matter what was the framework of the allegory, the inseparable ideas of something that was lost and afterwards recovered, as to its interpretation, and so teaching, as does Freemasonry at this day, by a similar system of allegorizing, that after the death of the body comes the eternal life of the soul. The inquiring Freemason will thus readily see the analogy in the symbolism of the Giblemites at Byblos and Hiram the Builder in his own initiation.

CABIRIC MYSTERIES.—The Cabiri was gods whose worship was first established in the Island of Samothrace, where the Cabiric Mysteries were practiced. The gods called the Cabiri were originally two, and afterwards four, in number, and are supposed by Bryant to have referred to Noah and his three sons, the Cabiric Mysteries being a modification of the Arkite worship. In these mysteries there was a ceremony called the "Cabiric Death," in which was represented, amid the groans and tears and subsequent rejoicings of the initiates, the death and restoration to life of Cadmillus, the youngest of the Cabiri. The legend recorded that he was slain by his three brothers, who afterwards fled with his virile parts in a mystic basket. His body was crowned with flowers and was buried at the foot of Mount Olympus. Clement of Alexandria speaks of the legend as the sacred mystery of a brother slain by his brethren.

There is much perplexity connected with the subject of these mysteries, but it is generally supposed that they were instituted in honor of Atys, the son of Cybele, or Demeter, of whom Cadmillus was but another name.

According to Macrobius, Atys was one of the appellations of the sun, and we know that the mysteries were celebrated at the vernal equinox. They lasted three days, during which they represented in the person of Atys Cadmillus, the enigmatical death of the sun in winter, and his regeneration in the spring.

In all probability, in the initiation, the candidate passed through a drama, the subject of which was the violent death of Atys. The "Cabiric Death" was in fact a type of the Hiramic, and the legend, so far as it can be understood from faint allusions of ancient authors, was very analogous in spirit and design to that of the third degree of Freemasonry.

Many persons annually resorted to Samothrace to be initiated into the celebrated mysteries, among who are mentioned Cadmus, Orpheus, Hercules and Ulysses. Jamblicus says in his life of Pythagoras that from those of Lemnos that sage derived much of his wisdom.

The Mysteries of the Cabirit were much respected among the common people, and great care was taken in their concealment. The priests made use of a language peculiar to the rites.

The mysteries were in existence at Samothrace as late as the eighteenth year of the Christian era, at which time the Emperor Germanicusembarked for that island to be instructed, but was prevented from accomplishing his purpose by adverse winds.

DIONYSIAN MYSTERIES.—These mysteries were celebrated throughout Greece and Asia Minor, but principally at Athens, where the years were numbered by them. They were instituted in honor of Bacchus, or, as the Greeks called him, Dionysus, and were introduced into Greece from Egypt. In these mysteries the murder of Dionysus by the Titans was commemorated. In this legion he is evidently identified with the Egyptian Osiris, who was slain by his brother Typhon. The aspirant in the ceremonies through which he passed, represented the murder of the god, and his restoration to life, which, says the Baron de Sacy, "were the subject of allegorical explanations altogether analogous to those which were given to the rape of Proserpine and the murder of Osiris. The commencement of the mysteries was signified by the consecration of an egg, in allusion to the mundane egg, from which all things were supposed to have sprung. The candidate having been first purified by water and crowned with a myrtle branch, was introduced into the Vestibule and there clothed in the sacred habiliments. He was then delivered to the conductor, who, after the mystic warning, "Depart hence, all ye profane," exhorted the candidate to exert all his fortitude and courage in the danger and trials through which he was about to pass.

He was then led through a series of dark caverns, a part of the ceremonies which Stobeus calls "a rude and fearful march through night and darkness." During this passage he was terrified by the howling of wild beasts, and other fearful noises; artificial thunder reverberated through the subterranean apartments, and transient flashes of lightning revealed monstrous apparitions to his sight. In this state of darkness and terror he was kept for three days and nights, after which they commenced the aphanism or mystical death of Bacchus. He was now placed on the pastes, or couch; that is, he was confined in a solitary cell, where he could reflect seriously on the nature of the undertaking in which he was engaged. During this time, he was alarmed with the sudden crash of water, which was intended to represent the deluge.

Typhon, searching after Osiris, or Dionysus (for they are here identical), discovered the ark in which he had been secreted, and tearing it violently asunder, scattered the limbs of his victim upon the waters. The aspirant now heard the lamentations which were instituted for the death of the god. Then commenced the search of Rhea for the remains of Dionysus. The apartments were filled with shrieks and groans; the initiated mingled with their howling of despair the frantic dances of the Corybantes; everything was a scene of distraction, until, at a signal from the hierophant, the whole drama is changed;—the mourning was turned to joy; the mangled body was found, and the aspirant was released from his confinement amid the shouts of, "We have found it; let us rejoice together!"

The candidate was now made to descend into

the infernal regions, where he beheld the torments of the wicked and the rewards of the virtuous. It was now that he received the lecture explanatory of the Rites, and was invested with the tokens which served the initiated as a means of recognition. He then underwent a lustration, after which he was introduced into the holy place, where he received the name of Epopt, and was fully instructed in the doctrines of the mysteries, which consisted in a belief in the existence of one God, and the future state of rewards and punishments.

These doctrines were inculcated by a variety of significant symbols. After the performance of these ceremonies, the aspirant was dismissed and the rites concluded with the pronunciation of the mystic words "knox ompax. Sainte Croix says that the murder of Dionysus by the Titans was only an allegory of the physical revolutions of the world; but these were in part in the ancient initiations, significant of the changes of life and death and resurrection.

DRUIDICAL MYSTERIES.—The Druids were a sacred order of priests who existed in Britain and Gaul, but whose mystical rites were practiced in most perfection in the former country, where the Isle of Anglesea was considered as their principal seat.

Druidism was divided into three orders or degrees, which were, beginning with the lowest, the Bards, the Prophets, and the Druids. Higgins thinks that the Prophets were the lowest order, but he admits that it was not generally allowed. The

constitution of the order was in many respects like
that of the Freemasons. In every country there was
an Arch-Druid, in whom all authority was placed.
In Britain it is said that there were under him
three arch-flamens or priests, and twenty-five
flamens.

There was an annual assembly for the
administration of justice and the making of laws,
and besides, four quarterly meetings which took
place on the days when the sun reached his
equinoxial and solstical points. The latter two
would very nearly correspond at this time with the
festival of St. John the Baptist, and St. John the
Evangelist. It was not lawful to commit their
ceremonies or doctrines to writing, and Caesar
says that they used the Greek letters, which was,
of course, as a cipher; but Higgins says that one of
the Irish Ogum alphabets, which Toland calls
secret writing, "was the original, sacred and secret
character of the Druids."

The places of worship, which were also places
of initiation, were of various forms: Circular,
because a circle was an emblem of the universe;
or oval, in allusion to the mundane egg, from
which, according to the Egyptians, our first
parents issued; or serpentine, because a serpent
was a symbol of Hu, the Druidical Noah; or
winged, to represent the motion of the Divine
Spirit; or cruciform, because a cross was the
emblem of regeneration. Their only covering was
the clouded canopy, because they deemed it
absurd to confine the omnipotent beneath a roof;
and they were constructed of embankments of
earth, and of unhewn stones, unpolluted with a

metal tool. Nor was any one permitted to enter their sacred retreats unless he bore a chain.

The ceremony of initiation into the Druidical Mysteries required much preliminary mental preparation and physical purification. The aspirant was clothed with the three sacred colors, white, blue and green. White as the symbol of light, blue of truth, and green of hope. When the rites of initiation were passed, the tri-colored robe was changed for one of green. In the second degree the candidate was clothed in blue, and having surmounted all the dangers of the third and arrived at the summit of perfection, he received the red tiara and flowing mantle of purest white. The ceremonies were numerous, the physical proofs painful, and the mental trials appalling.

They commenced in the first degree with placing the aspirant in a pastos, bed or coffin, where his symbolical death was represented, and they terminated in the third by his regeneration, or restoration to life from the womb of the giantess Ceridwin, and the committal of the body of the newborn to the waves in a small boat, symbolical of the ark. The result was, generally, that he succeeded in reaching the safe landing place; but if his arm was weak or his heart failed, death was the almost inevitable consequence. If he refused the trial through timidity, he was contemptuously rejected, and declared forever ineligible to participate in the sacred rites. But if he undertook it and succeeded, he was joyously invested with all the privileges of Druidism.

The doctrines of the Druids were the same as those doctrines entertained by Pythagoras. They taught the existence of one Supreme Being, a future state of rewards and punishment; the immortality of the soul, and metempsychosis, and the object of their mystic rites were to communicate these doctrines in symbolic language, an object and a method common alike to Druidism, to the Ancient Mysteries, and to modern Freemasonry.

ELEUSINIAN MYSTERIES.—Of all the mysteries of the ancient religions, those celebrated at the village of Eleusis, near the city of Athens, was the most splendid and the most popular. To them men came, says Cicero, from the remotest regions, to be initiated. They were also the most ancient, if we may believe St. Epiphanius, who traced them to the reign of Inachus, more than eighteen hundred years before the Christian era. They were dedicated to the goddess Demeter, the Ceres of the Romans, who was worshiped by the Greeks as the symbol of the prolific earth, and in them were scenically represented the loss, and the recovery of Persephone, and the doctrines of the unity of God and the immortality of the soul were esoterically taught. The learned Faber believed that there was an intimate connection between the Arkite worship and the Mysteries of Eleusis, but Faber's theory was that the Arkite rites, which he traced to almost all the nations of antiquity, symbolized in the escape of Noah, and the renovation of the earth, the doctrines of the resurrection and the immortal life. Plutarch says that the travels of Isis in search of Osiris, were not different from those of Demeter, in search of Persopine, and this view has been adopted by St. Croix, and by Creuzer, and hence we may well suppose that the recovery of the former at Byblos, and the latter in Hades, were both intended to symbolize the restoration of the soul after death to eternal life. The learned have generally admitted that when Virgil, in the sixth book of his Aeneid, depicted the descent of Eneus into hell," he intended to give a representation of the Elusion Mysteries.

The mysteries were divided into two classes, the lesser and the greater. The lesser mysteries were celebrated on the banks of the Ilisseus, whose waters supplied the means of purification of the aspirants. The greater mysteries were celebrated in the temple at Eleusis. An interval of six months occurred between them, the former taking place in March and the latter in September, which has led some writers to suppose that there was some mystical reference to the vernal and autumnal equinoxes. But, considering the character of Demeter as the goddess of agriculture, it might be imagined—although this is a mere conjecture—that the reference was to seed-time and harvest. A year, however, was required to elapse before the initiate in the lesser mysteries was granted admission into the greater.

In conducting the mysteries there were four officers, namely, first, the Hierophant, or explainer of the sacred things. As the pontifex maximus in Rome, so he was the chief priest of Atica. He presided over the ceremonies, and explained the nature of the mysteries to the initiated, as the Masters of all Lodges should do. Second, the

Dadouchus, or torch-bearer, which appears to have acted as the immediate assistant of the Hierophant. Third, the Hieroceryx, or sacred herald, who had the general care of the temple, guarded it from the profanation of the unitiated, and took charge of the aspirant during the trials of initiation. Fourth, the Epibomus, or altar-server, who conducted the sacrifices.

The ceremonies of initiation into the lesser mysteries were altogether purificatory, and intended to prepare the neophyte for his reception into the more sublime rite of the greater mysteries. This, an ancient poet, quoted by Plutarch, illustrates by saying that "Sleep is the lesser mysteries of the death." The candidate who desires to pass through this initiation entered the modest temple erected for that purpose on the borders of the Ilissus, and there submitted to the required ablutions, typical of moral purification. The Dadouches then placed his feet upon the skins of the victims which had been immolated to Jupiter. Hesychius says that only the left foot was placed upon the skins. In this position he was asked if he had eaten bread, and if he was pure, and his replies being satisfactory, he passed through other symbolic ceremonies, the mystical signification of which was given to him, an oath of secrecy having been administered the initiate. The lesser mysteries was called a mystes, a title which, being derived from a Greek word meaning to shut the eyes, signified that he was yet blind as to the greater truths thereafter to be revealed.

The greater mysteries lasted for nine days, and was celebrated partly on the Thracian plain which surrounded the temple, and partly in the temple of Eleusis itself, of this temple one of the most magnificent and the largest in Greece. Not a vestige is now left. Its antiquity was very great, having been in existence, according to Aristides the rhetorician, when the Dorians marched against Athens. It was burned by the retreating Persians under Xerxes, but immediately rebuilt, and finally destroyed with the city by Alarie, "the scourge of God," and all that is now left of Eleusis and its spacious temple is the mere site occupied by the insignificant Greek village of Lepina, an evident corruption of the ancient name.

The public processions on the plain and on the sacred way from Athens to Eleusis were made in honor of Demeter and Persephone, and made mystical allusions to events in the life of both and of the infant Iacchus. These processions were made in the day-time, but the initiation was nocturnal, and was reserved for the nights of the sixth and seventh days.

The herald opened the ceremonies of initiation into the greater mysteries by the proclamation, "Retire, O ye profane!" Thus were the sacred precincts tiled. The aspirant was clothed with the skin of a calf, an oath of secrecy was administered, and he was then asked, "Have you eaten bread?" the reply to which was, "I have fasted; I have drank the sacred mixture; I have taken it out of the chest. I have spun. I have placed it in the basket, and from the basket laid it in the chest." By this reply, the aspirant showed that he had been duly prepared by initiation into the lesser mysteries; for Clement of Alexandria says

that this formula was a shibboleth or password by
which the mystic, or initiates, into the lesser
mysteries were known as such, and admitted to the
epopteia or greater initiation. The gesture of
spinning wool, in imitation of what Demeter did in
the time of her affliction, seemed also to be used as
a sign of recognition.

The aspirant was now clothed in the sacred
tunic, and awaited in the vestibule the opening of
the doors of the sanctuary. What subsequently took
place must be left in great part to conjecture,
although modern writers have availed themselves
of all the allusions that are to be found in the
ancients. The temple consisted of three parts, the
megaron, or sanctuary, corresponding to the holy
place of the Temple of Solomon; the anactoron, or
holy of holies, and a subterranean apartment
beneath the temple. Each of these was probably
occupied at a different portion of initiation. The
representation of the infernal regions and the
punishment of the unitization impious were
appropriated to the subterranean apartment, and
was, as Sylvester de Saey says, an episode of the
drama which represented the adventures of Isis,
Osiris and Typhon, or of Demter, Persephone and
Pluto. This drama, the same author thinks,
represented the carrying away of Persephone, the
travels of Demeter in search of her lost daughter,
her descent-into hell, the union of Pluto with
Persephone, and was terminated by the return of
Demeter into the upper world and the light of day.

The representation of this drama commenced
immediately after the profane had been sent from
the temple. And it is easy to understand how the

groans and wailings with which the temple at one time resounded, might symbolize the sufferings and the death of man, and the subsequent rejoicings at the return of the goddess might be typical of the joy for the restoration of the soul to eternal life.

Others have conjectured that the drama of the mysteries represented in the deportation of Persephone to Hades by Pluto, the departure, as it were, of the sun, or the deprivation of its vivific power during the winter months, and her reappearance on earth, the restoration of the prolific sun in summer.

Others, again, tell us that the last act of the mysteries represented the restoration to life of the Zagreus, or Dionysus, by Demeter. Diodorus says the members of the body of Zagreus, lacerated by the Titans, was represented in the ceremonies of the mysteries as well as in the Orphic hymns, but prudently adds that he was not allowed to reveal the details to the unitiated. Whatever was the precise method of symbolism, it is evident that the true interpretation was the restoration from death to eternal life, and that the funeral part of the initiation to a loss, and the exultation afterwards to a recovery. Hence it was folly to deny the coincidence that exists between the Elusion drama and that enacted in the third degree of Masonry. It is claimed that the one was the uninterrupted successor of the other, but there must have been a common ideal source for the origin of both. The lesson, the design, the symbol and the method of initiation are the same. Having now, as Pinder says, "descended beneath the hollow earth and beheld those mysteries," the initiated ceased to be a mystes, or blind man, and was thenceforth called an epopt, a word signifying he who beholds.

The Elusion mysteries, which, by their splendor surpassed all contemporary institutions of the kind, were deemed of so much importance as to be taken under the special protection of the state, and to the council of five hundred were entrusted the observance of the ordinances which regulated them. By a law of Solon, the magistrates met every year at the close of the festival, to pass upon anyone who had violated or transgressed any of the rules which governed the administration of the sacred rites. Any attempt to disclose the esoteric ceremonies of initiation was punished with death. Plutarch tells us, in his life of Alcibiades, that that votary of pleasure was indicted for sacrilege because he had imitated the mysteries and shown them to his companions in the same dress as that worn by the Hierophant, and we get from Livy the following relation:

Two Acarnanian youths who had not been initiated accidentally entered the temple of Demeter during the celebration of the mysteries. They were soon detected by their absurd questions, and being carried to the managers of the temple, although it was evident that their intrusion was accidental, they were put to death for so horrible a crime. It is not, therefore, surprising that in the account of them we should find such uncertain and even conflicting assertions of the ancient writers, who hesitated to discuss publicly so forbidden a subject.

The qualifications for initiation were maturity of age and purity of life. Such was the theory, although in practice these qualifications were not always rigidly regarded. But the early doctrine was that none but the pure, morally and ceremonially, could be admitted to initiation. At first, too, the rite of admission was restricted to natives of Greece, but even in the time of Herodotus this law was dispensed with, and the citizens of all countries were considered eligible. So, in time, these mysteries were extended beyond the limits of Greece, and in the days of the Empire they were introduced into Rome, where they became exceedingly popular.

The scenic representation, the participation in secret signs and words of recognition, the initiation in a peculiar dogma, and the establishment of a hidden bond of fraternity, gave attraction to these mysteries, which lasted until the very fall of the Roman Empire, and exerted a powerful influence on the mystical associations of the Middle Ages.

The bond of union which connects them with modern institutions of Masonry is evident in the common thought which pervades and identifies both, though it is difficult and perhaps impossible to trace all the connecting links of the historic chain. We see the beginning and we see the end of one pervading idea, but the central point is hidden from us, to await some future discovery.

EGYPTIAN MYSTERIES.—Egypt has always been considered as the birthplace of the mysteries. It was there that the ceremonies of initiation were first instituted. It was there that truth was first vested in allegory and the dogmas of religion were first imparted under symbolic forms.

From Egypt, "the land of the winged globe," the land of science and philosophy, "peerless for stately tombs and magnificent temples—the land whose civilization was old and mature before other nations since called to empire had a name," this system of symbols was disseminated through Greece and Rome, and other countries of Europe and Asia, giving origin, through many intermediate steps, to that mysterious association which is now represented by the institution of Freemasonry.

To Egypt, therefore, Masons have always looked with peculiar interest, as the cradle of that mysterious science of symbolism, whose peculiar mode of teaching they alone, of all modern institutions, have preserved to the present day.

The initiation into the Egyptian Mysteries was of all the systems practiced by the ancients the most severe and impressive. The Greeks at Eleusis imitated it to some extent, but they never reached the magnitude of its forms, or the austerity of its discipline. The system had been organized for ages, and the priests, who alone were the hierophants—the explainers of the mysteries, or, as we should call them in Masonic language, the Masters of the Lodges—were educated almost from childhood for the business in which they were engaged. That "learning of the Egyptians" in which Moses is said to have been so skilled, was all-important in these mysteries. It was confined to the priests and to the initiates, and the trials of initiation through which the latter had to pass were so difficult to endure, that none but those who were stimulated by the most ardent thirst for knowledge dared to undertake them, or succeeded in submitting to them.

The priesthood in Egypt constituted a sacred caste, in which the sacerdotal functions were hereditary. They exercised also an important part in the government of the state, and the kings of Egypt were but the first subjects of its priests. They had originally organized and continued to control the ceremonies of initiation. Their doctrines were of two kinds; exoteric, or public, which were communicated to the multitude, and esoteric, or secret, which were revealed only to a chosen few, and to obtain them it was necessary to pass through an initiation which was characterized by severe trials of courage and fortitude.

The principal seat of the mysteries was at Memphis, in the neighborhood of the pyramid. They were of two kinds, the greater and the less; the former being the Mysteries of Osiris and Serapis, the latter those of Isis. The Mysteries of Osiris were celebrated at the autumnal equinox; those of Serapis at the summer solstice, and those of Isis at the vernal equinox. The candidate was required to exhibit proofs of a blameless life. For some days previous to the commencement of the ceremonies of initiation, he abstained from all unchaste acts, confined himself to an exceedingly light diet, from which animal food was rigorously excluded, and purified himself by repeated ablutions.

Apuleius, who had been initiated in all of them, thus alludes, with cautious reticence, to those of Isis: "The priest—all the profane being removed to a distance—taking hold of me by the hand, brought me into the inner recess of the sanctuary itself, clothed me in a new linen garment. Perhaps, curious reader, you would be eager to know what he then said or did. I would tell you, were it lawful for me to tell you. You should know it if it were lawful for you to hear. Both the ears that heard those things and the tongue that told them would reap the evil results of their rashness. Still, however, kept in suspense, as you probably are with religious longing, I will not torment you with long protracted anxiety. Hear, therefore, but believe what is truth. I approached the confines of death, and, having trod on the threshold of Proserpine, I returned there from, having been through all the elements. At midnight I saw the sun shining with its brilliant light, and I approached the presence of gods beneath and gods above, and stood near and worshiped them. Behold, I have related to you things of which, though heard by you, you must necessarily remain ignorant."

The first degree, as we may term it, of Egyptian initiation, was that in the Mysteries of Isis. What was its peculiar import, we are unable to say. Isis, says Knight, was among the later Egyptians the personification of universal nature. To Apuleius she says: "I am nature, the parent of all things, the sovereign of the elements, the primary progeny of time." Plutarch tells us that on the front of the temple of Isis were placed this inscription: "I, Isis, am all that has been, that is, or shall be, and no mortal hath ever unveiled me.'

Thus we may conjecture that the Isiac Mysteries were descriptive of the alternate decaying and renovating powers of Nature.

Higgins, it is true, says that during the mysteries of Isis were celebrated the misfortunes and tragical death of Osiris in a sort of drama; and Apuleius asserts that the initiations into her mysteries is celebrated as being a close resemblance to a voluntary death, with a precarious chance of recovery. But Higgins gives no authority for his statement, and that of Apuleius can not be constrained into any reference to the enforced death of Osiris, it is therefore probable that the ceremonies of this initiation were simply preparatory to that of the Osirian, and taught by instructions in the physical laws of nature the necessity of moral purification, a theory which is not incompatible with all the mystical allusions of Apuleius when he describes his own initiation.

The Mysteries of Serapis constituted the second degree of the Egyptian initiation. Of these rites we have but a scantly knowledge. Herodotus is entirely silent concerning them, and Apuleius, calling them "the nocturnal orgies of Serapes, a god of the first rank," only intimates that they followed those of Isis, and were preparatory to the last and greatest initiation. Serapis is said to have been only Osiris while in Hades; and hence the Serapian initiation might have represented the death of Osiris, but leaving the lesson of resurrection for a subsequent initiation. But this is merely a conjecture.

In the Mysteries of Osiris, which were a consummation of the Egyptian system, the lesson of death and resurrection was symbolically taught; and the legend of the murder of Osiris, the search for the body, its discovery and restoration to life, is scenically represented. This legend of initiation was as follows:

Osiris, a wise king of Egypt, left the care of his kingdom to his wife, Isis, and traveled for three years to communicate to other nations the arts of civilization. During his absence his brother Typhon formed a secret conspiracy to destroy him, and to usurp his throne. On his return Osiris was invited by Typhon to an entertainment, in the month of November, at which all the conspirators were present. Typhon produced a chest inlaid with gold, and promised to give it to any person present whose body would exactly fit it. Osiris was tempted to try the experiment, but had no sooner laid down in the chest, than the lid was closed and nailed down, and the chest thrown in the river Nile. The chest containing the body of Osiris was, after being for a long time tossed by the waves, finally cast up at Byblos, in Phenecia, and left at the foot of a tamarisk tree. Isis, overwhelmed with grief for the loss of her husband, set out on a journey, and traveled the earth in search of the body. After many adventures, she at length discovered the spot whence it had been thrown up by the waves, and returned with it in triumph to Egypt. It was then proclaimed with the most extravagant demonstrations of joy, that Osiris was raised from the dead, and had become a god.

Such, with slight variations of details by different writers, are the general outlines of the Osiric legend which was represented in the drama of initiation. Its resemblance to the Hiramic legend of the Masonic system will be readily seen, and its symbolism will be easily understood. Osiris and Typhon are the representatives of the two antagonistic principles—good and evil, light and darkness, life and death.

There is also an astronomical interpretation of the legend, which makes Osiris the sun, and Typhon the season of winter, which suspends the fecundating and fertilizing powers of the sun, or destroys life, to be restored only by the return of invigorating spring.

The sufferings and death of Osiris were the great mysteries of the Egyptian religion, his being the abstract idea of divine goodness. His death, his resurrection, and his subsequent office as judge of the dead in a future state look, says Wilkinson, like the early revelation of a future manifestation of the deity converted into a mythical fable.

Into these mysteries Herodotus, Plutarch and Pythagoras were initiated, and the former two have given brief accounts of them. But their own knowledge must have been extremely limited, for, as Celement of Alexandria tells us, the more important secrets were not revealed, even to all the priests, but to a select number of them only.

AMERICAN MYSTERIES.—Among the many evidences of a foreign state of civilization among the aborigines of this country which seem to prove their origin from the races that inhabit the Eastern Hemisphere, not the least remarkable is the existence of fraternities bound by mysteries, and claiming, like the Freemasons, to possess an esoteric knowledge, which they carefully conceal from all but the initiated. De Witt Clinton relates, on the authority of a respectable native minister, who has received the signs, the existence of such a society among the Iroquois. The number of the members was limited to fifteen, of whom six were to be of the Seneca tribe, five of the Oneidas, two of the Cayugas, and two of the Regis. They claim that their initiation has existed from the creation. The times of their meeting they kept a secret, and throw much mystery over all their proceedings.

Briton tells us, in his interesting and instructive work on the myths of the New World (p. 285), that among the red race of America "the priests formed societies of different grades of initiation, only to be entered by those willing to undergo trying ordeals, whose secrets were not to be revealed under the severest penalties.

The Algonkins had three such grades—the Waubno, the Meda, and the Jassakeed, the last being the highest. To this no white man has ever been admitted. All tribes appear to have been controlled by these secret societies. Alexander von Humboldt mentions one, called that of the Botuto, or Holy Trumpet, among the Indians of the Orinoco, whose members must vow celibacy and submit to severe scourging and fasts

AMERICAN RITE.—It has been proposed to give this name to the series of degrees conferred in the United States. The York Rite, which is the name by which they are usually designated, is certainly a misnomer, for the York Rite properly consists of only the degrees of Entered Apprentice, Fellow Craft, and Master Mason, including in the last degree the Royal Arch. This was the Masonry that existed in England at the time of the revival of the Grand Lodge in 1717. The abstraction of the Royal Arch from the Master's degree, and its location as a separate degree, produced the modification of the York Rite which now exists in England, and which should properly be called the Modern York Rite, to distinguish it from the Ancient York Rite, which consisted of only three degrees. But in the United States, still greater additions have been made to the rite, through the labors of Webb and other lecturers, and the influence insensibly exerted on the Order by the introduction of the Ancient and Accepted Rite into this country. The American modifications of the York Rite consist of nine degrees, viz.:

1.   Entered Apprentice.
2.   Fellow Craft.
3.   Master Mason, given in symbolic Lodges.
4.   Mark Master.
5.   Past Master.
6.   Most Excellent Master.
7.   Holy Royal Arch, given in chapters.
8.   Royal Master.
9.   Select Master, given in councils.

A tenth degree, called Super-excellent Master, is conferred in some councils as an honorary rather than a regular degree; but even as such it is represented by many Grand Councils. To these, perhaps, should be added three more degrees, namely, Knights of the Red Cross, Knight Templar, and Knight of Malta, which are given in commanderies, and are under the control of Grand Commanderies, or, as they are sometimes called. Grand Encampments. But the degrees of the commandery, which are also known as the degrees of chivalry, can hardly be called a part of the American Rite. The possession of the eighth and ninth degrees is not considered a necessary qualification for receiving them. The true American Rite consists only of the nine degrees above enumerated. There is no general Grand Lodge, or Grand Lodge of the United States; but there is a General Grand Chapter, and a Grand Encampment, to which the Grand Chapters and Grand Commanderies of some, but not all, of the States are subject.

YORK RITE.—This is the oldest of all the rites and consisted, originally, of only three degrees— the Entered Apprentice, the Fellow Craft and the Master Mason's. The last, including a part which contained the true word, but which was disrupted from it by Dunckerly in the latter part of the last century, and has never been restored. The rite in its purity does not now exist anywhere. The nearest approach to it is the St. Johns Masonry of Scotland, but the Master's degree of the Grand Lodge of Scotland is not the Master's degree of the

York Rite. When Dunckerly dismembered the third degree, he destroyed the identity of the rite. In 1813 it was apparently recognized by the United Grand Lodge of England, when it defined "pure Ancient Masonry to consist of three degrees, and no more; viz., those of Entered Apprentice, Fellow Craft, and Master Mason, including the Supreme Order of the Holy Royal Arch."

Had the Grand Lodge abolished the Royal Arch degree, which was then practiced as an independent order in England, and re-incorporated its secrets in the degree of Master Mason, the York Rite would have been revived. But by recognizing the Royal Arch as a separate degree, and retaining the Master's degree in its mutilated form, they repudiate the rite.

In the United States it has been the almost universal usage to call the Masonry there practiced the York Rite. But it has no better claim to this designation, than it has to be called the Ancient and Accepted Rite, or the French Rite, or the Rite of Schroder; it has no pretensions to the York Rite. Of its first three degrees, the Master Mason is the mutilated one which took the Masonry of England out of the York Rite, and it has added to these three degrees six others which were never known to the Ancient York Rite, or that which was practiced in England in the earlier half of the eighteenth century by the legitimate Grand Lodge.

The York Rite was that rite which was most probably organized or modified at the revival in 1717, and practiced for fifty years by the constitutional Grand Lodge of England. It consisted of only the three symbolic degrees, the last one, or the Master's, containing within itself the secrets now transferred to the Royal Arch. This rite was carried in its purity to France in 1725, and into America at a later period. About the middle of the eighteenth century the Continental Masons, and about the end of it the Americans, began to superimpose upon it those high degrees which, with the necessary mutilation of the third, have given rise to numerous other rites. But the Ancient York Rite, though no longer cultivated, must remain on the record of history as the oldest and purest of all the rites.

YORK LEGEND.—The city of York, in the north of England, is celebrated for its traditional connection with Masonry in that Kingdom. No topic in the history of Freemasonry has so much engaged the attention of modern Masonic scholars, or given occasion to more discussion, than the alleged facts of the existence of Masonry in the tenth century at the city of York, as a prominent point of the calling of a congregation of the Craft there in the year 926, of the organization of a general assembly, and the adoption of a constitution. Recently, the discovery of many old manuscripts has directed the labors of such scholars as Hughan, Woodford, Lyon and others, to the critical examination of the early history of Masonry. And that of York has particularly engaged their attention. It may be premised that, of all those who have subjected these legends to the crucible of historical criticism, Hughan, of Cornwall, in

England, must unhesitatingly be acknowledged as the ablest, the most laborious, and the most trustworthy investigator. He was the first and the most successful remover of the cloud of tradition which so long had obscured the sunlight of history. The legend which connects the origin of English Masonry at York in 926, is sometimes called the "York Legend;" sometimes the "Athelstane Legend." because the General Assembly said to have been held there, occurred during the reign of that king, and sometimes the "Edwin Legend," because that prince is supposed to be at the head of the Craft and have convoked them together to form a constitution.

The uninterrupted existence for several centuries of a tradition that such an assembly was held, requires that those who deny it should furnish some more satisfactory reason for their opinion than has yet been produced. And now the important question in Masonic literature is, whether it is a myth or a history—whether it is all or in any part fiction or truth—and if so, what portion belongs to the former, and what to the latter category. in coming to a conclusion on this subject, the question necessarily divides itself into three forms:

1. Was there an assembly of Masons held in or about the year 926, at York, under the patronage or by the permission of King Athelstane?

The Rev. Mr. Woodford has critically discussed this subject (in an essay on the connection of York with Freemasonry in England), and comes to this conclusion: "I see no reason, therefore, to reject so old a tradition that under Athelstane the operative

Masons obtained his patronage, and met in General Assembly." To that verdict, says Dr. Mackey, "I subscribe."

2. Was Edwin, the brother of Athelstane, the person who convoked that assembly?

Francis Drake, in his speech before the Grand Lodge of York, in 1726, said: "You know we can boast that the first Grand Lodge ever held in England was held in this city, where Edwin, the first Christian king of North Umbria, about the six hundredth year after Christ, and who laid the foundation of our cathedral, sat as Grand Master."

3. Are the constitutions which were adopted by that General Assembly now extant?

There is the strongest internal evidence that all the manuscripts, from the Hallmell to the Papworth, have a common original, from which they were copied with more or less accuracy, or on which they were framed with more or less modification. And this original is supposed to be the constitutions which must have been adopted at the General Assembly at York.

Dr. Mackey thinks the theory may safely be advanced on this subject, and which must be maintained until there are better reasons than we now have to reject it, that about the year 926, a General Assembly of Masons was held at York, under the patronage of Edwin, brother of Athelstane, at which assembly a code of laws was adopted, which became the basis on which all subsequent Masonic constitutions were framed.

LECTURES, HISTORY OF THE.—Each degree of Masonry contains a course of instruction in which the ceremonies, traditions and moral instruction appertaining to the degree are all set forth, each lecture, for the sake of convenience, and for the purpose of conforming to certain divisions in the ceremonies, is divided into sections, the number of which have varied at different periods, although the substance remains the same. It must be confessed that many of the interpretations given in the lectures are unsatisfactory to the cultivated mind, and seem to have been adopted on the principle of the old Egyptians, who made use of symbols to conceal, rather than to express their thoughts. Learned Masons have been, therefore, always disposed to go beyond the mere technicalities and stereotyped phrases of the lectures, and to look in the history and philosophy of the ancient religions, and the organization of the ancient mysteries for a true explanation of most of the symbols of Masonry, and there they have always been able to find this true interpretation. The lectures, however, serve as an introduction, or preliminary essay, enabling the student, as he advances in his investigation, to become acquainted with the symbolic character of the initiation. But if he ever expects to become a learned Mason, he must seek in other sources for the true development of Masonic symbolism. The lectures alone are but the primer of the science. Knowledge of these lectures, which must be communicated by oral teaching, constituted a very important part of a Masonic education, and until the great progress made within the present century in Masonic

literature, many "bright Masons" as they are
technically styled, could claim no other foundation
than such knowledge for their high Masonic
reputation. But some share of learning more
difficult to obtain, and more sublime in its
character than anything to be found in these oral
lectures, is now considered necessary to form a
Masonic scholar. Still, as the best commentary on
the ritual observances is to be found in the
lectures, and as they also furnish a large portion of
the secret mode of recognition, or that universal
language which has always been the boast of the
Institution, not only is a knowledge of them
absolutely necessary to every practiced Freemason,
but a history of the changes which they have from
time to time undergone, constitutes an interesting
part of the literature of the Order. Comparatively
speaking (comparatively in respect to the age of
the Masonic Institution), the system of Lodge
lectures is undoubtedly a modern invention. That
is to say, we can find no trace of any form of
lectures like the present before the middle, or
perhaps the close of the seventeenth century.
Examinations, however, of a technical nature,
intended to test the claims of the person examined
to the privileges of the Order, appear to have
existed at an early period. They were used until at
least the middle of the eighteenth century, but
were perpetually changing, so that the test of one
generation of Masons constituted no tests for the
succeeding one. Oliver very properly describes them
as being "something like the conundrums of the
present day—difficult of comprehension—admitting
only of one answer, which appeared to have no

direct correspondence with the question, and applicable only in consonance with the mysteries and symbols of the Institution."

But, when we speak of the lectures in the modern sense, as containing an expression of the symbolism of the Order, we may consider it as an established historical fact that the fraternity was without any such system until after the revival of 1717. Previous to that time, brief extemporary addresses and charges were used by the Masters of Lodges, which, of course, varied in excellence with the varied attainments and talents of the presiding officer.

A comparison of the primitive lectures, as they may be called, with those in use in America at the present day, demonstrates that a great many changes have taken place. There are not only omissions of some things, and additions of others, but sometimes the explanations of some points are entirely different in the two systems.

But lecture-making seems to have been a popular fancy at that early period of what may be called the Masonic renaissance. The Clare lectures did not very long occupy their authoritative position in the Order. Though longer and more elevated than those of Anderson, they were, in the course of a few years, found to be neither long enough, nor sufficiently elevated, for the increasing demands of Masonic purposes.

Accordingly, some time about the year 1770 the Grand Lodge of England authorized Thomas Dunckerly to prepare a new course of lectures which were to take the place of those of Martin Clair. To him is ascribed the adoption of the "lines parallel," as symbolical of the two Saints John; and he also introduced the theological ladder, with its three principal rounds—a beautiful and instructive symbol, that has been retained to the present day, but imperfectly explained. Webb, it is true, referred to its "three principal rounds." leaving room, by implication, for the addition of others. But Cross, who was wholly unacquainted with ancient symbolism, drew a picture, in which he absolutely made the rounds, three in number, and no more, thus fixing an incorrect theory on the Masonic mind. The Masonic ladder, like its prototype in all the mysteries, consists of seven rounds.

Above all, we are indebted to Hutchinson for restoring the ancient symbolism of the third degree, and for showing that, in all past time, its legend was but typical of a restoration from the grave; a thought that does not seem to have attracted the early lecturers, although always existing in the Masonic system. Even Webb, twenty-five years after Hutchinson's book appeared, could only find in the legend of the third degree "an instance of virtue, fortitude and integrity seldom equaled and never excelled in the history of man." And to teach this lesson only was the initiation preserved for years, as Dr. Mackey says, "Alas! for such lectures."

But in the last decennium of the eighteenth century, a lecture-maker did arise among the American Masons; and to Thomas Smith Webb we are indebted for our present system of lectures.

JACOB'S LADDER.—The introduction of
Jacob's ladder into the symbolism of speculative
Masonry is to be traced to the vision of Jacob,
which is thus substantially recorded in the twenty-
eighth chapter of the book of Genesis:

"When Jacob, by the command of his father
Isaac, was journeying towards Padanaram, while
sleeping one night on the bare earth for his couch,
and a stone for his pillow, he beheld the vision of a
ladder, whose foot rested on the earth and whose
top reached to heaven. Angels were continually
ascending and descending upon it, and promised
him the blessing of a numerous and happy
posterity. When Jacob awoke he was filled with
pious gratitude and consecrated the spot as the
house of God."

This ladder, so remarkable in the history of the
Jewish people, finds its analogue in all the ancient
initiations. Whether this is to be attributed simply
to a coincidence—a thing which but few scholars
would be willing to accept—or to the fact that these
analogies were all derived from a common fountain
of symbolism, or whether, as suggested by Oliver,
the origin of the symbol was lost among the
practices of the pagan rites while the symbol itself
was retained, it is impossible authentically to
determine. It is a fact, however, certain, that the
ladder as a symbol of moral and intellectual
progress existed almost universally in antiquity,
presenting itself either as a succession of steps, of
gates, of degrees, or in some other modified form.

The number of steps varied, although the favorite
one appears to be seven, in reference, apparently, to
the mystical character almost everywhere given to

that number. Thus in the Persian Mysteries of Mithras, there was a ladder of seven rounds, the passage through them being symbolical of the soul's approach to perfection. These rounds were called gates, and, in allusion to them the candidate was made to pass through seven dark and winding caverns, which process was called the ascent of the ladder to perfection. Each of these caverns was the representation of a world, or state of existence through which the soul was supposed to pass in its progress from the first world to the last, or the world of truth.

In the Mysteries of Brahma, we find the same reference to the ladder of seven steps. The seven steps were emblematical of the seven worlds which constituted the Indian universe. The lowest was the earth; the second, the world of pre-existence; the third, heaven; the fourth, the middle world, or intermediate region between the lower and upper worlds; the fifth, the world of births, in which souls were again born; the sixth, the mansion of the blessed, and the seventh or topmost round, the sphere of truth. Among the Kabbalists, the ladder was represented by ten Sephiroths, which, commencing from the bottom, were the kingdom, foundation, splendor, firmness, beauty, justice, mercy, intelligence, wisdom, and the crown by which we arrive at the En Soph, or the infinite.

In the higher Masonry we find the ladder of Kadosh, which consists of seven steps thus, commencing from the bottom—justice, equity, kindness, good faith, labor, patience and intelligence. The arrangements of these steps, for which we are indebted to modern ritualism, does not seem to be perfect, but yet, the idea of intellectual progress to perfection is carried out by making the topmost round represent wisdom, or understanding.

The Masonic ladder which is represented in the symbolism of the first degree ought really, says Mackey, to consist of seven steps which thus ascend: Temperance, fortitude, prudence. justice, faith, hope and charity; but the earliest examples of it present it only with three, referring to the three theological virtues, whence it is called the theological ladder. It seems, therefore, to have been settled by general usage that the Masonic ladder has but three steps.

As a symbol of progress, Jacob's ladder was early recognized. Picus of Mirandola, who wrote in the sixteenth century, in his oration, "De Hominis Dignitate," says that Jacob's ladder is the symbol of the progressive scale of intellectual communication betwixt earth and heaven, and upon the ladder, as it were, step by step, man is permitted with the angels to ascend and descend until the mind finds blissful and complete repose in the bosom of deity. The highest step he defines to be theology, or the study and contemplation of the deity in his own abstract and exalted nature.

"In the tracing board, the ladder has but three rounds; a change-from the old seven-stepped ladder of the mysteries, which, however, Preston corrected when he described it as having many rounds, but three principal ones."

In the Prestonian lecture, the ladder is said to rest on the Holy Bible, and to reach to the heavens.

This symbol is thus explained: "By the doctrines contained in the Holy Bible we are taught to believe in the divine dispensation of Providence, which belief strengthens our faith and enables us to ascend the first step; that faith naturally creates in us a hope of becoming partakers of some of the blessed promises therein revealed, which hope enables us to ascend the second step. But the third and last one being charity, comprehended the whole. And he who is possessed of this virtue in its ample sense, is said to have arrived to the summit of his profession, or more metaphorically, into the eternal mansion veiled from the mortal eye by the starry firmament." In the modern lectures the language is materially changed, but the idea and the symbolism are retained unaltered.

Dr. Mackey says, "The fact that Dunckerley derived his symbol from Ramsay; that Ramsay's ladder had seven steps, being the same as the Kadosh symbol; that in all the old initiations the number seven was preserved, and lastly; that Preston describes it as having 'many rounds or staves,' which point out as many moral virtues, but three principal ones, namely, faith, hope and charity, irresistibly lead us to the conclusion that the Masonic ladder should properly have seven steps, which represent the four cardinal and the three theological virtues."

SYMBOL.—A symbol is defined to be a visible sign, with which a spiritual feeling, emotion, or idea, is connected. It was in this sense that the early Christians gave the name of symbols to all rites, ceremonies and outward forms which bore a religious meaning. At a still earlier period the Egyptians communicated the knowledge of their esoteric philosophy in mystic symbols; in fact, man's earliest instruction was by means of symbols.

The word "symbol" is derived from a Greek verb, which signifies "to compare one thing with another," and hence a symbol, or emblem—for the two words are often used synonymously in Masonry—is the expression of an idea which is derived from the comparison, or contrast, of some object with a moral conception or attribute.

Thus, the plumb is the symbol of rectitude; the level of equality; the bee-hive of industry. The physical qualities of the plumb are compared or contrasted with the moral conception of virtue or rectitude of conduct. The plumb becomes to the Mason, after he has been taught its symbolic meaning, forever afterwards the visible expression of the idea, or uprightness of conduct.

To study and compare these visible objects, to elicit from them the moral ideas which they are intended to express—is to make oneself acquainted with the symbolism of Masonry.

The Egyptian priests were great proficient's in symbolism, and so were the Chaldeans, and so were Moses and the prophets, and the evangelist St. John has made much use of it in his vision on the Isle of Patmos.

In Freemasonry all the instructions in the mysteries are communicated in the form of symbols. Founded as a speculative science based on an operative art, it has taken the working tools of the profession which it spiritualizes. The terms of architecture, the Temple of Solomon, and everything connected with its traditional history and adopted them as symbols, it teaches its great moral and philosophical lessons by the system of symbolism. But its symbols are not confined to material objects, as were the hieroglyphics of the Egyptians. Its myths and legends are also for the most part symbolic; often a legend unauthenticated by history, distorted by anachronisms, and possibly abounding in pretensions, if viewed historically, or as a narrative of actual occurrence, when interpreted as a symbol, is found to impress the mind with some great spiritual and philosophical truth. The legends of Masonry are parables, and a parable is only a spoken symbol. By its utterance, says Adam Clark, "Spiritual things are better understood, and make a deeper impression on the attentive mind."

The science which is engaged in the investigation of the meaning of symbols and the application of their interpretation to moral, religious and philosophic instruction, is the science of symbolism. Therefore, in this sense, Freemasonry is certainly a science of symbolism.

KEY.—"The key," says Dr. Oliver, "is one of the most important symbols of Freemasonry; it bears the appearance of a common metal instrument, confined to the performance of one single act. But

the well-instructed brother beholds in it the symbol
which teaches him to keep a tongue of good report,
and to abstain from the debasing vices of slander
and defamation." Among the ancients the key was
symbolic of silence and circumspection, and thus
Sophocles alludes to it in the Edipus Colenius
(1051), where he makes the chorus speak of "the
golden key which had come upon the tongue of the
ministering hierophant in the Mysteries of
Eleusis." Callimachus says that the priestess of
Ceres bore a key as the ensign of her mystic office.
The key was in the Mysteries of Isis a hieroglyphic
of the opening or disclosing of the heart and
conscience in the kingdom of death, for trial and
judgment. In the old ritual of Masonry the key was
an important symbol, and Dr. Oliver regrets that it
has been abandoned in the modern system. In the
ritual of the first degree in the eighteenth century
allusion is made to a key by whose help the secrets
of Masonry are to be obtained, which key "is said to
hang and not to lie, because it is always to hang in
a brother's defense, and not to lie to his prejudice."
It was said to hang "by the thread of life at the
entrance," and was always connected with the
heart, because the tongue "ought to utter nothing
but what the heart dictated." And finally the key is
described as being "composed of no metal, but a
tongue of good report." In the ritual of the Master's
degree in the Adonhiram Rite, we find this
catechism:

"Q. What do you conceal?"

"A. All the secrets which have been entrusted to
me."

"Q. Where do you conceal them?"

"A. In the heart."

"Q. Have you a key to gain entrance there?"

"A. Yes, Right Worshipful."

"Q. Where do you keep it?"

"A. In a box of coral, which opens and shuts only with ivory keys."

"Q. Of what metal is it composed?"

"A. Of none; it is a tongue obedient to reason, which knows only how to speak well of those of whom it speaks in their absence as in their presence."

All of this shows that the key as a symbol was formerly equivalent to the modern symbol of the "instructive tongue" which however, with almost the same interpretation, has been conferred to the second or Fellow Craft's degree.

MOSAIC SYMBOLISM.—In the religion of Moses, more than any other which preceded or followed it, is symbolism the predominating idea. From the tabernacle, which may be considered the central point of the whole system, down to the vestments which clothe the servants at the altar, there will be found an underlying principle of symbolism. Long before the day of Pythagoras the mystical nature of numbers had been inculcated by the Jewish lawgivers, and the very name of God was constructed in symbolical form to indicate His eternal nature. Much of the Jewish ritual of worship delineated in the Pentateuch with so much precision as to its minutest details, would almost seem puerile were it not for the symbolic idea that it conveyed. So the fringes of the garments are

patiently described, not as decorations, but that by
them the people, in looking upon the fringe, might
"remember all the commandments of the Lord and
do them." Well, therefore, has a modern writer
remarked, that in the symbolism of the Mosaic
worship it is only ignorance that can find the
details trifling or the prescriptions minute; for if
we recognize the worth and beauty of symbolism,
we shall in vain seek in the Mosaic symbols for one
superfluous enactment, or one superstitious idea."

To the Mason, the Mosaic symbolism is very
significant, because from it Freemasonry has
derived and transmitted for its own uses, many of
the most precious treasures of its own symbolical
art. Indeed, except in some of the higher and
therefore more modern degrees, the symbolism of
Freemasonry is almost entirely deduced from the
symbolism of Mosaism. Thus the symbol of the
Temple, which persistently pervades the whole of
the ancient Masonic system comes to us directly
from the symbolism of the Jewish tabernacle. if
Solomon is revered by the Masons, as their
traditional Grand Master, it is because the Temple
constructed by him was the symbol of the divine
life to be cultivated in every heart. And this symbol
was borrowed from the Mosaic tabernacle, and the
Jewish thought that every Hebrew was to be a
tabernacle of the Lord has been transferred to the
Masonic system, which teaches that every Mason
is to be a temple of the Grand Architect. The papal
church, from which we get all ecclesiastical
symbolism, borrowed its symbology from the
ancient Romans. Hence, most of the high degrees
of Masonry, which partake of a Christian character,

are marked by Roman symbolism transmuted into Christian. But Craft Masonry—more ancient and more universal—finds its symbolic teaching almost exclusively in the Mosaic symbolism instituted in the wilderness.

If we inquire whence the Jewish lawgiver derived the symbolic system which he introduced into his religion, the history of his life will readily answer the question. Philojudaus says that "Moses was instructed by the Egyptian priests in the philosophy of symbols and hieroglyphs, as well as in the mysteries of the sacred animals."

The sacred historian tells us that he was "learned in all the wisdom of the Egyptians," and Manetho and other traditional writers, tell us that he was educated at Heliopolis as a priest under his Egyptian name of Osarsiph, and that there he was taught the whole range of literature and science which it was customary to impart to the priests of Egypt. When, then, at the head of his people, he passed away from the servitude of Egyptian taskmasters, it is not strange that he should have given a holy use to the symbols whose meaning he had learned in his ecclesiastic education on the bank of the Nile.

Thus it is that we find in the Mosaic symbolism so many identities with the Egyptian ritual. Thus the ark of the covenant, the breastplate of the high priest, the mitre and many others of the Jewish symbols will find their analogies in the ritualistic ceremonies of the Egyptians. Reghellini, who has written an elaborate work on "Masonry Considered as the Result of the Egyptian, Jewish and Christian Religion," says on the subject: "Moses in his mysteries, and after him Solomon, adopted a great part of the Egyptian symbols, which, after them, we Masons have preserved in our own."

ALL-SEEING EYE.—An important symbol of the Supreme Being, borrowed by the Freemasons from the nations of antiquity. Both the Hebrews and the Egyptians appear to have derived its use from that natural inclination of figurative minds to select an organ as a symbol of the function which it is intended peculiarly to discharge. Thus, the foot was often adopted as the symbol of swiftness, the arm of strength, and the hand of fidelity. On the same principle, the open eye was selected as the symbol of watchfulness, and the eye of God as the symbol of divine watchfulness and care of the universe. The use of the symbol in this sense is represented to be found in the Hebrew writers. Thus the Psalmist says, "The eyes of the Lord are upon the righteous;" and, "Behold he that keepeth Israel shall neither slumber nor sleep."

The Egyptians represented Osiris, their chief deity, by the symbol of open eyes, and placed this hieroglyphic of him in all of their temples. His symbolic name on the monuments was represented by the eye accompanying a throne, to which was sometimes added an abbreviated figure of the god, and sometimes what has been called a hatchet, or a presentation of a square. The All-Seeing Eye may then be considered as a symbol of God manifested in His omnipresence. His guardian and protecting character, to which Solomon alludes when he says: "The eyes of Jehovah are in every place, beholding the evil and the good." It is a symbol of the ominpresent Deity.

LIGHT.—Light is an important word in the Masonic system. It conveys a far more recondite meaning than it is believed to possess by the generality of readers. It is, in fact, the first of all the symbols presented to the neophyte, and continues to be presented to him in various modifications throughout all his future progress in his Masonic career, it does not simply mean, as might be supposed, truth or wisdom, but it contains within itself a far more abstruse allusion to the very essence of speculative Masonry, and embraces within its capacious signification all the other symbols of the Order. Freemasons are emphatically called the "sons of light," because they are, or are at least entitled to be, in possession of the true meaning of the symbol, while the profane or uninitiated have not received this knowledge, are, by parity of expression, said to be in darkness.

The connection of material light with this emblematic and mental illumination, was prominently exhibited in all the ancient systems of religious and esoteric mysteries. Among the Egyptians the hare was the hieroglyphic of eyes that are open, because that animal was supposed to have his eyes always open. The priests afterwards adopted the hare as the symbol of moral illumination revealed to the neophytes in the contemplation of the divine truth, and hence, according to Champollion, it was also the symbol of Osiris, their principal divinity, and the chief object of their mystic rites—thus showing the intimate connection that they maintained in their symbolic language between the process of initiation and the contemplation of divinity. On this subject a remarkable coincidence has been pointed out by M. Portal, in the Hebrew language. There the word for "hare" is arnebet, which seems to be composed of "aur, light" and "nabat, to see," so that the word which among the Egyptians was used to designate an initiation, among the Hebrews meant to see the light. If we proceed to an examination of the other systems of religion which were practiced by the other nations of antiquity, we shall find that light always constituted a principal object of adoration as the primordial source of knowledge and goodness, and that darkness was with them synonymous with ignorance and evil.

But as light not only came from God, but also makes man's way clear before him, so it was employed to signify moral truth, and pre-eminently that divine system of truth which is set forth in the Bible, from its earliest gleaming onward to the perfect day of the Great Sun of Righteousness. As light was thus adored as the source of goodness, darkness, which is the negative of light, was abhorred as the cause of evil, and hence arose the doctrine which prevailed among the ancients, that there were two antagonistic principles continually contending for the government of the world. Such was the dogma of Zoroaster, the great Persian philosopher, who, under the names of Ormuzd and Ahriman, symbolized these two principles of light and darkness.

Such was also the doctrine, though somewhat modified,

of Manes, the founder of the sect of Manichees, who describes God the Father as ruling over the kingdom of light, and contending with the powers of darkness.

In fact, in all the Ancient Mysteries, this reverence for light, as an emblematic representation of the eternal principle of good, is predominant. In the mysteries the candidate passed during his initiation through scenes of utter darkness, and at length terminated his trials by an admission into a splendidly illuminated sacellum, where he was said to have attained pure and perfect light, and where he received the necessary instructions which were to invest him with that knowledge of the divine truth which had been the object of all his labors.

DARKNESS.—Darkness has, in all the systems of initiation, been deemed a symbol of ignorance, and so opposed to light, which is the symbol of knowledge. Hence, the rule that the eye should not see until the heart has conceived the true nature of those beauties which constitute the mysteries of the Order. In the Ancient Mysteries the aspirant was always shrouded in darkness, as a preparation to the reception of the full light of knowledge. The time of this confinement in darkness and solitude varied in the different mysteries. Among the Druids the period was nine days and nights. In the Grecian Mysteries it was three times nine days; while among the Persians, according to Porphyry, it was extended to the almost incredible period of fifty days of darkness, solitude and fasting. Because, according to all the cosmogonies, darkness existed before light was created, darkness was originally worshiped as the first-born, as the progenitor of day, and the state of existence before creation. Freemasonry has restored darkness to its proper place as a state of preparation—the symbol of that ante-mundane chaos, from whence light issued at the divine command, of the state of nonentity before birth, and of ignorance before the reception of knowledge. Hence, in the Ancient Mysteries, the release of the aspirant from solitude and darkness was called the act of regeneration, and he was said to be born again, or to be raised from the dead, and in Masonry the darkness which envelops the mind of the uninitiated being removed by the bright effulgence of Masonic light, Masons are appropriately called "the sons of light."

In Dr. Oliver's "Signs and Symbols" there is a lecture "On The Mysterious Darkness of the Third Degree." This refers to the ceremony of enveloping the room in darkness when that degree is conferred—a ceremony once always observed," but now, in this country at least, frequently but improperly omitted. The darkness here is a symbol of death; the lesson is taught in the degree, while the subsequent renewal of light refers to that other and subsequent lesson of eternal life.

NIGHT.—Lodges all over the world meet, except on special occasions, at night. In this selection of the hours of the night and darkness for initiation, the usual coincidence will be found between the ceremonies of Freemasonry and those of the Ancient Mysteries, showing their evident derivation from a common origin.

In the Bacchoe of Euripides, that author introduces the god Bacchus, the supposed inventor of the Dionysian Mysteries, as replying to the question of King Pentheus, in the following words:

"Pentheus—By night or day, these sacred rites performs thou?

"Bacchus—Mostly by night, for venerable is darkness."

And in all the other mysteries the same reason was assigned for nocturnal celebrations, since night and darkness have something solemn and august in them which are disposed to fill the mind with sacred awe. And hence black, as an emblem of darkness and night, was considered as the color appropriate to the mysteries.

In the Mysteries of Hindustan, the candidate for initiation, having been duly prepared by previous purifications, was led at the dead of night to the gloomy cavern, in which the mystic rites were performed.

The same period of darkness was adopted for the celebration of the Mysteries of Mithras in Persia. Among the Druids of Britain and Gaul, the principal annual initiation commenced at "low twelve," or midnight of the eve of May-day. In short, it is indisputable that the initiations in all the Ancient Mysteries were nocturnal in their character.

The reason given by the ancients for this selection of night as the time for their initiation is equally applicable to the system of Freemasonry. "Darkness," says Oliver, "was an emblem of death, and death was a prelude to resurrection. It will be at once seen therefore in what manner the doctrine of the resurrection was inculcated and exemplified in these remarkable instances." Death and the resurrection were the doctrines taught in the Ancient Mysteries, and night and darkness were necessary to add to the sacred awe and reverence which these doctrines ought always to inspire in the rational and contemplative mind. The same doctrines form the very groundwork of Masonry; and as the Master Mason, to use the language of Hutchinson, "represents a man saved from the grave of iniquity and to the faith of salvation," darkness and light are the appropriate accompaniments to the solemn ceremonies which demonstrate this profession.

FREEMASONRY, HISTORY OF.—It is the opprobrium of Freemasonry that its history has never yet been written in a spirit of critical truth, that credulity and not incredulity has been the foundation on which all Masonic historical investigations have hitherto been built; that imagination has often "lent enchantment to the view;" that missing links in a chain of evidence have been frequently supplied by gratuitous invention; and that statements of vast importance have been carelessly sustained by the testimony of documents whose authenticity has not been proved. And this leads to the important question: How is the history of Freemasonry to be written, so that the narrative shall win the respect of its enemies, and secure the assent and approbation of its friends?

In the first place, we must begin by a strict

definition of the word Masonry. If we make it synonymous with Freemasonry, then must we confine ourselves closely to the events that are connected with the institution in its present form and organization. We may then say that Masonry received a new organization and a restoration in the beginning of the eighteenth century. We may trace this very institution, with an older but not dissimilar form, in the Masonic guilds of Europe, in the corporations of the stone-masons of Germany, in the traveling Freemasons of the Middle Ages, and connect it with the Colleges of Architects of Rome. Such a history will not want authentic memorials to substantiate its truth, and there will be no difficulty in conferring upon the Institution an enviable antiquity.

But if we confound the term Masonry with geometry, with architecture, or with moral science, we shall beget within the mind—equally of the writer and the reader—such a confusion of ideas as can never lead to any practical result. And yet this has been the prevailing error of great English writers on Masonry in the last and, with a few exceptions, even in the present century. At one moment they speak of Masonry as a mystical institution, which in its then existing form was familiar to their readers. Soon afterwards, perhaps on the same page, a long paragraph is found to refer, without any change of name, under the identical term Masonry, to the rise of architecture, to the progress of geometry, or perhaps to the condition of the moral virtues. Thus Preston, in his illustrations of Masonry, begins his section on the origin of Masonry by stating that "from the commencement of the world we may trace the foundation of Masonry." And he adds, "Ever since symmetry began, and harmony displayed her charms, our Order has had a being. But after reading through the entire chapter we find that it is not to Freemasonry, such as we know and recognize it, that the author has been referring, but to some great moral virtue, to the social feelings, to the love of man for man, which as inherent in the human heart, must have existed from the very creation of the race, and necessarily have been the precursor of civilization and the arts.

Oliver, who, notwithstanding the valuable services which he had rendered to Masonry, was unfortunately too much given to abstract speculations, has "out-heroded Herod," and in commenting on this passage of Preston, proclaims "that our science existed before the creation of this globe, and was diffused amidst the numerous systems with which the grand emporium of universal space is furnished," but on further reading we find that by speculative Masonry the writer means "a system of ethics founded on the belief of a God," and that in this grandiloquent sentence he does not refer to the Freemasonry of whose history he is professing to treat, but to the existence of such a belief among the sentient intelligences who, as he supposes, inhabit the planets and stars of the solar system. Anderson is more modest in his claims. He traces Masonry only to Adam in the garden of Eden, but soon we find that he, too, is treating of different things by the same name, and that the Masonry of the primitive patriarch is not the Freemasonry of our day, but geometry and architecture.

Now, Mackay says, "All this is to write romance, not history. Such statements may be said to be what the French call rhetorical flourishes, having much sound and no meaning." But when the reader meets with them in books written by men of eminence, professedly intended to give the true history of the Order, he either abandons in disgust a study which has been treated with so much folly, or he is led to adopt theories which he can not maintain, because they are absurd. In the former case, Freemasonry perhaps loses a disciple; in the latter he is ensnared by a delusion.

The true character of Freemasonry is much in its character like the history of a nation; it has its historic and its pre-historic era. In its historic era, the Institution can be regularly traced through various antecedent associations, similar in design and organization, to a comparatively remote period. Its connection with these associations can be rationally established by authentic documents, and by other evidences which no historian would reject. Thus dispassionately and philosophically treated, as though it were the history of an empire that was under investigation—no claim be advanced that can not be substantiated—no assertion made that can not be proved—Freemasonry—the word so used meaning, without evasion or reservation, precisely what everybody supposes it to mean—can be invested with an antiquity sufficient for the pride of the most exacting admirers of the society. And then, for the prehistoric era—that which connects it with the mysteries of the pagan world, and with the old priests of Eleusis, of

Samothrace, or of Syria—let us honestly say that we no longer treat of Freemasonry under its present organization, which we know did not exist in those days, but of a science, peculiar, and peculiar only, to the mysteries and to Freemasonry—a science which we may call Masonic symbolism, and which constitutes the very heart-blood of the ancient and modern institutions, and gave to them, while presenting a dissimilarity of form, an identity of spirit. And then, in showing the connection, and in tracing the germ of Freemasonry in these pre-historic days, although we shall be guided by no written narrative on which to rely, we shall find fossil thoughts embalmed in those ancient intellects precisely like the living ones which crop out in modern Masonry, and which, like the fossil shells and fishes of the old physical formations of the earth, show by their resemblance to living specimens, the graduated connection of the past with the present.

No greater honor could accrue to any man than that of having been the founder of a new school of Masonic history, in which the fictions and loose statements of former writers would be rejected, and in which the rule would be adopted that has been laid down as a vital maxim of all inductive science—in words that have been chosen as his motto by a recent powerful investigator of historical truth: "Not to exceed and not to fall short of facts; not to add and not to take away. To state the truth, the whole truth, and nothing but the truth."

RELIGION OF MASONRY.—There has been a needless expenditure of ingenuity and talent by a large number of Masonic orators and essayists, in the endeavor to prove that Masonry is not religion. This has undoubtedly arisen from a well intended but erroneous view that has been taken of the connection between religion and Masonry, and from the fear that if the complete disseverance of the two was not made manifest, the opponents of Masonry would be enabled successfully to establish a theory which they have been fond of advancing, "that the Masons were disposed to substitute the teachings of their Order for the truths of Christianity."

That Masonry is indebted solely to the religious element, which it contained for its origin and for its continual existence, can hardly be denied, when we consider that it includes a belief in the being and perfection of God, that a public profession of such faith is essentially necessary to gain admission into the fraternity, that no disbeliever in the existence of a God can be made a Mason.

The revelation of His will to man is technically called the spiritual, moral and Masonic trestle-board of every Mason, according to the rules and designs of which he is to erect the spiritual edifice of his eternal life. A state of reward and punishment is necessarily included in the very idea of an obligation, which without a belief in such a state, could have no binding force or efficacy.

And true goodness and piety of life is inculcated as the inevitable duty of every Mason from the inception of the first to the end of the very last

last degree he takes; and all the duties we owe to God, and to our fellow-men arise from and are founded on the principles of obedience to the Divine Will. It is the voice of the G. A. O. T. U. symbolized to us in every ceremony of our ritual that speaks to the true Mason, commanding him to fear God and love the brethren.

But some have assumed mistaken ground, in confounding the idea of a religious institution with that of the Christian religion, and in supposing, because Masonry teaches religious truth, that it is offered as a substitute for Christian truth and Christian obligation. But Freemasonry is not Christianity, nor a substitute for it. It is not intended to supersede it, or any other form of worship or system of faith. Although a man may be eminently religious without being a Mason, it is impossible that a Mason can be true and trusty to the Fraternity, unless he is a respecter of religion, and an observer of religious principles.

The mosque of the Mohammedan and the church or chapel of the Christian is but an embodiment of the same idea of temple worship in a different form. The Goths, the Celts, the Egyptians and the Greeks, however much they may have differed in the ritual, were all in the possession of priests and of temples. Masonry points its disciples to the path of righteousness, but it does not claim to be the "way, the Truth, and the life," but is ever searching after "the Truth" of eternal life. In so far, therefore, it can not become a substitute for Christianity, but its tendency is thitherward, and as a handmaid of religion it may, and often does, act as the porch that introduces its votaries into the temple of divine truth, but it does not propose any substitute for the virtues of the atonement, or the divine plan of human salvation from sin.

The Pharisees of old kept the law "blameless," yet the Master said, "Except your righteousness shall exceed the righteousness of the scribes and Pharisees, ye shall in no wise enter into the kingdom of heaven." Therefore it is evident that human nature, however pure and sinless it may have been in the beginning, or however highly developed by education and environments it may have become since, is, morally speaking, a temple in ruins. Both the Holy Scripture and human experience teach its imperfection.

Who ever found human nature truly dignified and exalted, until divine love had burnt out the dross of sin in the human heart, and then expanded it, so that it would reach out in its affections for God, and for sin-cursed humanity?

No one, however exalted his mind, can become truly noble and exalted, can learn the true secret of existence, and put into practice the divine equities of life without a proper conception of the life to come through a knowledge of the merits of the Lion of the Tribe of Judah, by the exercise of an implicit faith and trust in His power at the final day to raise the fallen temple of our immortal spirit into newness of a better life, to dwell in the Holy of Holies of the Great I Am. Then, how important that we should heed the exhortation of the great apostle, to "be not deceived; God is not mocked, for whatsoever a man sowed, that shall he also reap; for he that sowed to the flesh shall of the flesh reap corruption; but he that sowed to the spirit shall of the spirit reap life everlasting." But the religion of Masonry is not sectional. It admits men of every creed within its hospitable bosom, rejecting none and approving none for his peculiar faith. It is not Judaism, though there is nothing in it to offend a Jew. It is not Christian; but there is nothing in it repugnant to the faith of a Christian. Its religion is that general one of nature and primitive revelation—handed down to us from some ancient and patriarchal priesthood—in which all men may agree, and in which no men can differ; it inculcates the practice of virtue, but it supplies no scheme of redemption, teaching the Fatherhood of God, the brotherhood of man, and a future life, where the "True Word" or divine truth is the reward of a virtuous and holy life.

CIVILIZATION OF FREEMASONRY.—Those who investigate in the proper spirit the history of speculative Masonry, will be strongly impressed with the peculiar relation that exist between the history of Masonry and that of civilization. They both find these facts to be patent; that Freemasonry has ever been the result of civilization; that in the most ancient times the spirit of Masonry and the spirit of civilization have always gone together; that the progress of both has been with equal strides; that where there has been no appearance of civilization there has been no traces of Masonry, and finally, that where Masonry has existed in any of its forms, there it has been surrounded and sustained by civilization, which social conditions it in turn elevated and purified.

Speculative Masonry, therefore, seems to have been a necessary result of civilization. It is even in its primitive and most simple forms, to be found among no barbarous or savage people. Such a state of society has never been capable of introducing or maintaining its abstract principles of divine truth. But while speculative Masonry is the result of civilization, existing only in the bosom and never found among barbarous or savage races, it has, by a reactionary law of sociology, proved the means of extending and elevating the civilization to which it originally owed its birth. Civilization has always been progressive. That of Pelasgic Greece was far behind that which distinguished the Hellenic period of the same country. The civilization of the ancient world was inferior to that of the modern, and every country shows advancement in the moral, intellectual and social condition of mankind.

But in the progress of imperfection to perfection, the influence of those speculative systems that are identical with Freemasonry has always been seen and felt. Let us, for an example, look at the ancient heathen world and its impure religions. While the people of paganism bowed, in their ignorance, to a many-headed god, or rather worshiped at the shrine of many gods, whose mythological history and character must have exercised a pernicious effect on the moral purity of their worshipers, speculative philosophy, in the form of the "Ancient Mysteries," was exercising its influence upon a large class of neophytes and disciples, by giving this true symbolic interpretation of the old religious myths: In the adyta of their temples in Greece and Rome and Egypt; in the sacred caves in India, and in the consecrated groves of Scandinavia and Gaul and Britain, these ancient sages were secretly divesting the pagan faith of its polytheism, and of its anthromorphic deities, and were establishing a pure monotheism in its place, and illustrating, by a peculiar symbolism, the great dogmas—since taught in Freemasonry—of the unity of God and the immortality of the soul.

And in modern times, when the religious thought of mankind, under a better dispensation, has not required this purification, Masonry still in other ways exerts its influence in elevating the tones of civilization; for through its working the social feelings have been strengthened, the amenities and charities of life been refined and extended, and, as we have had reason to know and see, the very bitterness of strife and blood-guiltiness of war have been softened and oftentimes obliterated.

UNIVERSALITY OF MASONRY.—The boast of the Emperor Charles V., that the sun never set on his vast empire, may be applied with equal truth to the order of Freemasonry. From east to west, and from north to south, over the whole habitable globe, are our Lodges disseminated. Wherever the wandering steps of civilized man have left their footprints, there have our temples been established,. The lessons of Masonic love have penetrated into the wilderness of the West, and the red man of our soil has shared with his more enlightened brother the mysteries of our science; while the arid sands of the African desert have more than once been the scene of a Masonic greeting. Masonry is not a fountain, giving health and beauty to some single hamlet, and slaking the thirst of those only who dwell upon its humble banks; but it is a mighty stream, penetrating through every hill and mountain, and gliding through every field and valley of earth, bearing on its beneficent bosom the abundant waters of love and charity for the poor, the widow and the orphan of every land.

TUBAL CAIN.—Of Tubal Cain the sacred writings, as well as the Masonic legends gives us but scanty information. All that we hear of him in the book of Genesis is that he was the son of Lamech and Zilla, "and was an instructor of every artificer in brass and iron." The authorized version has, however, almost indelibly impressed the character of Tubal Cain as the father of artificers, and it is in this sense that he has been introduced, from a very early period, into the legendary history of Masonry.

The first Masonic reference to Tubal Cain is found in the "legend of the Craft," as follows:

"Before Noah's flood, there was a man called Lamech, as it is written in the Bible, in the fourth chapter of Genesis; and this Lamech had two wives, the one named Ada, and the other named Zilla; by his first wife, Ada, he got two sons, the one Jabel, and the other Jubal; and by the other wife he got a son and a daughter, and these four children founded the beginning of all the sciences in the world. The elder son, Jabel, founded the science of geometry, and he carried flocks of sheep and lambs into the fields, and first built houses of stone and wood, as it is noted in the chapter above named; and his brother Jubal founded the science of music. And the third brother, Tubal Cain, founded smith-craft, of gold, silver, copper, iron, and steel, and the daughter founded the art of weaving. And these children knew well that God would take vengeance for sin, either by fire or water, wherefore they wrote the sciences that they had found, on two pillars that they might be found after Noah's flood. The one pillar was marble, for that would not burn with fire, and the other was of brass, for that would not drown in water."

Similar to this is an old Rabbinical tradition, which asserts that Jubal, who was the inventor of writing as well of music, having heard Adam say that the universe would be twice destroyed, once by fire and once by water, inquired which catastrophe would first occur; but Adam refusing to inform him, he inscribed the system of music which he had invented, upon two pillars of stone and brick. A more modern Masonic tradition ascribes the construction of these pillars to Enoch.

To this account of Tubal Cain must be added the additional particulars recorded by Josephus, that he exceeded all men in strength, and was renowned for his warlike achievements.

The use of Tubal Cain as a significant word in the Masonic ritual is derived from the "Legend of the Craft," by which the name was made familiar to the operative and then to the speculative Masons, and it refers not symbolically, but historically to his scriptural and traditional reputation as an artificer. If he symbolized anything, it would be labor; and a Mason's labor is to acquire truth, and not worldly possessions.

HIRAM ABIF.—There is no character in the annals of Freemasonry, whose life is so dependent on tradition, as that of the celebrated architect of King Solomon's Temple.

Profane history is entirely silent in respect to his career, and the sacred records supply us with only very unimportant items. To fill up the space between his life and his death, we are necessarily compelled to resort to those oral legends which have been handed down from the ancient Masons to their successors, most of which were probably at first symbolical in their character; the symbol in the lapse of time having been converted into a myth, and the myth, by constant repetition, having assumed the formal appearance of a truthful narrative. Such has been the case in the history of all nations. But whatever may have been their true character, to the Mason at least they are interesting, and can not be altogether void of instruction.

Of this artist, whom Freemasons recognize, sometimes as Hiram the Builder, sometimes as the widow's son, but more commonly as Hiram Abif—the word Abif as an appellation, or surname, or title of honor and distinction, bestowed upon the chief builder of the Temple—the earliest account is found in the first book of Kings: "And King Solomon sent and fetched Hiram out of Tyre; he was a widow's son of the tribe of Naphtali, and his father was a man of Tyre, a workman in brass; and he was filled with wisdom and understanding, and cunning to work all works in brass, and he came to King Solomon and wrought all his work."

Upon the arrival of this celebrated artist at Jerusalem, which was in the year B. C. 1012, he was at once received into the intimate confidence of Solomon, and entrusted with the superintendence of all the workmen, both Tyrians and Jews, who were engaged in the construction of the building. He received the title of "Principal Conductor of the Work," an office which, previous to his arrival, had been filled by Adoniram, and, according to Masonic tradition, formed with Solomon and King Hiram of Tyre, his ancient patron, the Supreme Council of Grand Masters, in which everything was determined in relation to the construction of the edifice, and the government of the workmen.

The legend says: "It was the duty of Hiram Abif to superintend the workmen, and the reports of his officers were always examined with the most scrupulous exactness. At the opening of the day, when the sun was rising in the east, it was his constant custom, before the commencement of labor, to go into the Temple and offer up his prayers to Jehovah, for a blessing on the work; and in like manner when the sun was setting in the west, and after the labors of the day were closed, and the workmen had left the Temple, he returned his thanks to the Grand Architect of the Universe for the harmonious protection of the day. Not content with this devout expression of his feelings, he always went into the Temple at the hour of high twelve, when the men were called off from labor to refreshment, to inspect the work, to draw fresh designs upon the trestle-board, if such were necessary, and to perform other scientific labors,—never forgetting to consecrate the duties by solemn prayer. These religious customs were performed for the first six years in the secret recesses of the Lodge, and for the last year in the precincts of the most holy place."

While assiduously engaged in the discharge of these arduous duties, seven years passed rapidly away, and the magnificent Temple of Jerusalem was nearly completed. The Fraternity was about to celebrate the cape-stone with the greatest dem onstrations of joy; but, in the language of the venerable Book of constitutions, "their joy was soon interrupted by the death of their dear and worthy master, Hiram Abif." On the very day appointed for celebrating the cape-stone of the building, says one tradition, he repaired to his usual place of retirement at the usual hour, and did not return alive. On this subject we can say no more. This is neither the time nor place to detail the particulars of his death. It is enough to say that the circumstance filled the Craft with the most profound grief, which was deeply shared by his friend and patron, King Solomon, who, according to the Book of Constitutions, "after some time allowed to the Craft to vent their sorrow, ordered his obsequies to be performed with great solemnity and decency, and buried him in the Lodge near the Temple—according to the ancient usage among Masons—and long mourned his loss."

WORD.—When emphatically used, the expression "the Word" is in Masonry always referred to the third degree. The use of a word is of great antiquity. We find it in the Ancient Mysteries. In those of Egypt it is said to have been the Tetragrammaton. The German Stonemasons of the Middle Ages had one which, however, is supposed to be only a password, by which the traveling companion might make himself known in his professional wandering. Lyon shows that it existed in the sixteenth and subsequent centuries in the Scottish Lodges, and he says that "the word is the only secret that is ever alluded to in the minutes of Mary's Chapel, or in those of the Kilwinning, Atcheson's Haven, or Dumblane, or any other that we have examined, of a date prior to the erection of the Grand Lodge." Indeed, he thinks that the communication of this word constituted the only ceremony of initiation practiced in the operative Lodges. All that time there was evidently but one word for all the ranks of Apprentices, Craftsmen, and Masters. He thinks that the communication of the Mason word to the Apprentice under oath constituted the germ whence has sprung the symbolic Masonry. But it must be remembered that the learned and laborious investigations of Bro. Lyon refer only to the Lodges of Scotland. There is no sufficient evidence that a more extensive system of initiation did not prevail at the same time, or even earlier, in England and Germany. Indeed, Findel has shown that it did in the latter country, and it is difficult to believe that the system, which we know was in existence in 1717, was a sudden development out of a single word, and for which we are indebted to the inventive genius of those who were engaged in the revival of that period. Be this as it may, the evidence is conclusive that everywhere, and from the earliest times, there was a word. This, at least, is no modern usage.

But it must be admitted that this word, whatever it was, was at first a mere mark of recognition. Yet it may have had, and probably did have, a mythical signification, and had not been altogether arbitrarily adopted. The word given in the Sloane MS. No. 3329, which Bro. Hughan places at a date not posterior to 1700, is undoubtedly a corrupt form of that now in use, and with the signification of which we are well acquainted. Hence, we may conclude that the legend and the symbolism connected with it also existed at the same time, but only in a nascent and incomplete form.

The modern development of speculative Masonry into a philosophy has given a perfected form to the symbolism of the word no longer confined to use as a means of recognition, but elevated in its connection with the legend of the third degree, to the rank of a symbol.

So viewed, and by the scientific Mason it is now only so viewed, the word becomes the symbol of divine truth, the loss of which and the search for it constitute the whole system of speculative Masonry. So important is this word that it lays at the very foundation of the Masonic edifice. The word might be changed, as might a grip or sign, if it was possible to obtain the universal consent of the Craft, and Masonry would still remain unimpaired.

But were the word abolished or released from its intimate connection with the Hiramic legend, and with that of the Royal Arch, the whole symbolism of speculative Masonry would be obliterated. The Institution might withstand such an innovation, but its history, its character, its design, would belong to a newer and a totally different society. The word is what Dermott called the Royal Arch—"the marrow of Masonry."

WORD, TRUE.—Used in contradistinction to the lost word and the substituted word. To find it is the object of all Masonic search and labor. For as the Lost Word is the symbol of death, the True Word is the symbol of life eternal. It indicates the change that is always occurring—truth after error, light after darkness, life after death. Of all the symbolism of speculative Masonry, that of the True Word is the most philosophical and sublime.

LOST WORD.—The mystical history of Freemasonry informs us that there once existed a word of surpassing value, and claiming profound veneration; that this word was known to but few; that it was at length lost; and that a temporary substitute for it was adopted. But as the very philosophy of Masonry teaches that there can be no death without a resurrection—no decay without a subsequent restoration—on the same principle it follows that the loss of the word must suppose its eventual recovery.

Now, this it is, precisely, that constitutes the myth of the lost word and the search for it. No matter what was the word, no matter how it was lost, nor why a substitute was provided, nor when nor where it was recovered.

These are all points of subsidiary importance, necessary, it is true, for understanding the symbolism. The only term of the myth that is to be regarded in the study of its interpretation, is the abstract idea of a word lost and afterwards recovered.

The Word, therefore, is considered to be the symbol of divine truth; and all its modifications— the loss, the substitution, and recovery—are but component parts of the mythical symbol which represents a search after truth. In a general sense, the word itself being then the symbol of divine truth, the narrative of its loss and the search for its recovery becomes a mythical symbol of the decay and loss of the true religion among the ancient nations, at and after the dispersion on the plains of Shina, and of the attempts of the wise men, the philosophers, and priests, to find and to retain it in their secret mysteries and institutions, which have hence been designated as the spurious Freemasonry of antiquity.

But, there is a special or individual, as well as a general interpretation, and in this special or individual interpretation the word, with its accompanying myth of a loss, a substitute and a recovery, becomes a symbol of the personal progress of a candidate from his first initiation to the completion of his course, when he receives a full development of the mysteries.

SUBSTITUTE WORD.—This is an expression
of very significant suggestion to the thoughtful
Master Mason. If the word is, in masonry, a symbol
of divine truth; if the search for the word is a
symbol of the search for that truth; if the lost word
symbolizes the idea that divine truth has not been
found, then the substitute word is a symbol of the
unsuccessful search after divine truth and the
attainment of this life, of which the first Temple is
a type of what is only an approximation to it. The
idea of a substitute word and its history is to be
found in the oldest rituals of the last century, but
the phrase itself is of more recent date, being the
result of the fuller development of Masonic science
and philosophy. The history of this substitute word
has been an unfortunate one. Subjected from a
very early period to a mutilation of form, it
underwent an entire change in some rites, after the
introduction of the high degrees; most probably
through the influence of the Stuart Masons, who
sought by an entirely new word to give a reference
to the unfortunate representative of that house as
the similitude of the stricken builder. And so it has
come to pass that there are now two substitutes in
use, of entirely different form and meaning; one
used on the continent of Europe, and one in
England and this country.

It is difficult in this case, where almost all the
knowledge that we can have of the subject is so
scanty, to determine the exact time when, or the
way in which the new word was introduced. But
there is supposed to be abundant internal evidence
in the words themselves as to their appropriateness

and the language whence they came, as well as from the testimony of old rituals, to show that the word in use in the United States is the true word, and was the one in use before the revival in 1717.

Both of these words have, however, been translated by persons ignorant, says Mackey, of the language whence they are derived, so that the most incorrect and even absurd interpretations of their significations have been given. The word in universal use in this country has been translated as "rottenness in the bone," or the builder is dead," or by several other phrases equally as far from the true meaning.

Dr. Mackey says: "The correct word has been mutilated. Properly it consists of four syllables, for the last syllable, as it is now pronounced, should properly be divided into two. These four syllables compose three Hebrew words, which constitute a perfect and grammatical phrase appropriate to the occasion of their utterance. But to understand them, the scholar must seek the meaning of each syllable, and combine the whole."

JEHOVAH.—Jehovah is, of all the significant words of Masonry, by far the most important. Reghellini very properly calls it "the basis of our dogma and of our mysteries." The Hebrew it consisted of four letters, and hence called the Tetragrammaton, or four-lettered name; and because it was forbidden to a Jew, as it is to a Mason, to pronounce it, it is also called the ineffable or unpronounceable name.

For its history we must refer to the sixth chapter

of Exodus (verses 2, 3): "And God spoke unto Moses, and said unto him, I am the Lord. And I appeared unto Abraham, unto Isaac, and unto Jacob, by the name of God Almighty, but by my name Jehovah was I not known to them."

The first thing that attracts our attention in the investigation of this name is the ancient regulation, still existing, by which it was made unlawful to pronounce it. The Talmud in one of its treatises, the "Sanhedrim," which treats of the question, who of the Israelites shall have future life and who shall not, says: "Even he who thinks the name of God with the true letters forfeits his future life."

The last priest who pronounced it, says Rabbi Bechai, was Simon the Just. After the destruction of the city and Temple by Vespasian, the pronunciation of it ceased, for it was not lawful to pronounce it anywhere except in the Temple at Jerusalem, and thus the true and genuine pronunciation of the name was entirely lost to the Jewish people. Nor is it now known how it was originally pronounced. The Greeks called it Jao; the Romans Jova; the Samaritans always pronounced it Jahve. Hence some of the most learned of the Jewish writers even doubt whether Jehovah is the true pronunciation, and say that the recovery of the name is one of the mysteries that will be revealed at the coming of the Messiah. Among the Essenes, this sacred name, which was never uttered aloud, but always in a whisper, was one of the mysteries of their initiation, which candidates were bound by a solemn oath never to divulge. It is reported to have been, under a modified form, a password in the Egyptian Mysteries, and none,

Schiller, dare enter the temple of Serapis who did not bear on his breast or forehead the name Jao or Je-ha-ho, a name almost equivalent in sound to that of Jehovah, and probably of identical import, and no name was uttered in Egypt with more reverence. In Freemasonry, the Holy Name is the representative of the word, which is itself the symbol of the nature of God. To know the word is to know the true nature and essence of the Grand Architect. When the pronunciation of the name was first interdicted to the people is not certainly known. Leusden says it was a rabbinical prohibition, and was probably made at the Second Temple. The statement of the Rabbi Bechai, already cited, that the word was pronounced for the last time by Simeon, before the spoliation by the Roman Emperor Vespasian, would seem to indicate that it was known at the Second Temple, although its utterance was forbidden, which would coincide with the Masonic tradition that it was discovered while the foundation of the Second Temple was being laid. But the general opinion is that the prohibition commenced in the time of Moses, the rabbinical writers tracing it to the law of Leviticus already cited. This, too, is the theory of Masonry, which also preserves a tradition that the prohibition would have been removed at the First Temple, had not a well known occurrence prevented it. But this is not to be viewed as a historic statement; but only as a medium of creating a symbol. In Masonry, as in the Hebrew Mysteries, it was under the different appellation of the word, the true word, or the lost word, the symbol of the knowledge of divine truth, or the true nature of God.

That this name in its mystical use was not unknown to the Mediaeval Freemasons, there can be no doubt. Many of their architectural emblems show that they possessed this knowledge; nor can there be any more doubt that through them it came to their successors, the Freemasons of the beginning of the eighteenth century. No one can read Dr. Anderson's Defense of Masonry, written in 1730, without being convinced that this prominent actor in the revival was well acquainted with this name, although he is, of course, careful to make no very distinct reference to it, except in one instance. "The occasion," he says, "of the brethren searching so diligent for the Master was, it seems, to receive from him the secret word of Masonry, which should be delivered down to their posterity in after ages."

It is now conceded, from indisputable evidence, that the holy name was, in earlier years, and indeed, up to the middle of the last century, attached to the third degree, and then called the Master's word. Dr. Mackey says he had two tracing-boards of that degree, one an Irish one of the date of 1769, the other a Continental one of 1778, but apparently copies of some earlier one. Among the emblems displayed is a coffin, on which is inscribed, in capital letters, the word Jehovah. Hutchinson, who wrote in 1774, makes no reference to the Royal Arch, although that system had, by that time, been practically established in England. But in his lectures to Master Masons and on the third degree refers to "the mystic word, the Tetragrammaton." Oliver tells us distinctly that it was the Master's word until Dunckerley took it out of the degree and transferred it to the Royal Arch. That it was so on the Continent, we have the unmistakable testimony of Guillemain de St. Victor, who says that Solomon placed a medal on the tomb of Hiram "on which was engraved Jehova, the old Master's word, and which signifies the Supreme Being."

So far, then, these facts appear to be established: That this ineffable name was known to the operative Freemasons of the Middle Ages; that it was derived from them by the speculative Masons, who, in 1717, revived the Order in England; that they knew it as Master Masons, and that it continued to be the Master's word until late in that century, when it was removed by Dunckerley into the Royal Arch.

LION OF THE TRIBE OF JUDAH.—The connection of Solomon as the chief of the tribe of Judah, with the lion, which was the achievement of the tribe, has caused this expression to be referred, in the third degree, to him who brought life and immortality to light. The old Christian interpretation of the Masonic here prevails. And in Ancient Craft Masonry, all allusions to the lion, as the lion's paw, the lion's grip, etc., refer to the doctrine of the resurrection, taught by him who is known as "the lion of the tribe of Judah." The expression is borrowed from the Apocalypse: "Behold, the lion which is of the tribe of Judah, the root of David, hath prevailed to open the book and to loose the seven seals thereof." The lion was also a mediaeval symbol of the resurrection, the idea being founded on a legend. The poets of that age were fond of referring to the legendary symbol in connection with the scriptural idea of the "tribe of Judah." Thus Adam St. Victor, in a poem, says:

> "Thus the strong lion of Judah,
>   The gates of cruel death being broken,
>   Arose on the third day
>   At the loud sounding voice of the Father."

The lion was the symbol of strength and sovereignty, in the human-headed figures of the Nimrod gateway in Egypt. It was worshiped at the city of Leontopolis as typical of Dom, the Egyptian Hercules. Plutarch says that the Egyptians ornamented their temples with gaping lions' mouths, because the Nile began to rise when the sun was in the constellation of Leo. Among the Talmudists there was a tradition of the lion which has been introduced into the higher degrees of Masonry. But in the symbolism of Ancient Craft Masonry where the lion is introduced, as in the third degree, in connection with the "lion of the tribe of Judah," he becomes simply a symbol of the resurrection, thus restoring the symbology of a legend that the lion's whelp was born dead, and only brought to life by the roaring of its sire. The legend has been thus translated:

"Know that the lioness, if she bring forth a dead cub, she holds her cub and the lion arrives: he goes about and cries, till it revives on the third day. Know that the lioness signifies St. Mary, and the lion Christ, who gave himself to death for the

people. Three days he lay in the earth to gain our
souls. By the cry of the lion they understand the
power of God, by which Christ was restored to life
and robbed hell."

The phrase "lion of the tribe of Judah,"
therefore, when used in the Masonic ritual,
referred in its original interpretation to Christ,
him who "brought life and immortality to light."

DEATH.—The Scandinavians, in their Edda,
describing the residence of Death in hell, where she
was cast by her father, Johe, says that she there
possessed large apartments, strongly built and
fenced with gates of iron. Her halls is Grief; her
table, Famine; Hunger, her knife; Delay, her
servant; Faintness, her porch; Sickness, her pain,
her bed; and her tent, Cursing and Howling. But
the Masonic idea of death, like the Christian, is
accompanied with no gloom, because it is
represented only as a sleep, from whence we
awaken into another life. Among the ancients, sleep
and death were fabled as twins. Old Gorgias, when
dying, said: "Sleep is about to deliver me up to his
brother." But the death sleep of the heathen was a
sleep from which there was no awakening; the
popular belief was annihilation, and the poets and
philosophers fostered the people's ignorance, by
describing death as the total and irremediable
extinction of life. Thus Seneca says—and he was
too philosophic not to have known better—"that
after death there comes nothing;" while Virgil—
who doubtless had been initiated into the Mysteries
of Eleusis—nevertheless calls death "an iron sleep,

an endless night." Yet the Ancient Mysteries were based upon the dogma of eternal life, and their initiations were intended to represent a resurrection. Masonry, deriving its system of symbolic teaching from these ancient religious associations, presents death to the neophytes as a gate or entrance to eternal existence. To teach the doctrine of immortality is the great object of the third degree. In its ceremonies we learn that life here is the time of labor and that, working at the construction of a spiritual temple, we are worshiping the Grand Architect for whom we build that temple. But we learn also that when this life is ended, it closes only to open upon a newer and higher one, where in a second temple, and a purer Lodge, the Mason will find eternal truth. Death therefore, in Masonic philosophy, is the symbol of initiation completed, perfected, and consummated.

IMMORTALITY.—Very wisely has Max Muller said that "Without a belief in personal immortality, religion is surely like an arch resting on one pillar, like a bridge ending in an abyss," and he cites passages from the Vedas to show that to the ancient Brahmans the idea was a familiar one. Indeed, all the nations of the earth with whose religious faith we are acquainted, recognize the dogma, although sometimes in vague, and, perhaps, materialistic forms.

It was the professed teaching of the Ancient Mysteries where, in the concluding rites of their initiation, the restoration of the hero of their legend was a symbol of immortal life, so, too, the same doctrine is taught in a similar legendary and symbolic method in the third degree of Masonry.

And Deacon Mant thus describes the difference, in the teaching of this doctrine of immortality between what he calls—after the school of Oliver —the spurious and the true Masonry: "Whereas, the heathens had taught this doctrine only by the application of a fable to their purpose, the wisdom of the pious Grand Master of the Israelitish Masons took advantage of a real circumstance, which would more forcibly impress the sublime truths he intended to inculcate upon the minds of all brethren."

It will be doubted by some of our modern skeptics whether the Hiramic myth is entitled to more authenticity as a historic narrative than the Osiric, or the Dionysian; but it will not be denied that, while they all taught the same dogma of immortality, the method of teaching by symbolism was in all the same.

It is a well-established fact that each of the ancient religious mysteries, those quasi Masonic associations of the heathen world, was accompanied by a legend—which was always of a funeral character—representing the death by violence of the deity to whom it was dedicated, and his subsequent resurrection or restoration to life. Hence, the first part of the ceremonies of initiation was solemn and lugubrious in character, while the latter part was cheerful and joyous. And that these ceremonies and the legend were altogether symbolical, and the great truths of the unity of God and the immortality of the soul, were by them to be dramatically explained.

RESURRECTION. — The doctrine of a resurrection to a future and eternal life constitutes an indispensable portion of the religious faith of Masonry. It is not authoritatively inculcated as a point of dogmatic creed, but is impressively taught by the symbolism of the third degree. The dogma has existed among all nations from a very early period.

The Egyptians, in their mysteries, taught a final resurrection of the soul. Although the Jews, in escaping from their Egyptian bondage, did not carry the doctrine with them into the desert—for it formed no part of the Mosaic theology—yet they subsequently, after the captivity, borrowed it from the Zoroastrians. The Brahmans and Buddhists of the east, the Etruscans of the south, and the Druids and the Scandinavian Skals of the west, nursed the faith of a resurrection to a future life. The Greeks and the Romans subscribed to it, and it was one of the great objects of their mysteries to teach it. It is, as we all know, an essential part of the Christian faith, and was exemplified in His own resurrection, by Christ to his followers.

In Freemasonry a peculiar degree has been appropriated to teach it by an impressive symbolism. "Thus," says Hutchinson, "our Order is a positive contradiction to Judaic blindness and infidelity, and testifies our faith concerning the resurrection of the body."

We may deny that there has been a regular descent of Freemasonry, as a secret organization, from the mythical associations of the Eleusinians, the Samothracians, or the Dionysians; no one, however, who has carefully examined the mode in which the resurrection or restoration to life was taught by a symbol and a ceremony in the Ancient Mysteries, and how the same dogma is now taught in the Masonic initiation, can, without absolutely rejecting the evident concatenation of circumstances which lie patent before him, refuse his assent to the proposition that the latter was derived from the former. The resemblance between the Dionysian legend, for instance, and the Hiramic, can not have been purely accidental. The chain that connects them is easily found in the fact that the Pagan Mysteries lasted until the fourth century of the Christian era, and as the fathers of the church lamented, exercised an influence over the secret societies of the Middle Ages.

TEMPLE.—The symbolism of speculative Masonry is so intimately connected with temple building and temple worship that some notice of these edifices seems necessary. The Hebrews called a temple Beth, which literally signifies a house or dwelling, and finds its root in a word which signifies "to remain, or pass the night;" or hecal, an obsolete word, signifying "magnificent." So that they seem to have had two ideas in reference to a temple. When they called it Beth Jehova, or the "house of Jehovah," they referred to the continual presence of God in it, and when they called it hecal Jehovah, or the "place of Jehovah," they referred to the splendor of the edifice which was selected as His residence.

Masonry has derived its temple symbolism, as it has almost all its symbolic ideas, from the Hebrew type, and thus makes the temple a symbol of a Lodge. But of the Roman temple worship, it has not been neglectful, and has borrowed from it one of the most significant and important words in its vocabulary. The Latin word "specular" means to observe, to look around. When the augur, standing within the sacred precincts of his open temple on the Capitolian halls, watching the flight of birds, that from it he might deduce his auspices of good or bad fortune, he was said "speculari," to speculate, hence the word came at length to denote, like contemplate, from "templum," and investigation of sacred things, and thus we get into our technical language the title of "speculative Masonry," as distinguished by its religious design from operative, or practical Masonry.

The Egyptian temple was the real archetype of the Mosaic tabernacle, as that was of the temple of Jerusalem. The direction of an Egyptian temple was usually from east to west, the entrance being at the east. It was a quadrangular building, much longer than the width, and was situated in the western part of a sacred enclosure. The approach through this enclosure to the temple proper was frequently by a double row of sphinxes; in front of the entrance were a pair of obelisks, which will remind the reader of the two pillars at the porch of Solomon's Temple. The temple was divided into a spacious hall, the sanctuary where the great body of the worshipers assembled. Beyond it, in the western extremity, was the cell, or sekos, equivalent to the Jewish Holy of Holies, into which the priests only entered; and in the remotest part, behind a curtain, appeared the image of the god seated on his shrine, or the sacred animal which represented him.

GRECIAN TEMPLES, like the Egyptian and Hebrew, were places within an enclosure which was separated from the profane land around it, in early times by ropes, but afterwards by a wall. In temples connected with the mysteries, the cell was called the "adytum," and to it only the priests and the initiates had access, and we learn from Pausanias, that various stories were related of calamities that had befallen persons who had unlawfully ventured to cross the threshold.

ROMAN TEMPLES, after they emerged from their primitive simplicity, were constructed much upon the model of the Grecian. There was the same vestibule and cells, or "adytum," borrowed, as with the Greeks, from the holy and the most holy place of the Egyptians. Vitruvius says that the entrance of the Roman temple was, if possible, to the west, so that the worshipers, when they offered prayers, or sacrifices, might look towards the east; but this rule was not always observed.

It thus appears, notwithstanding what Montfaucon says to the contrary, that the Egyptian form of a temple was the type from which other nations borrowed their idea.

The Egyptian form of a temple was borrowed by the Jews, and with some modifications adopted by the Greeks and Romans, whence it passed over into modern Europe. The idea of a separation into a holy and a most holy place has everywhere been preserved. The same idea is maintained in the construction of Masonic Lodges, which are but imitations, in spirit, of the ancient temples.

TEMPLE, SYMBOLISM OF THE.—Of all the objects which constitute the Masonic science of symbolism, the most important, the most cherished by Masons, and by far the most significant, is the Temple of Jerusalem. The spiritualizing of the Temple is the first, the most prominent, and the most pervading of all the symbols of Freemasonry. It is that which most emphatically gives it its religious character. Take from Freemasonry its dependence on the Temple; leave out of its ritual all reference to that sacred edifice, and to the legends and traditions connected with it, and the system itself would at once decay and die, or at best, remain only as some fossilized bone, serving merely to show the nature of the once living body to which it had belonged. Temple worship is in itself an ancient type of the religious sentiment in its progress towards spiritual elevation. As soon as a nation emerged out of feticism, or the worship of visible objects, which is the most degrading form of idolatry, its people began to establish priesthood and to erect temples. The Goths, the Celts, the Egyptians, and the Greeks, however much they may have differed in the ritual, and in the objects of their polytheistic worship, were all in the possession of priests and of temples.

The Jews, complying with this law of our religious nature, first constructed their tabernacle, or portable temple, and then, when time and opportunity permitted, transferred their monotheistic worship to that more permanent edifice which towered in its magnificence above the pinnacle of Mount

Moriah. The mosque of the Mohammedan and the church or chapel of the Christian is but an embodiment of the same idea of temple worship in a simpler form.

The adaptation, therefore, of the Temple of Jerusalem, to a science of symbolism would be an easy task to the mind of those Jews and Tyrians who were engaged in its construction. Doubtless, at its original conception, the idea of this temple symbolism was rude and unembellished; it was to be perfected and polished only by future aggregations of succeeding intellects. And yet, no Biblical nor Masonic scholar will venture to deny that there was in the mode of building and in all the circumstances connected with the building of King Solomon's Temple, an apparent design to establish a foundation for symbolism.

The Freemasons have, at all events, seized with avidity the idea of representing in their symbolic language the interior and spiritual man by a material temple. They have the doctrine of the great Apostle of the Gentiles, who said, "Know ye not that ye are the temple of God, and that the spirit of God dwelleth in you?"

The great body of the Masonic Craft, looking only to this first Temple erected by the wisdom of King Solomon, make it the symbol of life; and as the great object of Masonry is the search after truth, they are directed to build up this temple as a fitting receptacle for truth when found, a place where it may dwell, just as the ancient Jews built up their great Temple as a dwelling place for Him who is the Author of all truth.

To the Master Mason, this Temple of Solomon is truly a symbol of human life; for, like life, it was to have an end. For four centuries it glittered on the hills of Jerusalem in all its gorgeous magnificence; now under some pious descendant of the wise King of Israel, the spot from whose altars arose the burnt-offerings to a living God, and now polluted by some recreant monarch of Judah to the service of Baal, until at length it received the divine punishment through the mighty King of Babylon, and having been despoiled of all its treasures, was burnt to the ground, so that nothing was left of all its splendor but a smoldering heap of ashes. Variable in its purposes, evanescent in its existence; now a gorgeous pile of architectural beauty, and anon a ruin over which the resistless power of fire has passed, it becomes a fit symbol of human life occupied in the search after divine truth, which is nowhere to be found; now sinning and now repentant; now vigorous with health and strength, and anon a senseless and decaying corpse.

Such is the symbolism of the first Temple, that of Solomon, as familiar to the class of Master Masons. But there is a second and higher class of the Fraternity—the Masons of the Royal Arch, by whom this temple symbolism is still further developed. This second class, leaving their early symbolism and looking beyond this Temple of Solomon, find in scriptural history another Temple, which, years after the destruction of the first one, was erected upon its ruins; and they have selected the second Temple, the Temple of Zerubbabel, as their prominent symbol; and as the first class of Masons find in their Temple the symbol of mortal life, limited and perishable, they, on the contrary, see in this second Temple, built upon the foundations of the first, a symbol of life eternal, where the lost truth shall be found, where new incense shall arise from a new altar and whose perpetuity their great Master had promised when, in the very spirit of symbolism, he exclaimed, "Destroy this temple, and in three days I will raise it up." And so to these two classes or orders of Masons the symbolism of the Temple presents itself in a connected and continuous form. To the Master Mason, the Temple of Solomon is the symbol of this life; to the Royal Arch Mason, the Temple of Zerubbabel is the symbol of the future life. To the former, his temple is the symbol of the search for truth; to the latter, his is the symbol of the discovery of truth; and thus the circle is complete and the system made perfect.

ZERUBBABEL.—In writing the life of Zerubbabel in a Masonic point of view, it is incumbent that reference should be made to the legends, as well as to the more strictly historical details of his eventful career. With the traditions of the Royal Arch and some other of the high degrees, Zerubbabel is not less intimately connected than is Solomon with those of symbolic or Ancient Craft Masonry. To understand these traditions properly, they must be placed in their appropriate place in the life of him who plays so important a part in

them. Some of these legends have the concurrent
support of Scripture; some are related by Josephus,
and some appear to have no historical foundation.
Without, therefore, vouching for their authenticity,
they must be recounted, to make the Masonic life
of the builder of the second Temple complete.

Zerubbabel, who in the book of Ezra, is called
"Sheshbazzar, the prince of Judah," was the
grandson of Jeconiah, who had been deposed by
Nebuchadnezzar, and carried as a captive to
Babylon. In him, therefore, was vested the regal
authority, and on him as such the command of the
returning captives was bestowed by Cyrus, who, on
that occasion, according to a Masonic tradition,
presented to him the sword which Nebuchadnezzar
had received from his grandfather, Jehoiachin.

As soon as the decree of the Persian monarch
had been promulgated to his Jewish subjects, the
tribes of Judah and Benjamin, with the priests
and Levites, assembled at Babylon, and prepared
to return to Jerusalem, for the purpose of
rebuilding the Temple. Some few from the other
tribes, whose love of their country and its ancient
worship had not been obliterated by the luxuries
of the Babylonian court, united with the followers
of Zerubbabel, and accompanied him to Jerusalem.
The greater number, however, remained, and
even the priests, who were divided into twenty-
four courses, only four courses returned, who,
however, divided themselves, each class into six,
so as again to make up the old number. Cyrus also
restored to the Jews the greater part of the sacred
vessels of the Temple which had been carried
away by Nebuchednazzar, and five thousand and

four hundred were received by Zerubbabel, the remainder being brought back many years after, by Ezra.

TEMPLE OF ZERUBBABEL.—For the fifty-two years that succeeded the destruction of Jerusalem by Nebuchadnezzar, that city saw nothing but the ruins of its ancient Temple. But in the year of the world 3468, and 536 B. C., Cyrus gave permission to the Jews to return to Jerusalem, and there to rebuild the Temple to the Lord. Forty-two thousand three hundred and sixty of the liberated captives returned under guidance of Joshua the high priest, Zerubbabel the prince or governor, and Haggai the scribe; and one year after, they laid the foundations of the second Temple. They were, however, much disturbed in their labors by the Samaritans, whose offer to unite with them in the building they had rejected.

Artaxerxes, having succeeded Cyrus on the throne of Persia, forbade the Jews to proceed with the work, and the Temple remained in an unfinished state until the death of Artaxerxes and the succession of Darius to the throne. As in early life there had been a great intimacy between this sovereign and Zerubbabel, the latter proceeded to Babylon, and obtained permission from the monarch to proceed with the labor. Zerubbabel returned to Jerusalem, and notwithstanding some further delays, consequent upon the enmity among the neighboring nations, the second Temple— or, as it may be called by way of distinction from the first, the Temple of Zerubbabel—was

completed in the sixth year of the reign of Darius,
515 years B. C., and just twenty years after the
commencement. It was then dedicated with all the
solemnities that accompanied the dedication of the
first. The general plan of this second Temple was
similar to that of the first. But it exceeded it in
almost every dimension by one-third. We are told
by Josephus, that "the priests and Levites and
elders of families were disconsolate at seeing how
much more sumptuous the old Temple was than
the one which, on account of their poverty, they
had just been able to erect."

The Jews also say that there were five things
wanting in the second Temple which had been in
the first, namely, the ark, the urim and thummin,
the fire from heaven, the divine presence or cloud
of glory, and the spirit of prophecy and power of
miracles.

Such are the most important events that relate
to the construction of this second Temple. But
there is a Masonic legend connected with it which,
though it may have no historical foundation, is yet
so closely interwoven with the Temple system of
Masonry that it is necessary that it should be
recounted. It was, says the legend, while the
workmen were engaged in making the necessary
excavations for laying the foundation, and while
numbers continued to arrive at Jerusalem from
Babylon, that three worn and weary sojourners,
after plodding on foot over the rough and devious
roads between the two cities, offered themselves to
the Grand Council as willing participants in the
labor of erection. Who these sojourners were we
have no historical means of discovering, but there

is a Masonic tradition that they were Hananiah, Mishael, and Azariah, three holy men who are better known to general readers by their Chaldaic names of Shadrach, Meshach, and Abed-nego, as having been miraculously preserved from the fiery furnace of Nebuchadnezzar. Their services were accepted, and from their diligent labors resulted that important discovery, the perpetuation and preservation of which constitute the great end and design of the Royal Arch degree.

As the symbolism of the first or Solomonic Temple is connected with and refers entirely to the symbolic degrees, so that of the second, or Temple of Zerubbabel, forms the basis of the Royal Arch in the York and American rites, and of several high degrees in other rites.

TEMPLE OF HEROD.—This was not the construction of a third temple, but only a restoration and extensive enlargement of the second, which had been built by Zerubbabel. To the Christian Mason it is interesting, even more than that of Solomon, because it was the scene of our Lord's ministrations, and was the Temple from which the Knight Templar's derived their name. It was begun by Herod seven years before Christ, finished A. D. 4, and destroyed by the Romans in A. D. 70, having subsisted only seventy-seven years.

GROUND-FLOOR OF THE LODGE.—Mount Moriah, on which the Temple of Solomon was built, is symbolically called the ground-floor of the Lodge, and hence it is said that "The Lodge rests on holy ground." This ground-floor of the

Lodge is remarkable for three great events, recorded in Scripture, and which are called "the three grand offerings of Masonry." It was here that Abraham prepared, as a token of his faith, to offer his beloved son Isaac—this was the first grand offering; it was here that David, when his people were afflicted with a pestilence, built an altar, and offered thereon peace-offerings and burnt-offerings to appease the wrath of God—this was the second grand offering; and lastly, it was here that, when the Temple was completed, King Solomon dedicated that magnificent structure to the service of Jehovah, with the offering of pious prayer and many costly presents—and this was the third grand offering.

This sacred spot was once the threshing-floor of Orman the Jebusite, and from him David purchased it for fifty shekels of silver, and another writer says for "six hundred shekels of gold." The Mosque of Omar now stands on the site of the Temple of Solomon.

TEMPLE OF SOLOMON.—The first Temple of the Jews was called "hecal Jehovah," or "Beth Jehovah," the palace or the house of Jehovah, to indicate its splendor and magnificence, and that it was intended to be the perpetual dwelling place of the Lord. It was King David who first proposed to substitute for the nomadic tabernacle a permanent place of worship for his people, but although he had made the necessary arrangements, and even collected many of the materials, he was not permitted to commence the undertaking, and the execution of the task was left to his son and successor, Solomon. Accordingly, that monarch laid the foundation of the edifice in the fourth year of his reign, 1012 years before Christ, and, with the assistance of his friend and ally, Hiram King of Tyre, completed it in about seven years and a half, dedicating it to the service of the Most High in the year 1004 B. C. This was the year of the world 3000, according to the Hebrew chronology, and although there has been much difference among chronologists in relation to the precise date, this is the one that has been generally accepted, and it is therefore adopted by Masons in their calculations of different epochs.

The Temple stood on Mount Moriah, one of the eminences of the ridge which was known as Mount Zion, and which was originally the property of Orman the Jebusite, who used it as a threshing-floor, and from whom it was purchased by David for the purpose of erecting an altar on it.

The Temple retained its original splendor for only thirty-three years. In the year of the world 3033, Shishak, King of Egypt, having made war upon Rehoboam, King of Judah, took Jerusalem and carried away the choicest treasures. From that time to the period of its final destruction, the history of the Temple is but a history of alternate spoliations and repairs, of profanations to idolatry and subsequent restorations to the purity of worship. One hundred and thirteen years after the conquest of Shishak, Joash, King of Judah, collected silver for the repairs of the Temple, and restored it to its former condition in the year of the world 3148. In the year 3264, Ahab, King of Judah,

robbed the Temple of its riches and gave them to
Teglath-Pileser, King of Assyria, who had united
with him in a war against the Kings of Israel and
Damascus. Ahaz also profaned the Temple by the
worship of idols. In 3276, Hezekiah, the son and
successor of Ahaz, repaired the portions of the
Temple which his father had destroyed, and
restored the pure worship. But fifteen years after,
he was compelled to give the treasures of the
Temple as a ransom to Sennacherib, King of
Assyria, who had invaded the land of Judah. But
Hezekiah is supposed, after his enemy had retired,
to have restored the Temple.

Manasseh, the son and successor of Hezekiah,
fell away to the worship of Sabanism, and
desecrated the Temple in 3306 by setting up altars
to the host of heaven. Manasseh was then
conquered by the King of Babylon, who in 3328
carried him beyond the Euphrates. But subsequently
repenting of his sins, he was released from captivity
and having returned to Jerusalem, he destroyed
the idols and restored the altar of burnt offerings.
In 3380, Josiah, who was then King of Judah,
devoted his efforts to the repairs of the Temple,
portions of which had been demolished or neglected
by his predecessors, and replaced the ark in the
sanctuary. In 3398, in the reign of Jehoiakim,
Nebuchadnezzar, King of Chaldea, carried a part of
the sacred vessels to Babylon. Seven years
afterwards, in the reign of Jehoniah, he took away
another portion, and finally in 3416, in the eleventh
year of the reign of Zedekiah, he took the city of
Jerusalem and entirely destroyed the Temple, and

carried many of its inhabitants in captivity to Babylon.

The Temple was originally built on a very hard rock, encompassed with frightful precipices. The foundations were laid very deep, with immense labor and expense. It was surrounded with a wall of great height, exceeding in the lowest part four hundred and fifty feet, constructed entirely of white marble. The body of the Temple was in length but ninety feet, or including the porch, one hundred and five, and its width but thirty. It was its outer court, its numerous terraces, and the magnificence of its external and internal decorations, together with its elevated position above the surrounding dwellings, which produced that splendor of appearance that attracted the admiration of all who beheld it, and gave a color of probability to the legend that tells us how the queen of Sheba, when it first broke upon her, exclaimed in admiration. "A most excellent master must have done this." The Temple itself, which consisted of the porch, the sanctuary, and the Holy of Holies, was but a small part of the edifice on Mount Moriah. It was surrounded with spacious courts and the whole structure occupied at least half a mile in circumference. Upon passing through the outer wall, you came to the first court, called the court of Gentiles, because the Gentiles were admitted into it, but were prohibited from passing farther. It was surrounded by a range of porticos, or cloisters, above which were galleries or apartments, supported by pillars of white marble.

Passing through the court of the Gentiles, you

entered the court of the children of Israel, which
was separated by a low stone wall and an ascent of
fifteen steps into the two divisions, the outer one
being occupied by the women, and the lower by the
men. Here the Jews were in the habit of resorting
daily for the purpose of prayer.

Within the court of the Israelites, and separated
from it by a wall of one cubit in height, was the
court of the priests; in the center of this court was
the altar of burnt-offerings, to which the people
brought their oblations and sacrifices, but none but
the priests were permitted to enter it. From this
court twelve steps ascended to the Temple strictly
so-called, that is, the porch, the sanctuary, and the
Holy of Holies. At the entrance of the porch was a
gate, made entirely of Corinthian brass. Beside
this gate there were two pillars, Jachin and Boaz.
From the porch you entered the sanctuary by a
portal which, instead of folding-doors, was
furnished with a magnificent veil of many colors,
which mystically represented the universe. The
breadth of the sanctuary was twenty cubits (30
feet), and its length forty. In the sanctuary were
placed the various utensils necessary for daily
worship of the Temple, such as the altar of incense,
on which incense was daily burnt by the officiating
priest; the ten golden candlesticks, and the ten
tables on which the offerings were laid previous to
the sacrifice.

The Holy of Holies, or innermost chamber, was
separated from the sanctuary by doors of olive,
richly sculptured and inlaid with gold and covered
with veils of blue, purple and scarlet, and the finest
linen. The size of the Holy of Holies was the same

as that of the porch, namely, twenty cubits square. It contained the ark of the covenant, which had been transferred into it from the tabernacle, with its overshadowing cherubim's and its mercy seat. Into the most sacred place the high priest alone could enter, and that only once a year, on the day of atonement.

The Temple, thus constructed, must have been one of the most magnificent structures of the ancient world. For its erection, David had collected more than four thousand millions of dollars, and one hundred and eighty-four thousand and six hundred men were engaged in building it for more than seven years, and after its completion it was dedicated by Solomon with solemn prayer and seven days fasting, during which time a peace-offering of twenty thousand oxen and six times that number of sheep was made, to consume which the holy fire came down from heaven.

In Masonry, the Temple of Solomon has played a most important part. Time was when every Masonic writer subscribed with unhesitating faith to the theory that Masonry was there first organized; that there Solomon, Hiram of Tyre, and Hiram Abif presided as Grand Masters over the Lodges which they had established; that there the symbolic degrees were instituted, and systems of initiation were invented, and that from that period to the present Masonry had passed down the stream of Time in unbroken succession and in unaltered form. But the modern method of reading Masonic history has swept away this edifice of imagination with as unsparing a hand, and as effectual a power as those with which the Babylonian king demolished the structure upon which they are founded. No writer, says Mackey, who values his reputation as a critical historian would now attempt to defend this theory.

Yet it has done it work. During the long period in which this hypothesis was being accepted as a fact, its influence was being exerted in molding the Masonic organization into a form closely connected with all the events and characteristics of the Solomonic Temple, so that now almost all of the symbolism of Freemasonry rests upon or is derived from the "House of the Lord" at Jerusalem. So closely are the two connected that to attempt to separate the one from the other would be fatal to the further existence of Masonry. Each Lodge is and must be a symbol of the Jewish Temple; each Master in the chair, a representative of the Jewish king, and every Mason a personation of the Jewish workmen.

Thus must it ever be while Masonry endures. We must receive the myths and legends that connect it with the Temple, not indeed as historical facts, but as allegories; not as events that have really transpired, but as symbols; and we must accept these allegories and these symbols for what their inventors really meant that they should be—the foundation of a science of morality.

GATES OF THE TEMPLE.—In the system of Freemasonry, the Temple of Solomon is represented as having a gate on the east, west and south sides, but none on the north. In reference to the historical Temple of Jerusalem, such representation is wholly incorrect. In the walls of the building itself there were no places of entrance except the door of the porch, which gave admission to the house.

But in the surrounding courts there were gates at every point of the compass. The Masonic idea of the Temple is, however, entirely symbolic. The Temple is to the speculative Mason only a symbol, not an historical building, and the gates are imaginary and symbolic also.

They are in the first place, symbols of the progress of the sun in his daily course, rising in the east, culminating to the meridian in the south, and setting in the west. They are also, in the allegory of life, which it is the object of the third degree to illustrate, symbols of the stages of manhood and old age, or more properly, of birth, life and death.

PILLARS OF THE PORCH.—The pillars most remarkable in Scripture history were the two erected by Solomon at the porch of the Temple. It has been supposed that Solomon in erecting these pillars had reference to the pillar of cloud and the pillar of fire which went before the Israelites in the wilderness, and that the right hand or south pillar represented the pillar of cloud, and that the left hand or north pillar represented that of fire. Solomon did not simply erect them as ornaments of the Temple, but as memorials of God's repeated promises of support to His people of Israel. For the pillar Jachin, derived from the word "jah," "jehovah," and "achin," "to establish," signifies that "God will establish His house of Israel." While the pillar Boaz, compounded of "in," "oaz," "strength," signifies that "In strength shall it be established." And thus were the Jews, in passing through the porch of the Temple, daily reminded of the abundant promises of God, and inspired with confidence in His protection and gratitude for His many acts of kindness to His chosen people.

The reader of the Scriptural account of these pillars will not be a little puzzled with the apparent discrepancies that are found in their height. Thus, in 1st Kings, 7:15: "He cast two pillars of brass of eighteen cubits high apiece;" 2nd Kings, 25:17: "The height of the one pillar was eighteen cubits;" Jer. 51:21: "And concerning the pillars, the height of one pillar was eighteen cubits;" 2nd Chro. 3:15: "Also he made before the house two pillars of thirty and five cubits high," which latter height, Whitson says, "would be contrary to all rules of architecture." Josephus (Antiq. lib. i., cap. 11) says: "Moreover, this Hiram made two hollow pillars whose outside were of brass, and the thickness of the brass was four fingers breadth and the height of the pillars was eighteen cubits" (27 feet). Dr. Mackey (Ency., p. 586) says, "The true description of these memorable pillars is simply this: Immediately within the porch of the Temple, and on each side of the door, were placed two hollow brazen pillars. The height of each was twenty-seven feet, the diameter about six feet, and the thickness of the brass three inches." In another place he says, "The discrepancy is easily reconciled by supposing, which indeed must have been the case, that in the book of Kings and where they are said to be eighteen cubits high, that the pillars are spoken of separately, and that in Chronicles their aggregate height is calculated, and the reason why in the latter book, their united length is placed at thirty-five cubits instead of thirty-six, which would be the double of eighteen, is because they are there measures as they appeared with the chapters upon them. Now half a cubit of each pillar was concealed in what Lightfoot calls "the whole of the chapter;" that is, half a cubit depth of the lower edge of the chapter covered the top of the pillar, making each pillar apparently only seventeen and a half cubits high, or the two thirty-five cubits, as laid down in the book of Chronicles.

The Masonic symbolism of the two pillars—Jachin and Boaz—may be considered, without going into minute details, as being two-fold. First, in reference to the name of the pillars; they are symbols of strength and stability of the institution. And then in reference to the ancient pillars of fire and cloud, they are symbolic of our dependence on the superintending guidance of the Grand Architect of the Universe, by which alone that strength and stability are secured.

HOLY OF HOLIES.—Every student of Jewish antiquity knows, and every Mason who has taken the third degree ought to know, what were the peculiar construction, character, and uses of the Sanctum Sanctorum, or Holy of Holies of King Solomon's Temple. Situated in the western end of the Temple, separated from the rest of the building by a heavy curtain, and enclosed on three sides by dead walls without aperture or windows, it contained the sacred ark of the covenant, and was secluded and set apart from all intrusion save of the high priest, who only entered it on certain solemn occasions. As it was the most sacred of the three parts of the Temple, so has it been made symbolic of a Master's Lodge, in which are performed the most sacred rites of initiation in Ancient Craft Masonry.

But as modern Hierologists have found in all the Hebrew rites and ceremonies the traces of more ancient mysteries from which they seem to have derived, or of which they have been modified, whence we trace also to the same mysteries most of the Masonic forms which, of course, are more immediately founded on the Jewish Scriptures, so we shall find in the ancient Gentile temples the type of this same Sanctorum, or Holy of Holies, under the name of Adytum; and, what is more singular, we shall find a greater resemblance between this Adytum of the pagan temple and the Lodge of Master Masons than we will discover between the latter and the Sanctum Sanctorum of Solomon's Temple. It will be curious and interesting to trace this resemblance and follow up the suggestions that it offers in reference to the antiquity of Masonic rites. The Adytum was the most retired and secret part of the ancient Gentile temple, into which, as into the Holy of Holies of the Jewish Temple, the people were not permitted to enter but which was accessible only to the priesthood. And hence the derivation of the word from the Greek, "adocin," "not to enter," "that which is not permitted to enter." Seclusion and mystery was always characteristic of the Adytum, and therefore, like the Holy of Holies, is never admitted of windows.

In the Adytum was to be found a taphos or tomb, and some relic or image or statue of the god to whom the temple was dedicated. The tomb reminds you of the characteristic feature of the third degree of Masonry; the image or statue of the god finds analogy in the ark of the covenant, and the overshadowing of cherubim.

It being supposed that temples owed their first origin to the reverence paid by the ancients to their deceased friends, and as it was an accepted theory that the gods were once men who had been deified on account of their heroic virtues, temples were perhaps in the beginning only stately monuments erected in honor of the dead. Hence, the interior of the temple was originally nothing more than a cell or cavity, that is to say, a grave, regarded as a place of deposit for the reception of a dead person interred; and therefore, in it was to be found the "soros" or coffin, and the "tapos" or tomb; or, among the Scandinavians, the barrow or mound grave. In time the statue or image of a god took the place of the coffin, but the reverence for the spot, as one of peculiar sanctity, remained, and the interior part of the temple became, among the Greeks the "sekos" or chapel; among the Romans the Adytum or forbidden place, and among the Jews the "kodesh kodashim," or Holy of Holies.

"The sanctity thus acquired," says Dudley in his Naology, "by the cell of interment, might really and with propriety be assigned to any fabric capable of containing the body of the departed friend, or relic, or even the symbol of the presence of existence, of a divine personage." And thus it happens that there was in every ancient temple an Adytum or Most Holy place.

There was in the Holy of Holies of the Jewish Temple, it is true, no tomb or coffin containing the relics of the dead. But there was an ark of the covenant which was the recipient of the rod of Aaron, and the pot of manna, which might well be considered the relics of the past life of the Jewish nation in the wilderness. There was an analogy easily understood, according to the principles of the science of symbolism. There was no statue or image of a god, but there were the sacred cherubim and, above all, the Shekinah, or Divine presence, and the bathcol, or voice of God.

But when Masonry established its system partly on the ancient rites, and partly on the Jewish ceremonies, it founded its third degree as the Adytum or Holy of Holies of all its mysteries; as the exclusive place, into which none but the most worthy—the priesthood of Masonry—the Masters of Israel, were permitted to enter, and then going back to the mortuary idea of the ancient temple, it recognized the reverence for the dead, which constitutes the peculiar characteristic of that degree. And therefore in every Lodge of Master Masons there should be found, either actually or allegorically, a grave, or tomb, and coffin, because the third degree is the inmost sanctuary, the kodesh kodashim, the Holy of Holies of the Masonic temple.

SPIRITUAL TEMPLE.—The French Masons
say, "We erect temples for virtue and dungeons for
vice," thus referring to the great Masonic doctrine
of a spiritual temple. There is no symbolism of the
Order more sublime than that in which the
speculative Mason is supposed to be engaged in the
construction of a spiritual temple, in allusion to
that material one which was erected by his
operative predecessor at Jerusalem; indeed, the
difference in this point of view between operative
and speculative Masonry is simply this; that while
the former was engaged in the construction on
Mount Moriah of a material temple of stones and
cedar and gold and precious stones, the latter is
occupied, from his first to his last initiation, in the
construction and adornment and the completion of
the spiritual temple of the body. The idea of
making the Temple a symbol of the body is not, it
is true, exclusively Masonic. It had occurred to the
first teacher of Christianity. Christ Himself
alluded to it when he said, "Destroy this temple,
and in three days I will raise it up," and St. Paul
extends the idea when he said, "Know ye not that
ye are the temple of God, and that the spirit of God
dwelleth in you?" And again he said in a more
positive form, "What, know ye not that your body is
the temple of the Holy Ghost which is in you,
which ye have of God, and ye are not your own?"

But the mode of treating this symbolism by
reference to the particular temple of Solomon and
to the operative art, engaged in its construction, is
an application of the idea peculiar to Freemasonry. Hitchcock, in his essay on Swedenborg,

thinks that the same idea was also shared by the Hermetic philosophers. He says, "With perhaps the majority of readers, the Temple of Solomon, and also the tabernacle, were buildings—very magnificent indeed, but still were buildings—for the worship of God. But some are struck with many portions of the account of their erection, admitting a moral interpretation, and while the buildings are allowed to stand (or to have stood once) visible objects, the interpreters are delighted to meet with indications that Moses and Solomon. in building these Temples, were wise in the knowledge of God and of man, from which point it is not difficult to pass on the moral meaning altogether, and affirm that the building which was erected without the noise of hammer, or axe, or any tool of iron, was altogether a moral building—a building of God, not made with hands. In short, many see in the story of Solomon's Temple a symbolic representation of MAN as the temple of God, with its Holy of Holies deep-seated in the center of the human heart.

DEDICATION OF THE TEMPLE.—There are five dedications of the Temple of Jerusalem which are recorded in Jewish history: First, the dedication of the Solomonic Temple, B. C. 1004; second, the dedication in the time of Hezekiah, when it was purified from the abominations of Ahaz, B. C. 726; third, the dedication of Zerubbabel's Temple, B. C. 513; fourth, the dedication of the Temple when it was purified after Judas Maccabeus had driven out the Syrians, B. C. 164; fifth, the dedication of Herod's Temple, B. C. 22. The fourth of these is still celebrated by the Jews in their "Feast of Dedication." The first only is connected with the Masonic ritual, and is commemorated in the Most Excellent Master's degree of the American Rite as the "celebration of the capestone."

This dedication was made by King Solomon in the year 3000, and lasted eight days, commencing in the month of Tisri, 15th day during the Feast of Tabernacles. The dedication of the Temple is called in the English system of lectures, "the third grand offering which consecrates the floor of a Mason's Lodge." The same lectures contain a tradition that on that occasion King Solomon assembled the nine Deputy Grand Masters in the holy place, from which all natural light had been carefully excluded, and which only received the artificial light which emanated from the east, west and south, and there made the necessary arrangements. The legend must be considered as a myth. A Scriptural account of the dedication is found in the eight chapters for the first book of Kings.

DEDICATION OF A LODGE.—Among the ancients every temple, altar, and statue, or sacred place, was dedicated to some divinity. The Romans, during the Republic, confined this duty to their churches, pretors, censors, or other chief magistrates, and afterwards to the emperors. According to the Papiran law, the dedication must have been authorized by a decree of the Senate and the people, and the consent of the College of Augurs. The ceremony consisted in surrounding the temple or object of dedication with garlands of flowers, while the vestal virgins poured on the exterior of the temple the lustral water. The dedication was completed by a formula of words uttered by the pontiff and the immolation of a victim, whose entrails were placed upon an altar of turf.

The dedication of a temple was always a festival for the people, and was annually commemorated. While the pagans dedicated their temples to different deities—sometimes to the joint worship of several—the monotheistic Jews dedicated their religious edifices to the one supreme Jehovah. Thus, David dedicated with solemn ceremonies the altar which he erected on the threshing-floor of Ornan the Jebusite, after the cessation of the plague which had afflicted the people, and Calmet conjectures that he composed the thirtieth psalm on this occasion.

The Jews extended this dedication even to their private homes, and Clark tells us in reference to a passage on this subject in the book of Deuteronomy, that "It was a custom in Israel to dedicate a new house to God with prayer, praise and thanksgiving, and this was done in order to secure the divine presence and blessing; for no pious or sensible man could imagine he could dwell safely in a house that was not under the immediate protection of God.6

According to the learned Selden, there is a distinction among the Jews between consecration and dedication; for sacred things were both consecrated and dedicated; while profane things, such as private dwelling-houses, were only dedicated. Dedication was therefore a less sacred ceremony than consecration. This distinction has also been preserved among Christians, many of whom, and in early ages all, consecrated their churches to the worship of God, but dedicated them to, or placed them under the especial patronage of some particular saint.

A similar practice prevails in the Masonic Institution; and therefore, while we consecrate our Lodges "to the honor of God's glory," we dedicate them to the patron saints of our Order. Tradition informs us that Masonic Lodges were originally dedicated to King Solomon, because he was the first Most Excellent Grand Master. In the sixteenth century, St. John the Baptist seems to have been considered as the peculiar patron of Freemasonry, but subsequently this honor was divided between the two saints, John the Baptist, and the Evangelist; and modern Lodges— in the country at least—are universally erected or consecrated to God, and dedicated to the Holy Saints John. In the Hemming lectures, dated in 1813, at the time of the union of the two Grand Lodges of England, the dedication was changed from the Saints John to King Solomon, and this usage now prevails very generally in England; but the ancient dedication to the Saints John has never been abandoned by the American Lodges. The formula in Webb which dedicates the Lodge "to the memory of the Holy St. John," was undoubtedly an inadvertence on the part of the lecturer, since in all of his oral teaching he adheres to the more general system, and described a Lodge is his esoteric work as being "dedicated to the Holy Saints John." This is now the universal practice, and the language used by Webb becomes contradictory and absurd when compared with the fact that the festivals of both saints are equally celebrated by the Order, and that the 27th of December is not a day of less observance in the Order than the 24th day of June. In one of the old lectures of the last century, this dedication to the two Saints John is thus explained:

"Q. Our Lodges being finished, furnished and decorated with ornaments, furniture and jewels, to whom were they consecrated?

"A. To God.

"Q. Thank you, brother; and can you tell me to whom they were first dedicated?

"A. To Noah, who was saved in the ark.

"Q. And by what name were the Masons then known?

"A. They were called Noachide, sages or wise men.

"Q. To whom were the Lodges dedicated during the Mosaic dispensation?

"A. To Moses, the chosen of God, and Solomon the son of David, King of Israel, who was an eminent patron of the Craft.

"Q. And under what name were the Masons known during that period?

"A. Under the name of Dionysians, Geometricians, or Masters in Israel.

"Q. But as Solomon was a Jew, and died long before the promulgation of Christianity, to whom were they dedicated under the Christian dispensation?

"A. From Solomon, the patronage of Masonry passed to St. John the Baptist.

"Q. And under what name were they known after the promulgation of Christianity?

"A. Under the names of Essenes, Architects, or Freemasons.

"Q. Why was the Lodges dedicated to St. John the Baptist?

"A. Because he was the forerunner of our Savior, and by preaching repentance and humiliation, drew the first parallel of the gospel.

"Q. Had St. John the Baptist any equal?

"A. He had; St. John the Evangelist.

"Q. Why is he said to be equal to the Baptist?

"A. Because he finished by his learning what the other began by his zeal, and drew the second line parallel to the former; ever since which time Freemason's Lodges in all Christian countries have been dedicated to the one or the other, or both of these worthy and worshipful men."

There is another old lecture, adopted into the Prestonian system, which still further develops these reasons for the Johanite dedication, but with slight variations in some of the details. But a more philosophical reason may be assigned for this dedication to the two Saints John. One of the earliest deviations from the pure religion of the Noachide was distinguished by the introduction of sun worship. The sun in the Egyptian Mysteries was symbolized by Osiris, the principal object of their rites, and whose name, according to Plutarch and Macrobius, signified the prince and leader, the soul of the universe, and the governor of the stars, Macrobius says that the Egyptians worshiped the sun as the only divinity; and they represented him under different forms, according to the different phases of his infancy at the winter solstice in December, his adolescence at the vernal equinox in March, his manhood at the summer solstice in June, and his old age at the autumnal equinox in September.

But it is a needless task to recite authorities or multiply instances to prove how intimately the sun, as a symbol, is connected with the whole system of Freemasonry. It is evident that the sun, either as an object of worship or of symbolization, has always formed an important part of what has been called the two systems of Freemasonry —the spurious and the pure.

To the ancient sun worshipers, the movements of the heavenly bodies must have been something more than mere astronomical phenomena; they were the actions of the deities whom they adored, and hence were invested with the solemnity of a religious character. But, above all, the particular periods when the sun reached his greater northern and southern declination, at the winter and summer solstices, by entering the zodiacal signs of cancer and Capricorn, marked as they would be by the most evident efforts on the seasons, and on the length of the days and nights, could not have passed unobserved; but, on the contrary, must have occupied an important place in their ritual. Now, these important days fell successively on the 21st of June and the 21st of December, hence those solstice periods were among the principal festivals observed by the pagan nations. The Druids always observed these festivals of midsummer and midwinter in June and December, the former for a long time celebrated by the Christian descendants of the Druids. "The eve of St. John the Baptist," variously called midwinter eve, was formerly a time of high observance among the English, as it still is in Catholic countries.

Our ancestors, finding that the church, according to its usage of purifying pagan festivals by Christian application, had appointed two days near those solstical periods, to the memory of two eminent saints, incorporated this festival by the lapse of a few days into the Masonic calendar, and adopted these worthies as patrons of our Order. To this change the earlier Christian Masons were the more persuaded by the peculiar character of these saints; St. John the Baptist by announcing the approach of Christ, and by the mystic ablution to which he subjected his proselytes; while the mysterious and emblematic nature of the Apocalypse assimilated the mode of instruction adopted by St. John the Evangelist to that practiced by the Fraternity.

We are thus led to the conclusion that the connection of the Saints John with the Masonic Institution is rather of a symbolic than of an historical character. In dedicating our Lodges to them we do not so much declare our belief that they were eminent members of the Order, as demonstrate our reverence for the great Architect of the Universe in the symbol of his most splendid creation, the great light of day.

In conclusion it may be observed that the ceremony of dedication is merely the enunciation of a form of words, and this having been done, the Lodge is this, by the consecration and dedication, set apart as something sacred to the cultivation of the principles of Masonry, under that peculiar system which acknowledges the two Saints John as its patrons. Royal Arch Chapters are dedicated to Zerubbabel, prince or governor of Judah; and Commanderies of Knights Templar's to St. John the Almoner. Mark Lodges should be dedicated to Hiram the Builder; Past Masters to the Saints John, and Most Excellent Masters, to King Solomon.

INNOVATIONS.—There is a well-known maxim of the law which says every innovation occasions more harm and disarrangement by its novelty, than benefit by its actual utility. This maxim is peculiarly applicable to Freemasonry, whose system is opposed to all innovations. Thus Dr. Dalcho says, in his Ahiman Rezon, "Antiquity is dear to the Mason's heart; innovation is treason, and saps the venerable fabric of the Order." In accordance with this sentiment, we find the installation charges of the Master of a Lodge affirming that "It is not in the power of any man, or body of men, to make innovations in the body of Masonry." By the "body of Masonry" is here meant, undoubtedly, the landmarks, which have always been declared to be unchangeable. The non-essentials, such as the local and general regulations, and the lectures, are not included in this term. The former are changing every day, accordingly as experience or caprice suggests improvement or alteration.

The most important of these changes in this

country has been the abolition of the quarterly communications of the Grand Lodge, and the substituting for them, except perhaps in a single State, of an Annual Communication. But after all, this is perhaps only a recurrence to first usages; for, although Anderson says that in 1717 the quarterly communications "were revived," there is no evidence extant that before that period the Masons ever met except once a year in their "Grand Assembly." If so, the change in 1717 was an innovation, and not that which has almost universally prevailed in America.

The lectures, which are but the commentaries on the ritual and the interpretation of the symbolism, have been subjected, from the time of Anderson to the present day, to repeated modifications. But, notwithstanding the repugnance of Masons to innovations, a few have occurred in the Order. Thus, in the schism which took place in the middle of the eighteenth century, and which resulted in the formation of the Grand Lodge of Ancients, as they called themselves in contradistinction to the regular Grand Lodge of England, which was styled the Grand Lodge of Moderns, the former body, to prevent the intrusion of the latter upon their meetings, made a change in some of the modes of recognition—changes which, although Dalcho has said that they amounted to no more than a dispute "whether the glove should be placed first upon the right hand or on the left" (Ahim. Rez., 193), were among the causes of continuous acrimony among the two bodies, which was only healed in 1813 by the partial sacrifice of principles on the part of the legitimate Grand Lodge, and have perpetuated differences which still exist among the English and American and the Continental Freemasons.

But the most important innovation which sprang out of this unfortunate schism is that which is connected with the Royal Arch degree. On this subject there has been two theories; one that the Royal Arch degree originally contained a part of the Master's degree, and that it was dissevered from it by the Ancients; the other, that it had never had any existence until it was invented by Ramsay and, adopted by Dermott for his Ancient Grand Lodge. If the first, which is the most probable and the most generally received opinion, be true, then the regular or Modern Grand Lodge committed an innovation in continuing the disseverance at the union in 1813. If the second be the true theory, then the Grand Lodge equally perpetuated an innovation in recognizing it as legal, and declaring, as it did, that "Ancient Craft Masonry consisted of three degrees, including the Holy Royal Arch." But, however the innovation may have been introduced, the Royal Arch degree has now become, so far as the York and American Rites are concerned, well settled and recognized as an integral part of the Masonic system.

About the same time there was another innovation attempted in France. The adherents of the Pretender, Charles Edward, sought to give to Masonry a political bias in favor of the exiled house of Stuarts, and for this purpose altered the interpretation of the great legend of the third degree, so as to make it applicable to the execution, or as they called it, the martyrdom of Charles I. But this attempted innovation was not successful, and the system in which the lesion was practiced has ceased to exist, although its workings are now and then seen in some of the high degrees, without, however, any manifest evil effect.

On the whole, the spirit of Freemasonry, so antagonistic to innovation has been successfully maintained, and an investigator of the system as it prevailed in the year 1717 and as it is maintained at the present day, will not refrain from wonder at the little change which has been brought about by the long cycle of near two centuries of its present form.

CRIMES, MASONIC.—In Masonry, every offence is a crime, because in every violation of a Masonic law there is not only sometimes an infringement of the rites of an individual, but always super induced upon this, a breach and violation of public rights and duties, which affect the whole community of the Order considered as a community.

The first class of crimes which are laid down in the constitutions as rendering their perpetrators liable to Masonic jurisdiction, are the offenses against the moral law. "Every Mason," says the old charge of 1772, "is obliged by his tenure to obey the moral law." The same charges continue the precepts by asserting that if he rightly understands the art, he will never be a stupid atheist nor an irreligious libertine. Atheism, therefore, which is the rejection of a superintending Creator, and irreligious libertine which, in the language of that day, signified a denial of all moral responsibility, are offences against the moral law, because they deny its validity and condemn its sanctions; and hence they are to be classed as Masonic crimes.

Again, the moral law inculcates love of God, love of our neighbor, and duty to ourselves. Each of these embraces other incidental duties which are obligatory on every Mason, and the violation of any one of which constitutes a Masonic crime.

The love of God implies that we should abstain from all profanity and irreverent use of His name. Universal benevolence is the necessary result of love of our neighbor, cruelty to one's inferiors and dependents, uncharitableness to the poor and needy, and a general misanthropical view of our duty as men to our fellow-beings, exhibiting itself in extreme selfishness and indifference to the comfort and happiness of all others, are offenses against the moral law, and, therefore, Masonic crimes.

Next to violations of the moral law, in the category of Masonic crimes, are to be considered the transgressions of the municipal law, or the law of the land. Obedience to constitutional authority is one of the first duties which are impressed upon the mind of the candidate, and hence he who transgresses the law of the government under which he lives violates the teachings of the Order, and is guilty of a Masonic crime. But the Order will take no cognizance of ecclesiastical or political offenses; and this arises from the very nature of the Society, which eschews all controversies about nation, religion, or state policy. Hence, apostasy, heresy and schisms, although considered in some governments as heinous offenses and subject to severe punishment, are not viewed as Masonic crimes.

Lastly, violations of the Landmarks and Regulations of the Order are Masonic crimes. Thus, disclosure of any of the secrets which a Mason has promised to conceal, disobedience and want of respect for Masonic superiors—those in authority —the bringing of "private piques or quarrels" into the Lodge, want of courtesy and kindness to the brethren, speaking calumniously of a Mason behind his back, or in any other way attempting to injure him, as by striking him, except in self-defense, or violating his domestic honor, is each a crime in Masonry. Indeed, every violation by a Mason of his Masonic obligations. The intemperate use of intoxicating drinks, gambling, profane swearing, denying the divine authority of the Bible, dishonest or fraudulent acts, disobeying the summons of a Lodge, defamation of character, drunkenness, false swearing, incest and adultery, keeping or cohabiting with a lewd woman, obtaining money from Masons or others under false pretenses, seduction, slander of a Mason's wife, to inform a candidate by whom he was blackballed, and willful abandonment of family, are offenses punishable by suspension or expulsion from the Order, according to the nature of the charge and the circumstances under which the offense was committed.

DEGREES.—The word "degree" in its primary meaning signifies "step." The degrees of Freemasonry are then the steps by which the candidate ascends from a lower to a higher degree of knowledge. It is now the opinion of the best scholars that the division of the Masonic system into degrees was the work of the revivalists of the beginning of the eighteenth century; that before that period there was but one degree, or rather one common platform of ritualism, and that the division into Masters, Fellows, and Apprentices was simply a division of ranks, there being but one initiation for all. In 1717 the whole body of the Fraternity consisted only of Entered Apprentices, who were recognized by the thirty-nine regulations compiled in 1720, as among the lawgivers of the Craft, no change in those regulations being allowed unless first submitted "even to the youngest apprentice." In the old charges, collected by Anderson, and approved in 1722, the degree of Fellow Craft is introduced as being a necessary qualification for Grand Master, although the word degree is not used. "No brother can be a Grand Master unless he has been a Fellow Craft before his election." And in the "Manner of Constituting a New Lodge," of the same date, the Master and Wardens are taken from "among the Fellow Crafts," which Dermott explains by saying that "they were called Fellow Crafts because the Masons of old times never gave any man the title of Master Mason until he had first passed the chair."

In the thirteenth of the Regulation of 1720, approved in 1721, the order or degrees of Master and Fellow Craft are recognized in the following words: "Apprentices must be admitted Masters and Fellow Crafts only in the Grand Lodge." Between that period and 1738 the system of degrees had been perfected, for Anderson, who in that year published the second edition of the Book of Constitutions, changed the phraseology of the old charges to suit the altered condition of things, and said, "A prentice, when of age and expert, may become an entered prentice or a Free-Mason of the lowest degree, and upon his due improvement, a Fellow Craft, and a Master Mason." No such words are found in the charges as printed in 1723. And if at that time the distinction of the three degrees had been as well defined as in 1738, Anderson would not have failed to insert the same language in his first edition. That he did not, leads to the presumption that the ranks of Fellow Craft and Master were not then absolutely recognized as distinctive degrees. The earliest ritual extant, which is contained in the Grand Mystery, published in 1725, makes no reference to any degree, but gives only what is supposed was the common initiation in use about that time. The division of the Masonic system into three degrees must have grown up between 1717 and 1730, but in so general and imperceptible a manner that we are unable, says Mackey, to fix the precise date of the introduction of each degree.

In 1717 there was evidently but one degree, or rather one form of initiation, and one catechism. Perhaps about 1721 the three degrees were introduced, but the second and third were not perfected for many years. Even as late as 1735, the Entered Apprentice degree contained the most prominent form of initiation, and he who was an Apprentice was, for all practical purposes, a Freemason. It was not until repeated improvements, by the adoption of new ceremonies and new regulations that the degree of Master Mason took the place it now occupies, having been confined at first to those who had passed the chair.

ENTERED APPRENTICE.—The first degree of Freemasonry, in all the rites, is that of Entered Apprentice. Like the lesser mysteries of the ancient initiations, it is in Masonry a preliminary degree, intended to prepare the candidate for the higher and fuller instructions of the succeeding degrees. It is, therefore, although supplying no valuable historical information, replete, in its lecture, with instructions on the internal structure of the Order. Until late in the seventeenth century, Apprentices do not seem to have been considered as forming any part of the confraternity of Free and Accepted Masons; for, although they are incidentally mentioned in the old constitutions of the fifteenth, sixteenth and seventeenth centuries, these records refer only to Masters and Fellows as constituting the Craft, and this distinction seems to have been one rather of position than of degree. The Sloan Manuscript, No. 3,329, which Findel supposes to have been written at the end of the seventeenth century, describes a just and perfect Lodge as consisting of "two Interprentices, two Fellow Crafts, and two Masters," which shows that by that time the Apprentices had been elevated to a recognized rank in the Fraternity. In the manuscript signed

"Manuscript Constitutions No. 4," the date of which is 1693, there is a still further recognition in what is there called "the Apprentice charge," one item of which is that "he shall keep council in all things spoken in Lodge or Chamber by any Masons, Fellows, or Freemasons." This indicates that they were admitted to a closer communion with the members of the Craft.

But, notwithstanding these recognitions, all the manuscripts up to 1704 show that only "Masters and Fellows" were summoned to the assembly. During all this time, when Masonry was in fact an operative art, there was but one degree in the modern sense of the word. Early in the eighteenth century, if not earlier, apprentices must have been admitted to the possession of this degree; for after what is called the revival of 1717 Entered Apprentices constituted the bulk of the Craft, and they only were initiated in the Lodge, the degree of Fellow Craft and Master Mason being conferred by the Grand Lodge. This is not left to conjecture. The thirteenth of the General Regulations approved in 1721, says that "Apprentices must be admitted Masters and Fellow Crafts only in the Grand Lodge, unless by a dispensation." But this having been found very inconvenient, on the 22nd of November, 1725, the Grand Lodge repealed the article, and decreed that the Master of a Lodge, with the Wardens and competent number of the Lodge, assembled in due form, can make Masters and Fellows at discretion. The mass of the Fraternity being at that time composed of Apprentices, they exercised a great deal of influence in the legislation of the Order, for although they could not represent their Lodge in the quarterly communications of the Grand Lodge— a duty which could be only discharged by a Master or a fellow—yet they were always permitted to be present at the grand feast, and no General Regulation could be altered or repealed without their consent; and, of course, in all the business of their particular Lodges, they took the most prominent part, for there were but few Masters or Fellows in a Lodge, in consequence of the difficulty and inconvenience of obtaining the degree, which could only be done at a quarterly communication of the Grand Lodge.

But as soon as the subordinate Lodges were invested with the power of conferring all the degrees, the Masters began to rapidly increase in numbers and in corresponding influence, and now the bulk of the Fraternity consisting of Master Masons, the legislation of the Order is done exclusively by them, and the Entered Apprentices and Fellow Crafts have sunk into comparative obscurity, their degrees being considered only as preparatory to the greater initiation of the Master's degree.

FREE-BORN.—In all the old constitutions, free birth is required as a requisite to the reception of Apprentices. Thue the Landsdown MS. says, "That the prentice to be able of birth, that is, free born." So it is in the Edinburg, Kilwinning, the York, the Antiquity, and in every other manuscript that has been so far discovered. And hence the modern constitutions framed in 1721 continue the regulation. After the abolition of slavery in the

West Indies by the British Parliament, the Grand
Lodge of England changed the word "free born"
into "free," but the ancient landmark never has
been removed in this country.

The non-admission of a slave seems to have
been founded upon the best of reasons, because, as
Freemasonry involves a solemn contract, no one
can legally bind himself to its performance who is
not a free agent and the master of his own actions.
That the restriction is extended to those who were
originally in a servile condition, but who may have
since acquired their liberty, seems to depend on the
principle that birth in a servile condition is
accompanied by a degradation of mind and
abasement of spirit which no subsequent
disenthralment can so completely efface as to
render the party qualified to perform his duties as
a Mason with that "freedom, fervency and zeal"
which we are said to have distinguished our
ancient brethren. "Children," says Oliver, "can not
inherit a free and noble spirit, except they be born
of a free woman."

The same usage existed in the spurious
Freemasonry of the mysteries of the ancient world.
There, no slave, or man born in slavery, could be
initiated, because the prerequisites imperatively
demanded that the candidate should not only be a
man of irreproachable manners, but also a freeborn
denizen of the country of which the mysteries were
celebrated.

Some Masonic writers have thought that in this
regulation, in relation to free birth, some al-elusion
is intended, both in the Mysteries and in
Freemasonry, to the relative conditions and

character of Isaac and Ishmael. The former—the
accepted one, to whom the promise was given—was
the son of a free woman; and the latter, who was
cast forth to have "his hand against every man and
every man's hand against him," was the child of a
slave. Wherefore we read that Sarah demanded of
Abraham, "Cast out this bond-woman and her son,
for the son of the bond-woman shall not be heir
with my son" (or with the son of the "free woman").
Dr. Oliver, in speaking of the grand festival with
which Abraham celebrated the weaning of Isaac,
says that he "had not paid the same compliment to
the weaning of Ishmael, because he was the son of
a bond-woman, and consequently could not be
admitted to participate in the Freemasonry of his
father, which could only be conferred on free men,
born of free women." The ancient Greeks were of
the same opinion, for they used the word, or "slave
manners," to designate any very great impropriety
of manners.

FREE-WILL AND ACCORD.—There is one
peculiar feature in the Masonic Institution that
must commend it to the respect of every generous
mind. In other associations it is considered
meritorious in a member to exert his influence in
obtaining applications for admission; but it is
wholly uncongenial with the spirit of our Order to
persuade any one to become a Mason. Whosoever
seeks a knowledge of our mystic rites, must first be
prepared for the ordeal in his heart; he must not
only be endowed with the necessary moral
qualifications which would fit him for admission into

our ranks, but he must come, too, uninfluenced by friends and unbiased by unworthy motives. This is a settled landmark of the Order, and therefore nothing can be more painful to a true Mason than to see this landmark violated by young and heedless brethren. For it can not be denied that it is sometimes violated, and the habit of its violation is one of those unhappy influences sometimes almost insensibly exerted upon Masonry by the existence of the many secret societies to which the present age has given birth, and which resemble Masonry in nothing except in having some sort of a secret ceremony of initiation. These societies are introducing into some parts of our country such phraseology as a "card" for a "demit," or "worthy" for "worshipful," or "brothers" for "brethren;" and there are some men who, coming among us imbued with the principles and accustomed to the usages of these modern societies in which the persevering solicitation of candidates is considered as a legitimate and even laudable practice, bring with them these preconceived notions, and consider it their duty to exert all their influence in persuading their friends to become members of the Craft.

Men who thus misunderstand the true policy of our Institution should be instructed by their older and more experienced brethren, that it is wholly in opposition to our laws and principles to ask any man to become a Mason, or to exercise any kind of influence upon the minds of others, except that of a truly Masonic life, and a practical exemplification of its tenets, by which they may be induced to ask admission into our Lodge. We must not seek; we are to be sought.

And if this were not an ancient law, imbedded
in the very cement that upholds our system, policy
would dictate an adherence to the voluntary usage.
We need not fear that our Institution will suffer
from a deficiency of members. Our greatest dread
should be that in its rapid extension less care may
be given to the selection of candidates than the
interests and welfare of the Order demand.

There can, therefore, be no excuse for the
practice of persuading candidates, and every hope
of safety is in avoiding such a practice. It should
always be borne in mind that the candidate who
comes to us not of his own "free-will and accord,"
but induced by the persuasion of his friends —no
matter how worthy he may be—violates, by so
coming, the requirements of our Institution on the
very threshold of its temple, and in ninety-nine
cases out of a hundred, fails to become imbued with
that zealous attachment to the Order which is
always absolutely essential to the formation of a
true Masonic character, because he was not "first
prepared" so as to apply of his "own free will and
accord."

APRON.—There is no one of the symbols of
speculative Masonry more important in its
teachings or more interesting in its history, than
the lamb skin, or white leather apron. Commencing
its lesson at an early period in the Masons' progress,
it is impressed upon his memory as the first gift
which he receives, the first symbol which is
explained to him, and the first tangible evidence

which he possesses of his admission into the Fraternity. Whatever may be his future advancement in the "royal art," into whatsoever deeper arcana his devotion to the mystic Institution, or his thirst for knowledge may subsequently lead him, with the lamb skin apron— his first investiture—he never parts. Changing perhaps its form and its decorations, and conveying at each step some new but still beautiful allusion, its substance is still there, and it continues to claim the honored title by which it was first made known to him on the night of his initiation as "the badge of a Mason."

We have the most satisfactory evidence that the use of the apron, or some equivalent mode of investiture, as a mystic symbol, was common to all the nations of the earth, from the earliest periods. In the Masonic apron two things are essential to the due preservation of its symbolic character—its color and its material.

The color of a Masonic apron should be pure, unspotted white. This color has in all ages and countries been esteemed an emblem of innocence and purity. It was this reference that a portion of the vestments of the Jewish priesthood was directed to be white. In the Ancient Mysteries the candidate was always clothed in white.

As to its material, a Mason's apron must be made of lamb skin. No other substance, such as linen, silk, or satin, could be substituted without entirely destroying the emblematic character of the apron, for the material of a Mason's apron constitutes one of the most important symbols of the profession. The lamb skin has always been considered as an appropriate embled of innocence, and hence we are taught, in the ritual of the first degree, that "by the lamb skin the Mason is reminded of that purity of life and conduct which is so essentially necessary to his gaining admission into the celestial Lodge above, where the Supreme Architect of the Universe forever presides."

The true apron of a Mason must then be of unspotted lamb skin, without device or ornament of any kind. The usage of the Craft in this country has, for a few years past, allowed a narrow edging of blue ribbon in the symbolic degrees, to denote the universal friendship which constitutes the bond of the Society, and of which virtue blue is the Masonic emblem. But this undoubtedly is an innovation, for the ancient apron was with-out any edging or ornament.

In this country there are now no distinctive decorations for the aprons in the symbolic degrees. The only mark of distinction is in the mode of wearing; and this differs in the different jurisdictions, some wearing the Master's apron turned up at the corner, and others the Fellow Craft's. The authority of Cross conclusively shows that he taught the former method, although the latter is now the more common usage.

As we advanced to the higher degrees, we find the apron varying in its decorations, and the color of its border, which are, however, always symbolical of some idea taught in the degree.

NORTHEAST CORNER.—In the "Institutes of Menu," the sacred book of the Brahmans, it is said, "If any one has an incurable disease, let him advance in a straight path towards the invincible northeast point, feeding on water and air till his mental frame totally decays, and his soul becomes united with the Supreme." It is at the same northeast point that those first instructions begin in Masonry which enables the true Mason to commence the erection of that spiritual temple in which, after the decay of his mortal frame, "his soul becomes united with the Supreme."

In the important ceremony which refers to the northeast corner of the Lodge, the candidate becomes as one who is, to all outward appearances, "a perfect and upright man and Mason"—the representative of a spiritual cornerstone—on which he is to erect his future moral and Masonic edifice.

This symbolic reference of the cornerstone of a material edifice to a Mason when, at his first initiation, he commences the moral and intellectual task of erecting a spiritual temple in his heart, is beautifully sustained when we look at all the qualities that are required to constitute a "well-tried, true and trusty" cornerstone. The squareness of its surface, emblematic of morality—its cubical form, emblematic of firmness and stability of character, and the peculiar finish and fineness of the material, emblematic of virtue and holiness, show that the ceremony of the northeast corner of the Lodge was undoubtedly intended to portray, in the consecrated language of symbolism, the necessity of integrity and stability of conduct, of truthfulness and uprightness of character, and of purity and holiness of life, which, just at that time and in that place, the candidate is most impressively charged to maintain.

ADVANCEMENT, HURRIED.—Nothing can be more certain than that the proper qualifications of a candidate for admission into the mysteries of Freemasonry and the necessary proficiency of a Mason who seeks advancement to a higher degree, are the two great bulwarks which are to protect the purity and integrity of our Institution. "Indeed, it is doubtful," says Mackey, which is the most hurtful, to admit an applicant who is unworthy, or to promote a candidate who is ignorant of his first lessons." The one affects the external, the other the internal character of the Institution. The one brings discredit upon the Order among the profane, who already regard us, too often with suspicion and dislike; the other introduces ignorance and incapacity into our ranks, and dishonors the science of Masonry in our own eyes. The one covers our walls with imperfect and worthless stones, which mar the outward beauty and impair the strength of our temple; the other fills our interior apartments with confusion and disorder, and leaves the edifice, though externally strong, both inefficient and inappropriate for its destined uses.

But to the candidate himself, a too hurried advancement is often attended with the most disastrous effects. As in geometry, so in Masonry, there is no "royal road" to perfection. A knowledge of its principles and its science, and consequently an acquaintance with its beauties can only be acquired by long and diligent study.

To the careless observer it seldom offers, at a hasty glance, much to attract his attention, or secure his interest. The gold must be deprived, by careful manipulation, of the dark and worthless ore which surrounds and envelops it, before the metallic luster and value can be seen and appreciated. Hence, the candidate, who hurriedly passes through his degree without a due examination of the moral and intellectual purposes of each, arrives at the summit of our edifice without a due and necessary appreciation of the general symmetry and connection that pervade the whole system.

The candidate thus hurried through the elements of our science and unprepared by a knowledge of its fundamental principles, for the reception and comprehension of the corollaries which are to be deduced from them, is apt to view the whole system as "a rude and indigested mass" of frivolous ceremonies and puerile conceits, whose intrinsic value will not adequately pay him for the time, the trouble and expense that he had incurred in his forced initiation. To him Masonry is as incomprehensible as was the veiled statue of Isis to its blind worshipers, and he becomes, in consequence, either a useless drone in our hive, or speedily retires in disgust from all participation in our labors—unless influenced by mercenary motives, which render him unworthy of Masonic respect or privileges.

But the candidate who, by slow and careful steps has proceeded through each apartment of our mystic temple, from its porch to its sanctuary, pausing in his progress to admire the beauties, and to study the uses of each, learning as he advances, "line upon line and precept upon precept," is gradually and almost imperceptibly imbued with so much admiration for the Institution, so much love for its principles, so much just appreciation of its designs as a conservator of divine truth, and an agent of human civilization, that he is inclined, on beholding, at least, the whole beauty of the finished building, to exclaim, as did the wondering Queen of Sheba: "A Most Excellent Master must have done all this."

The necessity of a full comprehension of the mysteries of our degrees, before any attempt is made to acquire those of a second, seems to have been thoroughly appreciated from the earliest times; and hence all the ancient constitutions have prescribed that "the Masters shall instruct the Apprentices faithfully, and make them perfect workmen."

TRUTH.—The real object of Freemasonry in a philosophical and religious sense, is the search for truth. This truth is therefore symbolized by the word. From the first entrance of the Apprentice into the Lodge, until his reception of the highest degree, this search is continued. It is not always found, and a substitute must sometimes be provided. Yet whatever be the labors he may perform, whatever the ceremonies through which he may pass, whatever the symbols in which he may be instructed, whatever the reward he may obtain, the true end of all is the attainment of truth. This idea of truth is not the same as that expressed in the lecture of the first degree, where Brotherly Love, Relief and Truth are there said to be the "three great tenets of a Mason's profession." In that connection, truth, which is called a "divine attribute, the foundation of every virtue," is synonymous with sincerity, honesty of expression, and plain dealing.

The higher idea of truth which pervades the whole Masonic system, and which is symbolized by the word, is that which is properly expressed to a knowledge of God, and is synonymous with the nature of God, implying His present, past and future existence.

FELLOW CRAFT.—The second degree of Freemasonry in all the rites is that of the Fellow Craft. The radical meaning of the word is, a fellow-workman, thus showing the origin of the title from an operative institution. Like the degree of Apprentice, it is only preparatory to the higher initiation of the Master; and yet it differs essentially from it in its symbolism. For, as the first degree was typical of youth, the second is supposed to represent the stage of manhood, and hence the acquisition of science is made its prominent characteristic; while the former is directed in all its symbols and allegorical ceremonies to the purification of the heart, the latter is intended by its lessons to cultivate the reasoning faculties and improve the intellectual powers.

Before the eighteenth century, the great body of the Fraternity consisted of Fellow Crafts, who are designated in all the old manuscripts as "Fellows." After the revival of 1717, the Fellow Crafts, who then first began to be called by that name, lost their prominent position, and the great body of the brotherhood was for a long time made up altogether of Apprentices, while the government of the Institution was committed to the Masters and Fellows, both of whom were made only in the Grand Lodge, until 1725, when the regulation was repealed, and subordinate Lodges were permitted to confer the two degrees.

WINDING STAIRS, LEGEND OF THE.—The Apprentice having entered within the porch of the Temple, has begun his Masonic life. But the first degree of Masonry, like the lesser mysteries of the ancient systems of initiation, is only a preparation and purification for something higher. The Entered Apprentice is the child of Masonry. The lessons which he receives are simply intended to cleanse the heart and prepare the recipient for the mental illumination which is to be given in the succeeding degrees. As a Fellow Craft, he has advanced another step, and as the degree is emblematical of youth, so it is here that the intellectual education of the candidate begins, and therefore here, at the very spot which separates the porch from the sanctuary, where childhood ends, and where manhood begins, he finds stretched out before him a winding stair, which invites him, as it were, to ascend, and which, as the symbol of discipline and instruction teaches him that here he must commence his Masonic labor, here he must enter upon those glorious, though difficult researches, the end of which is to be the possession of divine truth.

The winding stairs begin after the candidate has passed within the porch, and between the pillars of strength and establishment as a significant symbol, to teach him that as soon as he has passed beyond the years of irrational childhood and commenced his entrance upon manly life, the laborious task of self-improvement is the first duty that is placed before him. He can not stand still if he would be worthy of his vocation. His duty as an immortal being requires him to ascend, step by step, until he reaches the summit, where the treasures of knowledge await him.

The number of these steps in all systems has been odd, because odd numbers were considered more perfect than even ones. The odd number of steps was therefore to symbolize the idea of perfection, to which it was the object of the aspirant to attain.

As to the particular number of the stairs, this has varied at different periods. Tracing-boards of the last century have been found in which only five steps are delineated, and others in which they amount to seven. The Prestonian lectures used in England in the beginning of this century, gave the whole number as thirty-eight, dividing them into series of one, three, five, seven, nine, and eleven. The error of making an even number, which was a violation of the Pythagorean principle of odd numbers as a symbol of perfection, was corrected in the Hemming lectures, adopted at the union of the two Grand Lodges of England, by striking out eleven, which was also objectionable as receiving a sectarian explanation. In this country the number was still further reduced to fifteen, divided into three series of three, five, and seven. But the particular number of the steps, or the peculiar method of their division into series will not in any way affect the general symbolism of the whole legend.

The candidate, then, in the second degree of Masonry, represents a man starting forth on a journey of life, with the great task before him of self-improvement. For the faithful performance of this task, a reward is promised, which reward consists in the development of all his intellectual faculties, the moral and spiritual elevation of his character, and the acquisition of truth and knowledge. Now, the attainment of this moral and intellectual condition supposes an elevation of character, an ascent from a lower to a higher life, and a passage of toil and difficulty through rudimentary instruction, to the full fruition of wisdom. This is therefore beautifully symbolized by the winding stairs, at whose foot the aspirant stands ready to climb the toilsome steep, while at its top is placed "that hieroglyphic bright which none but craftsmen ever saw," as the emblem of divine truth.

And hence a distinguished writer has said that "these steps, like all the Masonic symbols, are illustrative of discipline and doctrine, as well as of natural, mathematical and metaphysical science, and open to us an extensive range of moral and speculative inquiry."

The total number of these steps in the American system is a significant symbol, because the letters of the holy name "JAH" were, in their numerical value, equal to fifteen, the fifteen steps in the winding stairs are therefore symbolic of the name of God. And we divide them into three section of three, five, and seven steps. At each of these divisions the candidate pauses to gather instruction from the symbolism, which each division presents to his attention. At the first pause he is instructed in the peculiar organization of the Lodge, the perfect points of his initiation, the duties he owes to God, his neighbor, and himself, which are presented to symbolize his upward progress in the cultivation of knowledge, and the erection of a spiritual temple in the search after truth.

Advancing in his progress, the candidate is invited, at the second pause, to contemplate another series of instruction. The human senses, as the appropriate channel through which we receive all our ideas of perception, and which, therefore, constitute the most important source of our knowledge, are here referred to as a symbol of intellectual cultivation.

But his motto will be "excelsior." Still must he go onward and forward. The stair is still before him; its summit is not yet reached, and still further treasures of wisdom are to be sought for, or the reward will not be gained, nor the middle chamber, the abiding place of truth, be reached.

In his third pause, he therefore arrives at the point in which the whole circle of human science is to be explained. This selection of the seven liberal arts and sciences as a symbol of the completion of human learning, was because

Masonry is an institution of the olden time, and
this selection of the liberal arts and sciences as a
symbol of the completion of human learning is one
of the most pregnant evidences that we have of its
antiquity.

In the seventh century, and for a long time
afterwards, the circle of instruction to which all the
learning of the most eminent schools and most
distinguished philosophers was confined, was
limited to what were then called the liberal arts
and sciences, and consisted of two branches—the
trivium and the quadrivium. The first included
grammar, rhetoric and logic. The latter
comprehended arithmetic, geometry, music and
astronomy. "These seven heads," says Enfield,
"were supposed to include universal knowledge."
So far, then, we are able to comprehend the true
symbolism of the winding stairs. They represent
the progress of an inquiring mind, with the toils
and labors of intellectual cultivation and study,
and the preparatory acquisition of all human
science, as a preliminary step to the attainment of
divine truth, which, it must be remembered, is
always symbolized in Masonry by the word. It will
be remembered that a reward was promised for all
this toilsome ascent of the winding stairs. Now,
what are the wages of a speculative Mason? Not
money, nor corn, nor wine, nor oil. All these are but
symbols. His wages are Truth, or that
approximation to it which will be most appropriate
to the degree in which he has been initiated. It is
one of the most beautiful, but at the same time
most abstruse doctrines of the science of Masonic
symbolism, that the Mason is ever to be in the

search of truth, but is never to find it. This divine truth, the object of his labors, is symbolized by the word, for which we all know he can only obtain a substitute; and this is intended to teach the humiliating but necessary lesson that the knowledge of the nature of God and of man's relation to Him, which knowledge constitutes divine truth, can never be acquired in this life. It is only when the portals of the grave open to us and give us an entrance into a more perfect life that this knowledge is to be attained. "Happy is the man," says the father of lyric poetry, "who descends beneath the hollow earth, having beheld these mysteries; he knows the end, he knows the origin of life."

The middle chamber is therefore symbolic of this life, where the symbol only of the word can be given, where the truth is to be reached by approximation only, and yet where we are to learn that that truth will consist of a perfect knowledge of the G. A. O. T. U. This is the reward of the inquiring Mason; in this consist the wages of a Fellow Craft. He is directed to the truth, but must travel farther and ascend still higher to attain it.

It is then, as a symbol, and a symbol only, that we must study the beautiful legend of the winding stairs. If we attempt to adopt it as a historical fact, the absurdity of its details stares us in the face, and wise men will wonder at our credulity. Its inventors had no desire to thus impose upon our folly; but offering it to us as a great philosophical myth, they did not for a moment suppose that we would pass over its sublime moral teachings to accept the allegory as a historical narrative without meaning, and wholly irreconcilable with the records of Scripture, and opposed by all the principles of probability. But to teach us that in the "middle chamber of life—in the full fruition of manhood—the reward is attained, and the purified and enlivened intellect is invested with the reward in the direction how to seek God and God's truth; to believe this is to believe and to know the true design of speculative Masonry, the only design which makes it worthy of a good and wise man's study.

Its historical details are barren, but its symbols and allegories are fertile with instruction.

SYMBOLIC DEGREES.—The first three degrees in Freemasonry are known by way of distinction as the symbolic degrees; the term "symbolic" is exclusively confined to the degrees conferred in a Lodge of the three primitive degrees, which Lodge, therefore, whether opened on the first, the second, or the third degrees, is always referred to as a "symbolic Lodge." As this distinctive term is of constant and universal use, it may be considered not altogether useless to inquire into its origin and signification.

The germ and nucleus of all Freemasonry is to be found in the three primitive degrees—the Apprentice, the Fellow Craft, and the Master Mason. They were at one time (under a modification, however, which included the Royal Arch), the only degrees known to and practiced by the Craft, and hence they are often called "Ancient Craft Masonry," to distinguish them from those comparatively modern additions which constitute what are designated as the "high degrees."

The striking pecularity of these primitive degrees is, that their prominent mode of instruction is by symbols. Not that they are without legends. On the contrary, they have each an abundance of legends, such, for instance, as the details of the building of the Temple, of the payment of wages in the middle chamber, or of the construction of the pillars of the porch. But these legends do not perform any very important part in the construction of the degree. The lessons which are communicated to the candidate in these primitive degrees are conveyed principally through the medium of symbols, while there is (at least in the working of the degree) but little traditional of legendary teaching, with the exception of the great legend of Masonry, the "Golden Legend" of the Order, to be found in the Master's degree, and which is itself a symbol of the most abstruse and solemn signification.

But even in this instance, interesting as are the details of the legend, they are only subordinate to the symbol. "Hiram the Builder" is the profound symbol of manhood laboring for immortality; and all the different points of the legend are simply clustered around it only to bring out the symbol in bolder relief. The legend is of itself inert; it is the symbol of the master workman that gives it life and true meaning.

Symbolism is, therefore, the prevailing characteristic of these primitive degrees; and it is because all the science, and philosophy, and religion of "Ancient Craft Masonry" is thus concealed from the profane, but unfolded to the initiate by symbols, that the first three degrees which comprise it are said to be symbolic.

Now, nothing of the kind is to be found in the degrees above and beyond the third, if we except the Royal Arch, which was originally a part of Ancient Craft Masonry, and was unnaturally torn from the Master's degree, of which it, as every Masonic student knows, constituted the complement and consummation. Take, for instance, the intermediate degrees of the American Chapter, such, for instance, as the Mark and Most Excellent Master. Here we find the symbolic feature ceasing to predominate, and the traditional or legendary taking its place. It is true that in these capitular degrees the use of symbols is not altogether abandoned. This could not well be, for the symbol constitutes the very essence of Freemasonry. The symbolic element is still to be discovered in these degrees, but only in a position subordinate to legendary instruction. As an illustration, let us consider the keystone in the Mark Master's degree. Now, no one will deny that this is, strictly speaking, a symbol, and a very important and beautiful one, too. It is a symbol of a fraternal covenant between those who are engaged in the common search after divine truth. But in the role which it plays in the ritual of this degree, the symbol, however beautiful and appropriate it may be, is in a manner lost sight of, and the keystone derives almost all its importance and interest from the traditional history of its construction, its architectural design, and its fate. It is as the subject of a legend, and not as a symbol, that it attracts attention. Now, in the third or Master's degree we find the trowel, which is a symbol of almost precisely the same import as the keystone. They both refer to a Masonic covenant; but no legend, nor tradition, nor history, is connected with the trowel. It presents itself simply and exclusively as a symbol. Hence we learn that symbols do not in the capitular, as in the primitive degrees of Masonry, strike the eyes, inform the mind, and teach the heart, in every part of the Lodge, and in every part of the ceremonial initiation. On the contrary, the capitular degrees are almost altogether founded on and composed of a series of events in Masonic history. Each of them has attached to it some tradition or legend which it is the design of the degree to illustrate, and the memory of which is preserved in its ceremonies and instructions. That most of these legends are themselves of symbolic signification, is not denied. But this is their interior sense; in their outward and ostensible meaning they appear before us simply as legends. To retain these legends in the memory of Masons appears to have been the primary design in the establishment of the higher degrees, and as the information intended to be communicated in these degrees is of a historical character, there can of course be but little room for symbols or for symbolic instruction, the profuse use of which would rather tend to an injury than to a benefit, by complicating the purposes of the ritual and confusing the mind of the aspirant.

The celebrated French writer Ragon objects to this exclusive application of the term "symbolic" to the first three degrees, as a sort of unfavorable criticism on the higher degrees, and as implying that the latter are entirely devoid of the element of symbolism. But he has mistaken the true import and meaning of the application. It is not because the higher or capitular and cryptic degrees are altogether without symbols—for such is not the case—that the term symbolic is withheld from them, but because symbolic instruction does not constitute their predominating characteristic, as it does in the first three degrees. And hence the Masonry taught in these three primitive degrees is very properly called symbolic Masonry, and the Lodge in which this Masonry is taught is known as a symbolic Lodge.

The science of symbolism is that which is engaged in the investigation of the meaning of symbols, and the application of their interpretation to moral, religious and philosophical instruction. In this sense, Freemasonry is essentially a science of symbolism. The English lectures define Freemasonry to be "a science of morality veiled in allegory and illustrated by symbols." Mackey says, "The definition would be more correct were it in these words: Freemasonry is a system of morality developed and inculcated by the science of symbolism.

The legends of Masonry are parables, and a parable is only a spoken symbol. By its utterance, says Adam Clark, "spiritual things are better understood, and make a deeper impression on the attentive mind." Hence Christ taught his disciples by parables, or moral fables—to teach more impressively the idea of good and evil in life and judgment. He used the parable of "the tares," and the parable of the "mustard seed" to symbolize the spread of the gospel, and that of the wicked husbandmen as a symbol of his "rejection by the Jews." And thus we have a great similarity in the teachings of Christ to His disciples, and the teachings of Moses to the children of Israel, in the wilderness. Therefore the necessity of a knowledge of symbolism to properly understand many portions of the Holy Scriptures. (See Apocalypse, Masonry.)

LEGEND OF THE THIRD DEGREE.—The most important and significant of the legendary symbols of Freemasonry is undoubtedly that which relates to the fate of Hiram Abif, commonly called, "by way of excellence," the Legend of the Third Degree. The first written record of this legend is probably that contained in the second edition of Anderson's constitutions, published in 1738, and is in these words:

"It (the Temple) was finished in the short space of seven years and six months, to the amazement of all the world, when the cape-stone was celebrated by the Fraternity with great joy. But their joy was soon interrupted by the sudden death of their dear master, Hiram Abif, whom they decently interred in the Lodge near the Temple, according to ancient usage." In the next edition of the same work, published in 1754, a few additional circumstances are related, such as the participation of King Solomon in the general grief, and the fact that the King of Israel "ordered his obsequies to be conducted with great solemnity and decency." With these exceptions, and the citations of the same passages made by subsequent authors, the narrative has always remained unwritten, and descended from age to age through the means of oral tradition. The legend has been considered of so much importance that it has been preserved in the symbolism of every Masonic rite. No matter how much the ingenuity or the imagination of the founders of the rites may have perverted or corrupted other symbols, abolishing the old and substituting new ones, the legend of the Temple Builder has ever been left untouched, to present itself in all the integrity of its ancient mythical form.

What then, is the signification of this symbol so important and so extensively diffused? What interpretation can we give to it that will account for its universal adoption? How is it that it has become so intimately interwoven with Freemasonry as to make, to all appearance, a part of its very essence, and to have been always deemed inseparable from it?

To answer these questions satisfactorily, it is necessary to trace, in a brief investigation, the remote origin of the Institution of Freemasonry, and its connection with the ancient systems of initiation. It was, then, the object of all the rites and mysteries of antiquity to teach the doctrine of the immortality of the soul. This dogma shining as an almost solitary beacon light in the surrounding gloom of pagan darkness, had undoubtedly been received from the ancient people, or priesthood, among whom it probably existed only in the form of an abstract proposition, or a simple and unembellished tradition. But, in the more sensual minds of the pagan philosophers and mystics, the idea, when presented to the initiates in their mysteries, was always conveyed in the form of a scenic representation. The influence, too, of the early Sabian worship of the sun and heavenly bodies, in which the solar orb was adored on its resurrection each morning from the apparent death of its evening setting, caused the rising sun to be adopted in the more ancient mysteries, as a symbol of the regeneration of the soul.

Thus, in the Egyptian Mysteries, we find a representation of the death and subsequent regeneration of Osiris; in the Phoenician, of Adonis; in the Syrian, of Dionysus; in all of which the scenic apparatus of initiation was intended to indoctrinate the candidate into the dogma of a future life.

It will be sufficient here to refer to the theory of Oliver, that through the instrumentality of the Tyrian workmen at the Temple of King Solomon, what he called the spurious, and pure branches of the Masonic system were united at Jerusalem, and that the same method of scenic representation was adopted by the latter from the former, and the narrative of the Temple Builder substituted for that of Dionysus, which was the myth peculiar to the mysteries practiced by the Tyrian workmen. The idea, therefore, proposed to be communicated in the myth of the Ancient Mysteries, was the same as that which is now conveyed in the Masonic legends of the third degree. Hence, then, Hiram Abif, in the Masonic system is the symbol of human nature, as developed in this life here and the life to come, and so, while the

Temple was the visible symbol of the world, its builder became the mythical symbol of man, the dweller and worker in that world.

Man, setting forth on the voyage of life, with faculties and powers fitting him for the due exercise of the high duties to whose performance he has been called, holds, if he be "a curious and cunning workman," skilled in all moral and intellectual purposes (and it is only of such men that the Temple Builder can be the symbol) within the grasp of his attainment, the knowledge of all that divine truth, imparted to him as the heirloom of his race—that race to whom he has been granted to look, with exalted countenance, on high; which divine truth is symbolized by the Word.

Thus provided with the word of life, he occupies his time in the construction of a spiritual temple, and travels onward in the faithful discharge of all his duties, laying down his designs upon the trestle-board of the future, and invoking the assistance and direction of God.

But, is his path always over flowery meads and through pleasant groves? Is there no hidden foe to obstruct his passage? Is all before him clear and calm, with joyous sunshine and refreshing zephyrs? Alas; not so. "Man is born to trouble as the sparks fly upward." At every "gate of life"—as the Orientals has beautifully called the ages—he is beset by peril. Temptation allure his youth; misfortune darkens the pathway of his manhood, and his old age is encumbered with infirmity and disease. But, clothed in the armor of virtue, he may resist the temptation; he may cast misfortunes aside, and rise triumphantly above them; but to the last—the direst, the most inexorable foe of his race he must eventually yield; and, stricken down by death, he sinks prostrate into the grave, and is buried in the rubbish of his sins and human frailty.

Here, then, in Masonry, is what was called the aphonism—concealment or disappearance in the Ancient Mysteries. The bitter but necessary lesson of death has been imparted; the living soul, with the lifeless body which encased it, has disappeared, and can nowhere be found. All is darkness, confusion, despair. Divine truth—the word—for a time is lost, and the Master Mason may now say, in the language of Hutchinson, "I prepared my sepulcher; I made my grave in the pollution of the earth. I am under the shadow of death." But if the mythic symbolism ended here with the lesson of death, then were the lesson incomplete. That teaching would be vain and idle; nay, more; it mould be corrupt and pernicious, which should stop short of the conscious and innate instinct for another existence, and hence the succeeding portion of the legend are intended to convey the sublime symbolism of a resurrection from the grave, and a new birth into a future life. The discovery of the body, which, in the initiations of the Ancient Mysteries was called the "euresis," and its removal from the polluted grave into which it had been cast, to an honored and sacred spot within the precincts of the temple, are all profoundly and beautifully symbolic of that great truth, the discovery of which was the object of all the ancient initiations, as it is almost the whole design of Freemasonry, namely, that when man shall have passed the gates of life, and have yielded to the inexorable fate of death, he shall then (not in the pictured ritual of an earthly Lodge, but in the realities of that eternal one of which the former is but an antitype) be raised at the omnificent word of the Grand Master of the Universe, from time to eternity— from the tomb of corruption to the chambers of hope—from the darkness of death to the celestial beams of life; and that his disembodied spirit shall be conveyed as near the Holy of Holies of the Divine Presence as humanity can ever approach to deity.

Such Dr. Mackey conceived to be the true interpretation of the legend of the third degree— which interpretation has been very generally adopted in this country. But elsewhere and by various writers, other interpretations have been made, very different in their character, although always agreeing in retaining the general idea of a resurrection, or regeneration, or a restoration of something from an inferior to a high sphere or function. Thus, some of the earlier continental writers have supposed the myth to have been a symbol of the destruction of the Order of the Templar's, looking upon its restoration to its original wealth and dignities as being prophetically symbolic. In some of the high philosophical degrees it is taught that the whole legend refers to the sufferings and death, with the subsequent resurrection of Christ. Hutchinson, who has the honor of being the earliest philosophical writer on Freemasonry in England, supposes it to have been intended to embody the idea of the decadence of the Jewish religion, and the substitution of the Christian in its place and on its ruins.

Dr. Oliver thinks it is typical of the murder of Abel and Cain, and that it symbolically refers to the universal death of our race through Adam, and the restoration to life in the Redeemer, according to the expression of the Apostle, "As in Adam we all die, so in Christ we all live."

Ragon makes Hiram a symbol of the sun, shorn of its vivifying rays and fructifying power by the three winter months, and its restoration to prolific heat by the season of spring.

And finally Des Etangs, adopting in part the interpretation of Ragon, adds to it another, which he calls the moral symbolism of the legend, and supposes that Hiram is no other than Eternal Reason, whose enemies are the vices that deprave and destroy humanity.

To each of these interpretations Dr. Mackey says, "It seems to me there are important objections, though perhaps to some less so than to others.

As to those who seek for an astronomical interpretation of the legend, in which the annual changes of the sun are symbolized, while the ingenuity with which they press their argument can not but be admired, it is evident that by such an interpretation they will yield all that Masonry has gained of religious development in passed ages, and fall back upon that corruption and perversion of Sabaism from which it was the object, even of the spurious Freemasonry of antiquity to rescue its disciples.

The Templar interpretation of the myth must at once be discarded if we would avoid the difficulties of anachronism, unless we deny that the legend existed before the abolition of the Order or Knights Templar's; and such a denial would be fatal to the antiquity of Freemasonry. As to the adoption of Christian reference, Hutchinson, and after him Oliver, profoundly philosophical as are the Masonic speculations of both, have, I am constrained to believe, fallen into a great error in calling the Master Masons' degree a Christian institution. It is true that it embraces within its scheme the great truths of Christianity upon the subject of the immortality of the soul and the resurrection of the body; but this was to be presumed, because Freemasonry is truth, and Christianity is truth; and all truth must be identical. But the origin of each is different; their histories or dissimilar. The creed of Freemasonry is the primitive one of Noah and his immediate descendants. If Masonry were simply a Christian institution, the Jews and the Moslem, the Brahman, and the Buddhist could not conscientiously partake of its illumination. But its universality is its boast; in its language citizens of every nation may converse; at its altars men of all religions may kneel; to its creed disciples of every faith may subscribe.

But the true ancient interpretation of the legend—the universal Masonic one—for all countries and for all ages, undoubtedly was that the fate of the Temple Builder is but figurative of the pilgrimage of man on earth, through trials and temptations, through sin and sorrow, until his eventful fall beneath the blow of death, and his final and glorious resurrection to another and an eternal life.

And now, in conclusion, a word of historical criticism may not be misplaced. It is not at all essential to the value of the symbolism that the legend shall be proved to be historical, whether considered as a truthful narrative of an event that actually transpired during the building of the Temple, or simply as a myth embodying the utterance of a religious sentiment; the symbolic lesson of life and death and immortality is still contained in its teachings, and commands our earnest attention.

ASSASSINS, OF THE THIRD DEGREE.— There are in Freemasonry a legend of certain unworthy Crafts who entered into a conspiracy to distort from a distinguished brother a secret of which he was the possessor. The legend is altogether symbolic, and when its symbolism is truly comprehended, it becomes supremely beautiful. By those who look at it as having the pretension of an historical fact, it is sometimes considered an absurdity. But it is not thus that the legends and symbols of Masonry must be read, if we would learn their true spirit. To behold the goddess in all her glorious beauty, the veil that conceals her statue must be withdrawn. Masonic writers who have sought to interpret the symbolism of the legend of the conspiracy of the three assassins, have not agreed always in the interpretation, although they have finally arrived at the same result; namely, that it has a spiritual signication. Those who trace speculative Masonry to the ancient solar worship, of whom Ragon may be considered as the exponent, find in this legend a symbol of the conspiracy of the three winter months, to destroy the life-giving heat of the sun. Those who, like the disciples of the Rite of Strict Observance, trace Masonry to a Templar origin, explain the legend as referring to the conspiracy of the three renegade knights who falsely accused the Order, and thus aided King Phillip and Pope Clement to abolish Templarism and to slay its Grand Master. Hutchinson and Oliver, who labored to give a Christian interpretation to all the symbols of Masonry, referred the legend to the crucifixion of the Messiah, the type of which is, of course, the slaying of Abel by his brother Cain, Others, of whom the Chevalier Ramsay was the leader, sought to give it a political significance; and, making Charles I. the type of the Builder, symbolized Cromwell and his adherents as the conspirators.

The Masonic scholars whose aim has been to identify the modern system of Freemasonry with the Ancient Mysteries, and especially with the Egyptian, which they supposed to be the germ of all the others, interpret the conspirators as the symbol of the evil principle, or Typhon, slaying the good principle, or Osiris; or, when they refer to the Zoroastiv Mysteries of Persia, as Ahriman contending against Ormuzd. And lastly, in the philosophic degrees, the myth is interpreted as signifying the war of Falsehood, Ignorance and superstition against Truth. Of the supposed names of their assassins there is hardly any end of variations, for they materially differ in all the principal rites. Thus, we have the three JJJ in the York and American Rites. In the Adonhiramite system we have Romvel, Gravelot and Abiram. In the Scottish Rite we find the names given in the old rituals as Jubelum Akirop, sometimes Abiram; Jubelo Romvel, and Jubela Gravelot. Schterke and Oterfut are in some of the German rituals, while other Scottish rituals have Abiram, Romvel and Hobhem. In all of these names there is a manifest corruption, and the patience of many Masonic scholars have been well nigh exhausted in seeking for some plausible and satisfactory derivation.

Abibalk was the supposed chief assassin, Akirop one of the ruffians, and Oterfut assassin at the west gate.

MASTER MASON.—In all the rites of Masonry, no matter how variant may be their organization in the high degrees, the Master Mason constitutes the third degree. In form this degree is also everywhere substantially the same, because its legend is an essential part of it, and as on that legend the degree must be founded, there can nowhere be any important variation, because the tradition has at all times been the same. The Master Masons degree was originally called the summit of Ancient Craft Masonry; and so it must have been before the disseverance from it of the Royal Arch—by which is meant, not the ritual, but the symbolism of Arch Masonry.

But under its present organization the degree is actually incomplete, because it needs a complement that is only to be supplied in a higher one. Hence its symbolism is necessarily restricted, in its mutilated form, to the first Temple and the present life, although it gives the assurance of a future one.

As the whole system of Craft Masonry is intended to present the symbolic idea of man passing through the pilgrimage of life, each degree is appropriated to a certain portion of that pilgrimage. If, then, the first degree is a representation of youth, the time to learn, and the second of manhood, the time to work, the third is symbolic of old age, with its trials and sufferings and its final termination in death. The time for toiling is now over—the opportunity to learn has passed away—the spiritual temple that we have all been striving to erect in our hearts is now nearly completed, and the wearied workman awaits only the word of the Grand Master of the Universe to call him from the labors of earth to the eternal refreshments of heaven. Hence this is by far the most solemn and sacred of the degrees of Masonry, and it has, in consequence of the profound truths which it inculcates, been distinguished by the Craft as the sublime degree.

As an Entered Apprentice, the Mason was taught those elementary instructions which were to fit him for further advancement in his profession, just as the youth is supplied with that rudimentary education which is to prepare him for entering on the active duties of life. As a Fellow Craft he is directed to continue his investigations in the science of the Institution, and to labor diligently in the tasks it prescribes, just as the man is required to enlarge his mind by the acquisition of new ideas and to extend his usefulness to his fellow-creatures. But as a Master Mason he is taught the last, the most important and the most necessary truths; that, having been faithful to all his trusts, he is at last to die, and to receive the reward of his fidelity.

It was the simple object of all the ancient rites and mysteries, practiced in the very bosom of pagan darkness, shining as a solitary beacon light in all the surrounding gloom, and cheering the philosopher in his weary pilgrimage of life, to teach the immortality of the soul. This is still the great design of the third degree of Masonry. This is the scope and aim of its ritual. The Master Mason represents the man, when youth, manhood, old age, and life itself, have passed away as fleeting shadows, yet raised from the grave of iniquity and quickened into another and a better existence. By its legend and all its ritual it is implied that we have been redeemed from the death of sin and the sepulcher of pollution. "The ceremonies and the lectures," says Dr. Crucifix, "beautifully illustrate the all-energizing subject, and the conclusion we arrive at is that youth, properly directed, leads us to honorable and virtuous maturity, and that the life of man, regulated by morality, faith and justice, will be rewarded at its closing hour, by the prospect of eternal life."

Masonic historians have found much difficulty in settling the question as to the time of the invention and composition of this degree. The theory that at

the building of the Temple of Jerusalem the Craft
were divided into three or more degrees being only
a symbolic myth, must be discarded in any
historical discussion of the subject. The real
question at issue is whether the Master Mason's
degree, as a degree, was in existence among the
operative Freemasons before the eighteenth
century, or whether we owe it to the revivalists of
1717. Brother Wm. J. Hughan, in a very able
article on the subject, published in 1873 in the
Voice of Masonry, says that "So far as evidence
respecting its history goes no further back than the
early part of the last century; the evidence,
however, is all of a negative character There is
none that the degree existed in the seventeenth
century or earlier, and there is none that it did not.
All the old manuscripts speak of Masters and
Fellows. But these might have been, and probably
were, only titles of rank." The Sloane manuscript,
No. 3,329, speaks, it is true, of modes of recognition
peculiar to Masters and Fellows, and also of a
Lodge consisting of Masters and Fellows and
Apprentices. But even if we give to this manuscript
its earliest date, that which is assigned to it by
Findel, near the end of the seventeenth century, it
will not necessarily follow that these Masters,
Fellows and Apprentices had each a separate and
distinct degree.

Indeed, it refers only to one Lodge, which was,
however, constituted by three different ranks, and
it records but one oath, so that it is possible that
there was only one common form of initiation. The
first positive historical evidence that we have of

the existence of a Master's degree is to be found in the General Regulations, by Payne, in 1720. It is there declared that Apprentices must be admitted Masters and Fellow Crafts only in the Grand Lodge. The degree was then in existence. But this record would not militate against the theory advanced by some, that Desagulaiers was its author in 1717. Dermott asserts that the degree, as we now have it, was the work of Desagulaiers and seven others, who, being Fellow Crafts, but not knowing the Master's part, boldly invented it, that they might form a Grand Lodge. He intimates that the true Master's degree existed before that time, and was in the possession of the Ancients. But Dermott's testimony is absolutely, says Mackey, "worth nothing, because he was a violent partisan and because his statements are irreconcilable with other facts."

If the Ancients were in possession of the degree which had existed before 1717, and the Moderns were not, where did the former get it, since they sprang out of the latter? Documentary evidence yet wants to settle the precise time of the composition of the third degree as we now have it.

But it would not be prudent to oppose, too pointedly, says Mackey, the theory that it must be traced to the second decade of the eighteenth century. The proofs, as they arise day by day from the resurrection of old manuscripts, seem to incline that way.

But the legend is thought to be of much older date. It may have made a part of the general initiation. And some have no doubt that, like the

similar ones of the Compagnons de la Tour, in
France, it existed among the operative guilds of the
Middle Ages as an esoteric narrative. Such a
legend, all the histories of the Ancient Mysteries
prove to us, belongs to the spirit of initiation. There
would have been no initiation worth preservation,
without it.

FREE AND ACCEPTED.—The title of "Free
and Accepted Masons" was first used by Dr.
Anderson in the second edition of the Book of
Constitutions, published in 1738, the title of which
is "The History and Constitutions of the Most
Ancient and Honorable Fraternity of Free and
Accepted Masons." In the first edition, of 1723, the
title was "The Constitutions of the Freemasons."
The newer title continued to be used by the Grand
Lodge of England, in which it was followed by
those of Scotland and Ireland; and a majority of the
Grand Lodges of this country has adopted the same
style, and call themselves Grand Lodges of Free
and Accepted Masons. The old lectures formerly
used in England give the following account of the
origin of the term:

"The Masons who were selected to build the
Temple of Solomon were declared Free, and were
exempted, together with their descendants, from
imposts, duties, and taxes. They had also the
privilege to bear arms.

"At the destruction of the Temple by
Nebuchadnezzar, the posterity of these Masons
was carried into captivity with the ancient Jews.
But the good will of Cyrus gave them permission to
erect a second Temple, having set them at liberty

for that purpose. It is from this epoch that we bear the name of Free and Accepted Masons."

The title most generally assumed by the English and American Grand Lodges is, Ancient Free and Accepted Masons.

COVENANT OF MASONRY.—As a covenant is defined to be a contract or agreement between two or more parties on certain terms, there can be no doubt that when a man is made a Mason he enters into covenant with the Institution. On his part he promises to fulfill certain promises and to discharge certain duties, for which, on the other part, the Fraternity bind themselves by an equivalent covenant of friendship, protection and support.

This covenant must, of course, be repeated and modified with every extension of the terms of agreement on both sides. The covenant of an Apprentice is different from that of a Fellow Craft, and the covenant of the latter from that of a Master Mason. As we advance in Masonry our obligations increase, but the covenant of each degree is not the less paramount and binding because that of a succeeding one has been superadded. The second covenant does not impair the sanctity of the first.

This covenant of Masonry is symbolized and sanctioned by the most important and essential of all the ceremonies of the Institution. It is the very foundation stone which supports the whole edifice, and unless it is properly laid, no superstructure can with any safety be erected. It is indeed the covenant that makes the Mason.

A matter so important as this, in establishing the relationship of a Mason with the Craft—this baptism, so to speak, by which a member is inaugurated into the Institution—must, of course, be attended with the most solemn and binding ceremonies. Such has been the case in all countries. Covenants have always been solemnized with certain solemn forms and religious observances, which gave them a sacred sanction in the minds of the contracting parties. The Hebrews especially invested their covenants with the most imposing ceremonies.

The parties entering into covenant first selected a proper animal, such as a calf, a kid, a sheep, or a pig. The "throat was then cut across" with a single blow, so as to completely divide the wind-pipe and the arteries. This was the first ceremony of the covenant. The second was to "tear open the breast," to take from thence the heart and vitals, and if on inspection the least imperfection was discovered, the body was considered unclean, and thrown aside for another. The third ceremony was to "divide the body in twain," and to place the two parts to the north and south, so that the parties to the covenant might pass between them, coming from the east and going to the west. The carcass was then left as a prey to the wild beasts of the field and the vultures of the air, and thus the covenant was ratified.

In the book of Jeremiah, 34:18-20, God says: "And I will give the men that have transgressed my covenant, which they have made before me, when they cut the calf in twain and passed between the parts thereof. I will even give them, the princes of Judah and Jerusalem, into the hand of their enemies, and into the hand of them that seek their life; and their dead bodies shall be for meat unto the fowls of the heaven and to the beasts of the earth."

AID AND ASSIST.—The duty of aiding and assisting, not only all worthy distressed Master Masons, but their widows and orphans also, "wheresoever dispersed over the face of the globe," is one of the most important obligations that is imposed upon every brother of the "mystic tie" by the whole scope and tenor of the institution. The regulations for the exercise of this duty are few, but rational. In the first place, a Master Mason who is in distress has a greater claim, under equal circumstances, to the aid and assistance of his brother, than one who, being in the Order, has not attained that degree, or who is altogether a profane—not a Mason. This is strictly in accordance with the natural instincts of the human heart, which will always prefer a friend to a stranger, or, as it is rather energetically expressed in the language of Long Tom Coffin: "A messmate before a shipmate, a shipmate before a stranger, and a stranger before a dog." And it is also strikingly in accordance with the teaching of the Apostle of the Gentiles, who has said, "As we have opportunity, therefore let us do good to all men, especially unto them who are of the household."

But this exclusiveness is only to be practiced under circumstances which would make a selection imperatively necessary; where the grant of relief to the profane would incapacitate us from granting similar relief to him who is "of the household." But the earliest symbolic lessons of the ritual teach the Mason not to restrict his benevolence within the narrow limits of the Fraternity, but to acknowledge the claims of all men who need it, to assistance.

Inwood has beautifully said: "The humble condition both of property and dress, of penury and want, in which you were received into the Lodge, should make you at all times sensible of the distress of poverty; and all you can spare from the call of nature, and the due care of your family, should only remain in your possession as a ready sacrifice to the necessities of an unfortunate, distressed brother. Let the distressed cottage feel the warmth of your Masonic zeal, and, if possible, exceed even the unabating ardor of Christian charity. At your approach, let the orphan cease to weep, and in the sound of your voice let the widow forget her sorrow."

But there is another aspect in which this subject may be considered; namely, in that peculiar and technical one of Masonic aid and assistance due from one Mason to another. Here there is a duty declared, a correlative right inferred; for it is the duty of one Mason to assist another. It follows that every Mason has the right to claim that assistance from his brother. It is this duty that the obligations of Masonry are especially intended to enforce. The symbolic ritual of Masonry which refers, as, for instance, in the first degree, to the virtue of benevolence, refers to it in the general virtue which all men should practice. But when the Mason reaches the third degree, he discovers new obligations which restrict and define the exercise of this duty to aid and assist. So far as his obligations control him, the Mason, as a Mason, is not legally bound to extend his aid beyond the just claimants of his own Fraternity. To do good to all men is, of course, inculcated and recommended; to do good to the household is enforced and made compulsory by legal enactment and sanction.

Now, as there is here, on one side, a duty, and on the other side a right, it is proper to inquire what are the regulations or laws by which this duty is controlled and this right maintained. The old charges, of 1722, say: "But if you discover him to be a true and genuine brother, you are to respect him accordingly, and if he is in want, you must relieve him if you can, or direct him now he may be relieved. You must employ him some days, or else recommend him to be employed. Prefer a poor brother, who is a good man and true, before any other people in the same circumstances." This written law agrees with the unwritten law of our Order, and from the two we may deduce the following principles: First, the applicant must be a Master Mason, or a Master Mason's widow or orphan. Second, the applicant must be worthy. We are to presume that every Mason is "a good man and true," until the Lodge which has jurisdiction over him has pronounced to the contrary. Every Mason who is "in good standing," that is, who is a regularly contributing member of a Lodge, is to be considered as "worthy" in the technical sense of the term. An expelled, a suspended, or a non-affiliated Mason does not meet the required condition of "a regular, contributing member." Third, the giver is not expected to exceed his ability in the amount of relief. And lastly, in granting relief or assistance, the Mason is to be preferred to the profane. He must be placed "before any other people in the same circumstances." These are the laws which regulate the doctrine of Masonic aid and assistance. They are often charged by the enemies of Masonry with a spirit of exclusiveness. But it has been shown that they are in accordance with the exhortation of the Apostle, who would do good unto all, but "especially to those who are of the household;" and they have the warrant of the law of nature, for everyone will be ready to say, with that kindest-hearted of men, Charles Lamb, "I can feel for all indifferently, but I can not feel for all alike. I can be a friend to a worthy man who, upon another account, can not be my mate or fellow. I can not like all people alike." And so as Masons; while we should be charitable to all persons in need or distress, there are only certain ones who can claim the aid and assistance of the Order, or of its disciples, under the positive sanction of Masonic law.

HONORS, GRAND.—The Grand Honors of Masonry are those public acts and gestures by which the Craft have always been accustomed to express their homage, their joy, or their grief, on memorable occasions. In the symbolic degrees of the Ancient Rite, they are of two kinds, the private and public, which are used on different occasions and for different purposes.

The private Grand Honors of Masonry are performed in a manner known only to Master Masons, since they can only be used in a Master's Lodge. They are practiced by the Craft only on four occasions: When a Masonic hall is to be consecrated, a new Lodge to be constituted, a Master-elect to be installed, or a Grand Master or his Deputy to be received on an official visitation to a Lodge. They are used at all these ceremonies as tokens of congratulation and homage. And as they can only be given by Master Masons, it is evident that every consecration of a hall, or construction of a new Lodge, every installation of a Worshipful Master, and every reception of a Grand Master must be done in the third degree. It is also evident from what has been said, that the mode and manner of giving the private Grand Honors can only be personally communicated to Master Masons. They are among the things forbidden to be divulged.

The public Grand Honors, as their name imports, do not partake of this secret character, They are given on all public occasions. In the presence of the profane as well as the initiated. They are used at the laying of cornerstones of public buildings, or in other services in which the ministration of the Fraternity is required, especially in funerals. They are given in the following manner: Both arms are crossed on the breast, the left uppermost, and the open palms of the hands sharply striking the shoulders; they are then raised above the head, the palms striking each other, and then made to fall smartly upon the thighs. This is repeated three times, and, as there are three blows given each time, namely, on the breast, on the palms of the hands, and on the thighs, making nine concussions in all, the Grand Honors are technically said to be given "by three times three." On the occasion of funerals, each one of these honors is accompanied by the words, "the will of God is accomplished; so mote it be," audibly pronounced by the brethren. These Grand Honors of Masonry have undoubtedly a classical origin, and are but the imitation of the plaudits and acclamations practiced by the ancient Greeks and Romans in their theaters, their senates, and their public games. There is abundant evidence in the writings of the ancients, that in the days of the empire the Romans had circumscribed the mode of doing homage to their emperors and great men when they made their appearance in public, and of expressing their approbation of actors at the theater, within as explicit rules and regulations as those that govern the system of the Grand Honors in Freemasonry. This was not the case in the earlier ages of Rome, for Ovid, speaking of the Sabines, says, that "when they applauded, they did so without any rules of art."

The ancient Romans had carried their science on this subject to such an extent as to have divided these honors into three kinds, differing from each other in the mode in which the hands were struck against each other, and in the sound that thence resulted.

The Freemasons, however, have altogether preserved the ancient custom of applause, guarding and regulating its use by as strict, though different rules as did the Romans, and thus showing as another evidence of the antiquity of the Institution, that the Grand Honors of Freemasonry are legitimately derived from the "plausus," or applauding, practiced by the ancients on public occasions.

In the higher degrees, and in other rites, the Grand Honors are different from those of Ancient Craft Masonry in the American Rite.

UNWORTHY MEMBERS.—That there are men in our Order whose lives and characters reflect no credit on the Institution, whose ears turn coldly from the beautiful lessons of morality, whose hearts are untouched by its soothing influences of brotherly kindness, whose hands are not open to the deeds of charity, is a fact which we can not deny, although he may be permitted to express our grief while we acknowledge its truth. But these men, though in the Temple, are not of the Temple; they are among us, but are not with us; they belong to our household, but they are not of our faith; they are of Israel, but the are not Israel; we have sought to teach them but they would not be instructed; seeing, they have not perceived, and hearing, they have not understood the symbolic language in which our lessons of wisdom are communicated. The fault is not with us that we have not given, but with them, that they have not received. And, indeed, hard and unjust would it be to censure the Masonic Institution because, partaking of the infirmity and weakness of human wisdom and human means, it has been unable to give strength and perfection to all who come within its pale. The denial of a Peter, the doubting of a Thomas, or even the betrayal of a Judas, could cast no reproach on that holy band of apostles of which each formed a constituent part. "Is Freemasonry answerable," says Dr. Oliver, "for the misdeeds of an individual brother? By no means. He has had the advantage of Masonic instruction, and has failed to profit by it. He has enjoyed Masonic privileges, but has not possessed Masonic virtues."

Such a man it is our duty to reform or to dismiss; but the world should not condemn us if we fail in our attempt at reformation. God alone can change the heart. Masonry furnishes precepts and obligations of duty which, if obeyed, must make its members wiser, happier men; but it claims no power of regeneration. Condemn where our Institution is evil, but not where our pupils are dull and deaf to our lessons, for in so doing you condemn the holy religion which you profess. Masonry prescribes no principles that are opposed to the sacred teaching of the Divine Lawgiver, and sanctions no acts that are not consistent with the strictest morality and the most faithful obedience to government and the laws; and while this continues to be its character, it can not, without the most atrocious injustice, be made responsible for the acts of its unworthy members.

Of all human societies, Freemasonry is undoubtedly, under all circumstances, the fittest to form the truly good man. But, however well conceived may be its laws, they can not completely change the natural disposition of those who ought to observe them. In truth they serve as lights and guides; but as they can only direct men by restraining the impetuosity of their passions, these last too often become dominant, and the Institution is forgotten.

FOREIGN COUNTRY.—The lecture of the third degree begins by declaring that the recipient was induced to seek that sublime degree "that he might perfect himself in Masonry, so as to travel in foreign countries, and work and receive wages as a Master Mason."

Thousands have head this ritual expression without dreaming for a moment of its hidden or spiritual meaning; or, if they think of any meaning at all, they content themselves by interpreting it as referring to the actual travels of the Masons, after the completion of the Temple, into the surrounding countries in search of employment, whose wages were to be the gold and silver which they could earn by the exercise of their skill in the operative art. But the true symbolic meaning of the foreign country into which the Master Mason travels in search of wages, is far different.

The symbolism of this life terminates with the Masters degree. The completion of that degree is the lesson of death and the restoration to a future life, where the True Word, or Divine Truth, not given in this, is to be received as the reward of a life worthily spent in its search.

Therefore, we can understand, as the lost word

is the symbol of death, so is the True Word the symbol of life eternal; and Heaven, the future life, the higher state of existence after death, is the foreign country to which the Master Mason is traveling, there to receive his wages in the reception of that TRUTH which is typified in the Masonic system under the mystical expression of the True Word, which can be imparted only in that better country, and where alone we can fully possess that Divine Truth of Masonic search which is the "Master's wages," implying in its signification a true knowledge of Jehovah, through faith in the Lion of the Tribe of Judah, which is synonymous with the salvation of the immortal soul.

WASHINGTON, GEORGE.—The connection of George Washington with Freemasonry is a source of pride to every. American Mason, at least. We can thus call the "Father of his Country" a brother. While the friends of the Institution have felt that the adhesion to it of a man so eminent for virtue was a proof of its moral and religious character, the opponents of Masonry being forced to admit the conclusion, have sought to deny the premises, and, even if compelled to admit the fact of Washington's initiation, have persistently asserted that he never took any interest in it, disapproved of its spirit, and at an early period of his life abandoned it. The truth of history requires that these misstatements should be met by a brief recital of his Masonic career.

Washington was initiated in 1752, in the Lodge at Fredericksburg, Virginia, and the records of the Lodge, still in existence, presents the following entries on the subject. The first entry is thus:

"Nov. 4th, 1752. This evening Mr. George Washington was initiated as an Entered Apprentice."

On the 3rd of March in the following year, "Mr. George Washington" is recorded as having passed a Fellow Craft; and on the 4th of the succeeding August, the record of the transactions of the evening states that "Mr. George Washington," and others, whose names are mentioned, have been raised to the sublime degree of a Master Mason.

There is ample evidence that during the Revolutionary War, while he was Commander-in-Chief of the American armies, he was a frequent attendant on the meetings of military Lodges. Captain Hugh Maloy, a revolutionary veteran, declared that on one of these occasions he was initiated in Washington's marquee, the chief himself presiding at the ceremony. Brother Scott, a Past Grand Master of Virginia, asserts that Washington was in frequent attendance on the communications of the brethren.

We next hear of Washington's official connection in the year 1788. Lodge No. 39, at Alexandria, which had hitherto been working under the Grand Lodge of Pennsylvania, in 1788 transferred its allegiance to Virginia. On May 29, in that year, the Lodge adopted the following resolution: "The Lodge proceeded to the appointment of Master and Deputy Master to be recommended to the Grand Lodge of Virginia, when George Washington, Esq., was unanimously chosen Master."

Timothy Bigelow, who, in a eulogy delivered before the Grand Lodge of Massachusetts, two months after Washington's death, and eleven after his appointment as Master, made the following statement:

"The information received from our brethren who had the happiness to be members of the Lodge over which he presided for many years, and of which he died the Master, furnishes proof of his persevering zeal for the prosperity of the Institution. Constant and punctual in his attendance, scrupulous in his observance of the regulations of the Lodge, and solicitous at all times, to communicate light and instruction, he discharged the duties of the chair with uncommon dignity and intelligence in all the Mysteries of our Art."

But incidents like these are not all that are left to us to exhibit the attachment of Washington to Masonry. On repeated occasions he has announced, in his letters and addresses to various Masonic bodies, his profound esteem for the character, and his just appreciation of the principles of that Institution into which, at so early an age, he had been admitted. And during his long and laborious life, no opportunity was presented of which he did not avail himself to evidence his esteem for the Institution.

Thus, in writing to the officers and members of St. David's Lodge at Newport, R. L., in 1791, he uses this language:

"Being persuaded that a just appreciation of the principles on which the Masonic Fraternity is founded must be promotive of private virtue and public prosperity, I shall always be happy to advance the interests of the Society, and to be considered by them a deserving brother."

In a letter addressed in November, 1798, only thirteen months before his death, to the Grand Lodge of Maryland, he has made this explicit declaration of his opinion of the Institution:

"So far as I am acquainted with the doctrines and principles of Freemasonry. I conceive them to be founded in benevolence, and to be exercised only for the good of mankind. I can not, therefore, upon this ground, withdraw my approbation from it."

Now I close with the language of Clinton: "Washington would not have encouraged an institution hostile to morality, religion, good order and public welfare.

TEXAS.—Freemasonry was introduced in Texas by the formation of a Lodge at Brazoria, which met for the first time, December 27, 1835. The dispensation for this Lodge was granted by J. H. Holland, Grand Master of Louisiana, and in his honor the Lodge was called Holland Lodge No. 36. It continued to meet until February, 1836, when the war with Mexico put an end to its labors for the time. In October, 1837, it was reopened at Houston, a charter having in the interval been issued for it by the Grand Lodge of Louisiana. In the meantime two other Lodges had been chartered by the Grand Lodge of Louisiana: Milam, No. 40, at Nacogdoches, and McFarlane, No. 41, at San Augustine. Delegates from these Lodges met at Houston, December 20, 1837, and

organized the Grand Lodge of the Republic of
Texas, Anson Jones being elected Grand Master.

The introduction of Royal Arch Masonry into
Texas was accomplished with some difficulties in
1838. The General Grand Chapter of the United
States granted a charter for a Chapter at San
Felipe de Austin. The members, finding it
impractical to meet at that place, assumed the
responsibility of opening it at Galveston, which
was done June 2, 1840. This irregular action was,
on application, healed by the General Grand
Chapter. Subsequently this body united with two
illegal Chapters in the Republic to form a Grand
Chapter. This body was declared illegal by the
General Grand Chapter, and Masonic intercourse
was prohibited. The Chapter at Galveston
submitted to the decree, and the so-called Grand
Chapter of Texas was dissolved. In 1850 the Grand
Chapter of Texas was duly established.

NINEVEH.—The capital of the ancient
Kingdom of Assyria, and built by Nimrod. The
traditions of its greatness and the magnificence of
its buildings were familiar to the Arabs, the Greeks,
and the Romans. The modern discoveries of Rich,
of Botta, and other explorers, have thrown much
light upon its ancient condition, and have shown
that it was the seat of much architectural
splendor and of a profoundly symbolical religion,
which had something of the characteristics of the
Mithraic worship. In the mythical relations of the
old constitutions, which make up the legend of
the Craft, it is spoken of as the ancient birthplace
of Masonry, where Nimrod, who was the

builder, and "was a Mason and loved well the Craft," employed 60,000 Masons to build it, and gave them a charge "that they should be true;" and this, says the Harleian MS., was the first time that any Mason had any charge of Craft.

ORIGINAL POINTS OF MASONRY.—The old English lectures, which were abrogated by the United Grand Lodge of England in 1813, when it adopted the system of Hemming, contained the following passage:

"There are in Freemasonry twelve original points which form the basis of the system, and comprehend the whole ceremony of initiation. Without the existence of these points, no man ever was, or can be, legally and essentially, received into the Order. Every person who is made a Mason must go through these twelve forms and ceremonies, not only in the first degree, but in every subsequent one."

Hence it will be seen that our ancient brethren deemed the "Twelve Original Points of Masonry." as they were called, of the highest importance to the ceremony of initiation, any they consequently took much pains and exercised much ingenuity in giving them a symbolical explanation. But as by the decrees of the Grand Lodge they no longer constitute a part of the English ritual, and were never introduced into this country, where the "four perfect points" constitute an inadequate substitute, there can be no impropriety in presenting a brief explanation of them.

The ceremony of initiation, when these points constituted a portion of the ritual, was divided into twelve parts, in allusion to the twelve tribes of Israel, to each of which one of the points was referred, in the following manner:

1. The opening of the Lodge was symbolized by the tribe of Reuben, because Reuben was the first-born of his father Jacob, who called him "the beginning of his strength." He was, therefore, appropriately adopted as the emblem of that ceremony which is essentially the beginning of every initiation.

2. The preparation of the candidate was symbolized by the tribe of Simeon, because Simeon prepared the instruments for the slaughter of the Shechemites; and that part of the ceremony which relates to offensive weapons was used as a token of our abhorrence for the cruelty exercised on that occasion.

3. The report of the Senior Deacon referred to the tribe of Levi, because, in the slaughter of the Shechemites, Levi was supposed to have made a signal or report to Simeon his brother, with whom he was engaged in attacking these unhappy people while unprepared for defense.

4. The entrance of the candidate into the Lodge was symbolized by the tribe of Judah, because they were the first to cross the Jordan and enter the promised land, coming from the darkness of servitude, as it were, of the wilderness into the light and liberty of Canaan.

5. The prayer was symbolized by the tribe of Zebulum, because the blessing and prayer of Jacob were given to Zebulum in preference to his brother Issachar.

6. The circumambulation referred to the tribe

of Issachar, because, as a thriftless and indolent tribe, they required a leader to advance them to an equal elevation with the other tribes.

7. Advancing to the altar was symbolized by the tribe of Dan, to teach us, by contrast, that we should advance to truth and holiness as rapidly as that tribe advanced to idolatry, among whom the golden serpent was first set up to receive adoration.

8. The obligation referred to the tribe of Gad, in allusion to the solemn vow which was made by Jephthah, judge of Israel, who was of that tribe.

9. The intrusting the candidate with the mysteries was symbolized by the tribe of Asher, because he was then presented with the rich fruits of Masonic knowledge, as Asher was said to be the inheritor of fatness and royal dainties.

10. The investiture of the lamb skin, by which the candidate is declared free, referred to the tribe of Naphtali, which was invested by Moses with a peculiar freedom, when he said, "O, Naphtali, satisfied with favor and full with the blessing of the Lord, possess thou the west and the south."

11. The ceremony of the northwest corner, of the Lodge, referred to Joseph, because, as this ceremony reminds us of the most superficial part of Masonry, so the two half-tribes of Ephram and Manasseh, of which the tribe of Joseph was composed, were accounted to be more superficial than the rest, as they were descendants of the grandsons only of Jacob.

12. The closing of the Lodge was symbolized by the tribe of Benjamin, who was the youngest of the sons of Jacob, and thus closed his father's strength.

Such were the celebrated twelve original points of Freemasonry of the ancient English lectures. They were never introduced into this country, and they are now disused in England. But it will be seen that, while some of the allusions are perhaps abstruse, many of them are ingenious and appropriate. It will not, perhaps, be regretted that they have become obsolete; yet it can not be denied that they added something to the symbolism and to the religious reference of Freemasonry. At all events, they are matters of Masonic antiquity, and as such are not unworthy of attention.

SCOTTISH RITE.—French writers call this the "Ancient and Accepted Rite," but as the Latin constitutions of the Order designate it as the "Ancient and Accepted Scottish Rite," that title has now been very generally adopted as the correct name of the rite.

The Primitive Scottish Rite claims to have been established in 1770, at Namur, in Belgium, by a body called the Melopoliten Grand Lodge of Edinburg. But according to Clavel, it was the invention of one Marchat, an advocate of Nivelles, who organized it in 1818, at Namur, beyond which city, and the Lodge of "Bonne Amitie" it scarcely ever extended, and consisted of thirty-three degrees, which rite, Mackey says, "appears to have been founded upon the Rite of Perfection, with an intermixture of the Strict Observance of Hund the Adronhiramite, and some other rites."

But the organization of the "Ancient and

Accepted Scottish Rite," according to Mackey, is briefly this:

In 1758, a body was organized in Paris, called the "Council of Emperors of the East and West." This Council organized a rite called the "Rite of Perfection," which consisted of twenty-five degrees, the highest of which was "Sublime Prince of the Royal Secret." In 1761 this Council granted a patent or deputation to Stephen Morin, authorizing him to propagate the rite in the Western Continent. In the same year, Morin arrived at the city of St. Domingo, where he commenced the dissemination of the rite, and appointed many Inspectors, both for the West Indies and for the United States. Among others, he conferred the degrees on M. Hayes, with a power of appointing others when necessary. Hayes accordingly appointed Isaac Da Costa, Deputy Inspector-General for South Carolina, who, in 1783, introduced the rite into that State by the establishment of a Grand Lodge of Perfection in Charleston. Other Inspectors were subsequently appointed, and in 1801, a Supreme Council was opened in Charleston by John Mitchell and Frederick Dalcho.

There is abundant evidence in the Archives of the Supreme Council, that up to that time the twenty five degrees of the Rite of Perfection were alone recognized. But suddenly, with the organization of the Supreme Council, there arose a new rite, fabricated by the adoption of eight more of the Continental high degrees, so as to make the thirty-third, and not the twenty-fifth degree, the summit of the rite.

Although one of the youngest of the Masonic rites, having been established not earlier than the year 1801, it is at this day the most popular and the most extensively diffused. Supreme Councils or governing bodies of the rite are to be found in almost every civilized country of the world, and in many of them it is the only Masonic obedience.

FRENCH RITE.—The French or Modern Rite is one of the three principal rites of Freemasonry. It consists of seven degrees; three symbolic, the Apprentice, Fellow Craft, and Master's degrees; and four high degrees, viz., the Elect, Scotch Master, Knight of the East, and Rose Croix. This rite is practiced in France, in Brazil and in Louisiana. It was founded in 1786, by the Grand Orient of France, who, unwilling to destroy entirely the high degrees which were then practiced by the different rites, and yet anxious to reduce them to a smaller number and to greater simplicity, extracted these degrees out of the Rite of Perfection, making some few slight modifications.

There has been a multitude of rites, called Masonic. Ragon supplies us with the names of a hundred and eight, under the different titles of rites, orders, and academies. But many of them are un-Masonic, being merely of a political, social, or literary character. Some of them have lived only with their authors, and died when their parental energy in fostering them ceased to exert itself. Others have had a more permanent existence, and still continue to divide the Masonic family, furnishing, however, only diverse methods of attaining to the same great end—the acquisition of Divine Truth by Masonic light.

LEGEND OF THE ROYAL ARCH DEGREE.— Much of this legend is a myth, having very little foundation, and of it none in historical accuracy. But underneath it all there lays a profound stratum of philosophical symbolism. The destruction and the rebuilding of the Temple by the efforts of Zerubbabel and his compatriots, the captivity and the return of the captives, are matters of sacred history; but many of the details have been invented, and introduced for the purpose of giving form to a symbolic idea. And this idea, expressed in the symbolism of the Royal Arch, is the very highest form of that which the ancient mystagogues called the "euresis," or the discovery. There are some portions of the legend which do not bear directly on the symbolism of the second Temple as a type of the second life, but which still have an indirect bearing on the general idea. This particular legend of the three weary sojourners is undoubtedly a mere myth, there being no known historical testimony for its support; but it is evidently the enunciation symbolically of the religious and philosophical idea that divine truth may be sought and won only by successful perseverance through all the dangers, trials and tribulations of life, and that it is not in this, but in the next life, that it is fully attained. The legend of the Royal Arch of the Scottish Rite is more usually called the legend of Enoch.

CONCLUSION.—The primitive Freemasonry of Noah and his descendants prior to the Flood, being corrupted by the introduction of a spurious Freemasonry during the building of the Tower of Babel on the plains of Shina, those primitive and highly instructed priests secretly taught such as they could induce to forsake idolatry, and accept the original precepts of Noah; and owing to the corruptions then existing, they were compelled to form secret societies, and introduce a system of recognition by the adoption of certain signs and pass-words, and a symbolic mode of instruction, symbolically teaching the existence of a future life, and the immortality of the soul, always presenting the idea to the initiate in the form of a scenic representation, just as it is now presented in the highest degree of symbolic Masonry.

Therefore it has been truly said to be folly to deny the coincidence that exists between the Osirian drama and that enacted in the third degree of Masonry.

By this confinement of the doctrine of a future life and the immortality of the soul to a secret knowledge, guarded by the most rigid rites, could they only expect to preserve them from the superstitious innovations of the world as it then existed.

While Freemasonry has borrowed much of its symbols from the Arkite worship and more modern institution, it has come down to us unchanged in its original design of teaching divine truth by a mythical initiation and secret symbols, and is still progressing in the natural and legitimate development of the religious sentiment that gave it birth.

Therefore it may be truly said that speculative Masonry is pre-eminently the great Auxiliary of Christianity; both being of divine origin, they have advanced hand in hand, and side by side, for two thousand years, over all opposing forces, to that high degree of intellectual and moral development that demands universal consideration and respect. While the one demands a belief and trust in God, the other further demands love and obedience to the Creator of our being, from Whom all blessings flow.

While the one was the religion symbolically taught for thousands of years before the light of Christianity dawned upon the world, teaching the existence of a future life, to be gained by a proper search for divine truth, which was veiled in allegory and illustrated by symbols; the other teaches what that truth is, and that it can only be gained by the erection of a spiritual temple in our own hearts, through faith in the Lion of the Tribe of Judah; and there is no symbol of the Order more sublime than that in which the speculative Mason is supposed to be engaged in the erection of a spiritual temple. History teaches us that the spiritualizing of the Temple of Jerusalem is most pervading of all the symbols of Freemasonry, prevading the whole Masonic system, emphatically giving it its religious character.

Doubtless, as this symbolism of the temple comes directly to us from the Jewish tabernacle or portable temple, which Moses by divine command erected in the wilderness, in which was put the mercy-seat upon the ark of the testimony in the most holy place, that God might dwell among His people Israel; it makes the Solomonic Temple the symbol of the divine life to be cultivated in every heart, and in a general sense, this same temple is viewed as a type of that spiritual temple formed by the aggregation of the whole Order in which each Mason is a stone.

Thus we can understand that the Jewish thought, that every Hebrew was to be a tabernacle of the Lord—as taught by the Apostle Paul when he said to his Jewish brethren, "Know ye not that ye are the temples of God, and that the spirit of God dwelleth in you?"—has been transformed to the Masonic system, which teaches that every Mason should be a temple of the Grand Architect of the Universe.

Now, as the great object of Freemasonry is the search after divine truth, each Mason is directed to build up his earthly temple as a fit receptacle for truth when found, which should be the chief concern of every Mason, taking for his guide the great light of our faith and practice. Whereunto we do dwell to take heed as unto a light that shines in a dark place, until the day dawn, and the day-star arise in our hearts, to give us the light of the glory of God in the face of Jesus Christ, who brought life and immortality to light.

> May we to God let memory cling,
>   Before desire shall fail or wane,
> Or ever be loosed life's silver string,
>   Or bowl at fountain be rent in twain;
> For man to his long home doth go,
>   And mourners group around his urn;
> Our dust to dust again must flow,
>   And spirits unto God return.

INDEX.

www.ingramcontent.com/pod-product-compliance
Lightning Source LLC
Chambersburg PA
CBHW062200270326
41930CB00009B/1593